Engineering Revolution

ENGINEERING REVOLUTION

The Paradox of Democracy Promotion in Serbia

Marlene Spoerri

PENN

UNIVERSITY OF PENNSYLVANIA PRESS

PHILADELPHIA

Published by
University of Pennsylvania Press
Philadelphia, Pennsylvania 19104-4112
www.upenn.edu/pennpress

Printed in the United States of America on acid-free paper
1 3 5 7 9 10 8 6 4 2

Library of Congress Cataloging-in-Publication Data
Spoerri, Marlene.
Engineering revolution : the paradox of democracy promotion
in Serbia / Marlene Spoerri.—1st ed.
    p. cm.
Includes bibliographical references and index.
ISBN 978-0-8122-4645-2 (hardcover : alk. paper)
1. Democratization—Serbia. 2. Democratization—Government
policy—Serbia. 3. Democratization—International cooperation—
Serbia. 4. Regime change—Serbia. 5. Political parties—Serbia.
6. Serbia—Politics and government—1992–2006. I. Title.
DR2051.S66 2014
320.9497109'0511—dc23
                                        2014009314

For my father, Max Spoerri

CONTENTS

ABBREVIATIONS

AMS   Alfred Mozer Stichting (Netherlands)
AOS   Associated Opposition of Serbia
BMZ   Federal Ministry for Economic Cooperation and Development (Germany)
BTI   Bertelsmann Transformation Index
CANVAS   Centre for Applied Nonviolent Action and Strategies
CEE   Central and Eastern Europe
CeSID   Center for Free Elections and Democracy
CSCE   Conference on Security and Cooperation in Europe
CIA   Central Intelligence Agency (United States)
CIPE   Center for International Private Enterprise
DA   Democratic Alternative
DANIDA   Danish International Development Agency (Denmark)
DC   Democratic Center
DEKO   Democratic Coalition
DEPOS   Democratic Movement of Serbia
DF   Democratic Forum
DHSS   Christian Democratic Party of Serbia
DOS   Democratic Opposition of Serbia
DS   Democratic Party
DSS   Democratic Party of Serbia
EC   European Commission
EPP   European People's Party
EU   European Union
FES   Friedrich-Ebert-Stiftung (Germany)
FNS   Friedrich-Naumann-Stiftung (Germany)
FOIA   Freedom of Information Act
FRY   Federal Republic of Yugoslavia
G17   G17 Plus

GOTV   Get-Out-the-Vote
GSS   Civic Alliance of Serbia
HBS   Heinrich-Böll-Stiftung (Germany)
HSS   Hanns-Seidel-Stiftung (Germany)
ICG   International Crisis Group
ICTY   International Criminal Tribunal for the former Yugoslavia
IDEA   Institute for Democracy and Electoral Assistance
IREX   International Research & Exchanges Board (United States)
IRI   International Republican Institute (United States)
JSO   Special Operations Unit
JUL   Yugoslav Left Party
KAS   Konrad-Adenauer-Stiftung (Germany)
LDP   Liberal Democratic Party
LP   Liberal Party
MI6   British Secret Intelligence Service (United Kingdom)
MP   Member of Parliament
NATO   North Atlantic Treaty Organization
ND   New Democracy
NDI   National Democratic Institute for International Affairs (United
          States)
NED   National Endowment for Democracy (United States)
NGO   Nongovernmental Organization
NIMD   Netherlands Institute for Multiparty Democracy (Netherlands)
NRP   National Radical Party
NS   New Serbia
OSCE   Organization for Security and Co-operation in Europe
OSI   Open Society Institute
OTI   USAID's Office of Transition Initiatives
Otpor   Resistance
PVT   Parallel Vote Tabulation
RLS   Rosa-Luxemburg-Stiftung (Germany)
RP   Roma Party
RPU   Roma Party "Unity"
RTS   Radio Television of Serbia
SAA   Stabilization and Association Agreement
SD   Social Democracy
SDB   State Security Service
SDP   Social Democratic Party

SDU	Social Democratic Union
SEED	Support for East European Democracy
SI	Socialist International
SIDA	Swedish International Development Cooperation Agency (Sweden)
SLS	Serbian Liberal Party
SNS	Serbian Progressive Movement
SPO	Serbian Renewal Movement
SPS	Socialist Party of Serbia
SRS	Serbian Radical Party
SSJ	Party of Serbian Unity
SSP	Serbian St. Sava Party
SVM	Alliance of Hungarians from Vojvodina
SWOT	Strengths, Weaknesses, Opportunities, and Threats
UNDP	United Nations Development Program
UNMIK	United Nations Mission in Kosovo
URS	Union of Roma of Serbia
USAID	United States Agency for International Development (United States)
USDO	United Serbian Democratic Opposition
USIP	United States Institute of Peace (United States)
WFD	Westminster Foundation for Democracy (United Kingdom)
ZES	For a European Serbia

Introduction

The past decade has not been kind to the world's democracy promoters. In Egypt, foreigners delivering aid to political parties have been arrested, their offices ransacked, and their efforts to leave the country denied. In Belarus, Uzbekistan, the United Arab Emirates, and Zimbabwe, democracy aid practitioners have been banned, forced to set up shop in neighboring states. In Russia, a controversial bill imposing strict controls on foreign-funded nongovernmental organizations (NGOs) was signed into law in 2012 after years of state-sanctioned harassment of foreign democracy promoters. That same year, Russian authorities dealt a final blow to America's largest aid agency—the U.S. Agency for International Development—forcing it to close its offices there for good.

These are not isolated incidents. Instead, they are part of an international trend—a global "backlash" against democracy promotion (Carothers 2006a, see also Gershman 2006; NED 2006). Convinced that foreign aid organizations threaten their grip on power, authoritarian-leaning governments from Moscow to Cairo have cracked down on democracy aid. They have done so, in part, because of the electoral revolutions that swept across Eastern Europe at the close of the twentieth century.

Starting in Bulgaria and Romania, then moving to Slovakia, the Balkans, and later engulfing the former Soviet republics, the late 1990s witnessed a spate of popular, peaceful uprisings that upended nondemocratic regimes long thought infallible (Bunce and Wolchik 2011; McFaul 2005). As the stunning displays of "people power" gained prominence, their origins were attributed not simply to domestic heroics but to something more ostensibly ominous: external intervention. Foreign money and tacticians were rumored to have swayed electoral outcomes and indoctrinated anti-regime activists. Western meddling, in particular, was blamed for inciting revolution and regime change. As a result, today's authoritarian leaders are taking preemptive steps to ensure that unwanted intrusions by outsiders are not repeated.

At the center of the backlash lie the political party foundations. Empowered with a mission to promote democracy in newly democratic and authoritarian states, organizations such as the National Democratic Institute for International Affairs (NDI) and the International Republican Institute (IRI) from the United States, as well as Germany's Konrad-Adenauer-Stiftung (KAS) and Friedrich-Ebert-Stiftung (FES), have offered assistance to political parties and electoral organizations in struggling states. Given their desire to influence the work and conduct of political parties, these organizations and their funders—chiefly, the U.S. and Western European governments—stand accused not simply of promoting democracy but of meddling in the internal affairs of sovereign states—arming political parties and civil society organizations with the knowledge, resources, and skills needed to counteract authoritarianism.

For all the musings of dictators, little is known about the effectiveness of such assistance. Wary of drawing the ire of authoritarian leaders or risking the impatience of Western taxpayers, groups like the NDI and IRI have kept a low profile. As a result, we know little about how—or if—these groups and the governments that fund them effectively influence democracy abroad. This book answers those questions.

On the basis of more than 150 interviews with activists and politicians, political party aid professionals, diplomats, and scholars, and extensive archival research, including access to thousands of pages of previously unreleased donor reports and declassified CIA documents obtained through the Freedom of Information Act (FOIA), *Engineering Revolution* explores the role of foreign aid in bringing down dictators and building democratic political parties in nondemocratic and newly democratic regimes. It does so by focusing on a case that has long fascinated scholars and practitioners: Serbia—a country that has entered history as "democracy promotion legend" (Mendelson 2004: 88).

Serbia as Democracy Promotion Legend

Serbia is located in the remnants of what was once the multiethnic federation of Yugoslavia. Unlike most postcommunist states, Yugoslavia's transition from one-party to multiparty rule was mired not only in contention but, ultimately, in bloodshed. In 1990, new rights to self-empowerment transformed into demands for self-determination. Before long, most of Yugoslavia's six constituent republics—which included Bosnia, Croatia, Macedonia, Montenegro, Slovenia, and Serbia (along with the Serbian province of Kosovo)—voiced calls for independence. By 1992, the federation was embroiled in a protracted civil war that would leave millions as refugees and 140,000 people dead.[1]

The Serbia that emerged from these wars was weak and insular.[2] Its economy was in shambles and its politics tyrannized by Slobodan Milošević, a staunch autocrat branded "Europe's last dictator." Over the course of ten years, Milošević oversaw Serbia's transition to a semi-authoritarian state in which political opposition was hampered, independent media was stifled, and competitive elections were stolen.

Despite these obstacles, however, on 5 October 2000 a democratic Serbia emerged. After a decade in power, Milošević was forced to cede ground to Serbia's fledgling democratic forces. To the surprise of many, Milošević's resignation came not amid a hail of bullets or a violent coup d'état but through a wave of peaceful public protests that extended from small towns and villages to the heart of Serbia's capital of Belgrade.[3] Strategically organized and avowedly nonviolent,[4] 5 October 2000 was hailed as a "Bulldozer Revolution" and would allegedly serve as inspiration for democratic revolutionaries from Kiev to Cairo and Tbilisi to Tunis.

The United States and its allies were quick to take credit for Milošević's fall. Within weeks of Milošević's ouster, a common narrative emerged in which one explanatory factor loomed large: foreign intervention. Of all the forms of intervention—and there were many—it was democracy assistance in the form of training, grants, and material resources to political parties, independent media, and civil society organizations that won the greatest praise. Donors of such assistance eagerly branded "their" Serbian experiment as an emblem of aid's utility. The distributors of U.S. aid to Eastern Europe credited their assistance for having played a "key role" in regime change by strengthening democratic political parties and equipping Serbia's citizens with "the tools needed to liberate themselves" (SEED 2001: 1, 149). Similarly, the Office of Transition Initiative (OTI) identified its assistance as one of but three factors accounting for the "surprising and extraordinary defeat of Milošević" (Cook and Spalatin 2002: 2).

The self-congratulatory accounts of donors were bolstered by evidence presented in both the media and academic scholarship. In the United States, the *Washington Post* reported that "U.S.-funded consultants played a crucial role behind the scenes in virtually every facet of the anti-Milošević drive."[5] In Germany, *Der Spiegel* applauded the "massive political and material support from Berlin" for having "contributed to the fact that opposition groups and parties could develop the strength to force Milošević to surrender."[6] Scholars and analysts were similarly impressed, going so far as to call such assistance "crucial to the birth of democracy in Serbia" (Cevallos 2001: 4) and among U.S. foreign policy's "greatest success" stories (Traub 2008: 82).[7]

Integral to this narrative was one highly controversial form of democracy aid: assistance designed to target political parties and electoral processes—a form of aid known among the development community as "political party assistance." Long ranked among the most contentious forms of democracy assistance, political party aid was said to be key to Milošević's ouster, enabling everything from opposition unity and the fine-tuning of electoral messages to the breadth of Serbia's Get-Out-the-Vote (GOTV) campaign and the stellar quality of election monitoring. Without party aid, many believe, "opposition parties would not have succeeded in toppling the Milošević regime" (Kumar 2004: 24). The perceived success of political party assistance in bolstering Serbia's anti-Milošević candidates and electoral processes has been heralded as proof that "partisan assistance can and does promote peace and democracy" (Kumar 2004).

The bold assertions of aid's success in Serbia are striking in at least two respects. First, there is the issue of its otherwise unremarkable reputation. Democracy aid is generally believed to be only modest in impact—its influence on the democratization of political parties in new and nondemocracies is thought minimal at best (Burnell 2000a; Burnell and Gerrits 2010; Carothers 2006a; Kumar 2005). Second, despite the many accolades it has received in Serbia, party assistance was and remains a highly contested form of foreign assistance—one that risks politicizing a development industry that longs to be seen as apolitical. Given the low esteem in which many parties are held (in new democracies and established democracies alike), donors have been reluctant to assist parties directly. In fact, until Serbia, many eschewed party aid altogether.[8]

The perceived success of party aid in Serbia helped change such perceptions. Inspired by party aid's ostensibly transformative impact in the Balkans, assistance to Serbia's anti-Milošević forces quickly emerged as a blueprint for how aid should and could be orchestrated in other authoritarian regimes.

Exporting the Serbian Model

Among the first regimes to receive the Serbia treatment was Belarus. As the dust settled on Milošević's exit in late 2000, donors hoped that Belarus, a former Soviet stronghold with strong ties to Russia, would emulate Serbia's success. To outside observers, Alexander Lukašenko's iron-fisted presidency was eerily reminiscent of Milošević's reign. And so, the aid community rapidly set about developing an aid program "in exile," mimicking that witnessed in Serbia.

Belarus would quickly prove a disappointment. Lukašenko's grip on power proved more enduring, and the opposition to his rule less widespread and organized than was the case in Serbia in 2000. But if Belarus failed to live up to the high expectations of the democracy promotion community, similar ventures in Georgia in 2003 and Ukraine in 2005 more than made up for it. In both of these countries, democracy promoters would seek to brand a model of "electoral revolution" in which party aid loomed large.

Lessons learned from Serbia would soon be applied beyond Europe's borders. Within months of Milošević's fall, young Serbs from the anti-Milošević youth movement Otpor traveled to authoritarian strongholds in Asia, Africa, and the Middle East, relying on Western funding and training to export a model of revolution allegedly tried and tested in Milošević's Serbia.

Serbian aid practitioners—who had taken part in training-of-trainers programs in Serbia in the run-up to Milošević's ouster and become employees of NDI and IRI—went on to replicate that assistance in Egypt, Tunisia, Iraq, and elsewhere, becoming resident directors and senior program officers for the American party institutes' offices throughout the Middle East, Asia, and Africa. The aid enterprise forged in Serbia, it was thought, could provide a model for the delivery of aid in other authoritarian and post-authoritarian countries.

For all the accolades thrust upon the model forged in Serbia, however, its export rests on an important but largely untested assumption: that party assistance—and democracy assistance more generally—worked in Serbia. Scholars, members of the media, Western governments, authoritarian leaders, and aid practitioners have overwhelmingly presumed this to be true. Moreover, they have often gone several steps further—assuming that Western aid was critical and even determinative for Milošević's unseating and the rise of democracy in Serbia.

The evidence suggests otherwise. As the following chapters will show, democracy took root in Serbia not because of but, in large part, *in spite of* Western intervention. It is not just that party assistance—and democracy assistance more broadly—did not work. Rather, it is that foreign meddling often *hurt* Serbia, undermining the prospects for Milošević's fall throughout the 1990s and lessening the chances that democracy would take hold in the years that followed his political exit.

The Argument

The following chapters put forward three main arguments. The first is that the aid enterprise in Serbia in 2000 rested on a single, clear goal: regime change. *Engineering Revolution* will show that, for a few short months, the world's aid community was aligned along the singular goal of enabling Serbia's opposition to unseat Milošević. Although the ambition to facilitate regime change may not, in retrospect, appear groundbreaking (particularly in the aftermath of the war in Iraq in 2003), it is difficult to underestimate precisely how significant it was at the close of the twentieth century.

Prior to Serbia, democracy assistance had been used in dozens of countries in Latin America, Eastern Europe, Africa, and Asia to support civil society groups, election monitors, independent media, and more. Much of that work was modest and, ultimately, limited in impact (Carothers 1999). Serbia, however, represented a new direction for democracy assistance, the goal of which was not "democracy" as such but rather that of replacing a sitting head of state. Ultimately, Serbia would usher in a new era for a more politicized democracy assistance agenda in which aid providers were not merely neutral arbiters of a political process but active proponents working to advance a particular political outcome. The goal was regime change.

This brings us to this book's second argument, which regards the effectiveness of the democracy assistance agenda in Serbia. Although Serbia is frequently heralded as the quintessential example of "aid done right," the evidence offered in the following chapters points to a different conclusion. While modestly helpful in facilitating Milošević's ouster in 2000, aid was *not* a determining factor in supporting democracy in Serbia. Most important, it was not an exclusively positive contributor to Serbia's transition to democracy. To the contrary, especially in the post-Milošević period, democracy aid often conflicted with the needs of Serbian democracy. Although aid may at times have helped democracy, it also (and arguably, more often) hindered it.

Therein lies the third argument, which is related to the causes of aid's varied outcomes. As will be shown, democracy assistance is frequently viewed from binary perspectives. On the one hand, advocates embrace democracy assistance as a tool through which established democracies selflessly work to support democracy abroad. On the other hand, critics see democracy assistance as a tool of Western imperialism, intent not on supporting legitimate democratic aspirations but on crafting political outcomes. This book argues for a more nuanced perspective. It shows that aid's varied effects are in large part a consequence of its varied and, at times, incompatible goals: to facilitate democracy abroad and, simultaneously, to support the foreign policy interests of donor states. When these goals coincide, democracy assistance has the capacity to do real good. When they do not, however, democracy assistance can become subservient to the demands of foreign policy considerations. Unfortunately, this does not always work to democracy's benefit. Nor does it bolster the perceived credibility of the democracy aid agenda as a neutral proponent of democracy everywhere.

Contribution to the Literature

The democracy assistance agenda is built on an important assumption: that external actors can influence democracy abroad for the better. Yet for all the millions of dollars devoted to democracy assistance, there is by no means a consensus on the validity of this assumption.

To the contrary, there is enormous dissension on this topic. For many decades it was presumed that external actors could do remarkably little good to support democracy abroad. Until the 1990s, scholars were convinced that democratization was an exclusively domestic affair, facilitated by factors like socioeconomic development, a strong middle class, or a participatory civic culture (see Almond and Verba 1963; Lipset 1959; Moore 1966; O'Donnell, Schmitter, and Whitehead 1986).

It was only with the end of the Cold War that scholars began to reassess such assumptions. Among the first to do so was Samuel Huntington. In *The Third Wave*, Huntington (1991: 85) concluded that "democratization in a country may be influenced, perhaps decisively, by the actions of governments and institutions external to that country." Laurence Whitehead (1996: 3)—also a major thinker in the field of democratization studies—later made similar, albeit more modest claims, noting the powerful effects of international influences on all but a handful of contemporary democracies. More recently, Thomas Carothers, a leading authority on external influences on democratization, has argued that while in most cases external efforts to support democracy are marginal to political outcomes, in some—like Serbia's—they can be

more than that (Carothers 2001). Larry Diamond (2008a: 34), also a leading
scholar on democracy, has stressed that "international factors can play an
important role in facilitating democratization." Bruce Russet (2008: 64) has
taken this several steps further, arguing that "in particular instances international influences are important, and sometimes critical."

    Engineering Revolution contributes to the exploration of such influences
by examining a case where external actors are perceived to have been critical
toward the realization of democracy. In so doing, it seeks to help establish if
and how external actors can support democracy abroad, for better or worse,
through the delivery of assistance explicitly designed to bolster democracy.
Yet this book distinguishes itself from past studies on democracy and aid in
Serbia, in three major respects.[9]

    First, *Engineering Revolution* focuses in large part on political parties. Al-
though it was a politician who defeated Milošević at the ballot box in September 2000 and an eighteen-party political alliance that helped make that
possible, the role of political parties have been largely overlooked in studies
on democracy's development in Serbia. In particular, many Western accounts
of the fall of Milošević have focused on the role of the youth movement,
Otpor, in mounting a massive get-out-the-vote (GOTV) campaign in the
months leading to Milošević's fall.[10] Although not discounting the significance
of this bottom-up approach to helping explain the ouster of Milošević, this
book argues that concentrating on youth alone greatly underestimates the
multiplicity of actors—including political elites—that combined to facilitate
democracy's ascent in Serbia in 2000 and beyond. For better and for worse,
political parties have been instrumental in Serbia's political development
throughout the postcommunist period. Their successes and failures have had
a profound impact on the democratic trajectory that Serbia has followed and
the troubles that continue to plague Serbian politics today. Understanding
how external democracy aid has influenced such parties thus goes some way
in understanding how foreign actors have influenced Serbian democracy.

    This book's second contribution is found in its time-frame. Most Western
studies of Serbian democracy have focused on just a short time-frame—in
most instances, the years or months leading up to Milošević's fall in October
2000. This has caused scholars to overlook the events that occurred before
and after aid's most impressive accomplishments. Instead of focusing solely
on the months immediately before Milošević's resignation, this book offers an
in-depth account of the decades that preceded and followed Milošević's fall.
In examining the years between 1990 and 2010, it avoids the habit of focusing

only on success and offers a more nuanced analysis of aid done right *and* wrong.

This book's third contribution is its comprehensive examination of *all* the actors involved in party aid in Serbia. To date, the majority of Western studies on Serbia have focused on American democracy assistance. The role of European assistance, through the work of FES or KAS, has received far less attention. Moreover, many of these studies have focused exclusively on the accounts of aid providers, opting to sidestep the perspectives of aid recipients and domestic actors who were denied such assistance. This book corrects this by relying on the full spectrum of actors involved in the foreign aid effort in Serbia.

I conducted more than 150 interviews for the purposes of this research.[11] This included interviews with both European and American aid providers, Serbian aid recipients, nonrecipient parties, journalists, and scholars. The book relies on the perspectives not only of party aid practitioners but also on those of diplomats, government officials, state security personnel, covert operatives, members of the European Commission (EC), and for-profit party consultants. It also draws on the public and internal documents of party aid providers, including the American party institutes, the German *Stiftungen*, and smaller European party foundations, like the Alfred-Mozer-Stichting (AMS). Where necessary, I used the Freedom of Information Act (FOIA) to get the inside story on the aid that was and was not provided to Serbian democrats, whether through internal practitioner reports or CIA analyses.

In addition, I consulted party manifestoes and statutes, media reports, historical overviews, relevant memoirs, and academic literature concerning the time periods in question—the combination of which provide rare insight into the thoughts, concerns, objectives, and regrets of those involved in aiding Serbia's political parties in the run-up to and aftermath of Milošević's electoral defeat.

Chapter Overview

This book includes an overview of the literature on party aid, analysis of Serbia's political landscape, and original empirical information. To set the stage for an analysis of party aid's effects in Serbia, Chapter 1 examines the state of political parties and political party aid in new democracies and authoritarian states. Its ambition is to elucidate the link between party aid, political parties, and democracy in an effort to show how party aid attempts to influence not only political party development but also democratization processes more generally. After exploring the contributions political parties are thought to make to democracy and authoritarianism, Chapter 1 explores the world of political party aid, in particular what party aid is, who is involved, and the propositions that comprise what scholars know (or think they know) about party aid.

Most of the empirical research relating to party aid in Serbia is introduced in Chapters 2, 3, and 4. Each of these chapters hones in on a different period in political party aid history. Chapter 2 explores the absence of party aid between 1990 and 1996 and what this meant for Serbia's opposition parties that had hoped to bring democracy to Serbia. Chapter 3 examines the initiation of political party aid in 1997 and its transformation in the months and years leading to Milošević's ouster in October 2000 and the parliamentary victories of the Democratic Opposition of Serbia (DOS) in December 2000. Chapter 4 traces the evolution of party aid in the aftermath of democracy's onset in Serbia, from the beginning of democratic politics in 2001 to the acceptance of Serbia as a European Union (EU) candidate country in 2012. Each of these empirical chapters is divided into four sections: the first, outlining the contours of the political system during that period; the second, providing an analysis of the challenges afflicting the political party system at that time; the third, offering an in-depth examination of how donors and practitioners of party aid sought to respond to such challenges; and the fourth, analyzing the impact of aid during the period in question.

Chapter 5 provides an overarching analysis of party aid's impact throughout the whole of Serbia's postcommunist period. After introducing aid's ambiguous record of achievement, it reflects on the implications of the achievements of political party aid. It concludes by looking beyond Serbia, in an attempt to draw lessons that might be applied to future interventions in other semi-authoritarian and newly democratic contexts.

CHAPTER ONE

Promoting Democracy and Aiding
Political Parties Abroad

Writing in the years following the fall of Milošević, democracy aid scholar Sarah Mendelson (2004: 88) predicted that aid to Serbia's democrats would make history. And so it would. Scholars and practitioners have celebrated Serbia as democracy promotion at its best. It has been seen to "reveal the hollowness of the cliché that 'democracy can't be imposed by outsiders.'"[1] And its perceived success has given rise to an industry tasked with "exporting revolution" as a result of which, Serbia has gone on to influence cases of regime change spanning from Georgia and Ukraine to Egypt and Libya.

But if the promotion of democracy has been celebrated in Serbia, it was certainly not with precedent. To the contrary, governments have been promoting democracy (in name, if not in practice) for more than a century. Today democracy promotion serves as an integral component of foreign policy on both sides of the Atlantic. And although it has traditionally been the prerogative of large Western powers like the United States and Germany, in recent years the field of providers has widened to include smaller European states, such as Sweden, the Netherlands, and Slovakia; multilateral organizations, including the Organization for Security and Co-operation in Europe (OSCE) and the European Commission; and even large NGOs like George Soros's Open Society Foundations and Freedom House.

Yet, although the promotion of democracy was not unprecedented in Serbia, the profound impact of democracy assistance was. Before Serbia, democracy aid was regarded as a helpful but largely benign tool that could help countries ease their way toward democracy. In Serbia, by contrast, democracy assistance was—for the first time—viewed as critical to the toppling of a dictator.

Like donors, authoritarian leaders from Russia's Vladimir Putin and Belarus' Alexander Lukašenko to Zimbabwe's Robert Mugabe and Egypt's Hosni Mubarak took lessons from Milošević's fall. One such lesson was that democracy assistance posed an existential threat to dictatorship.

To understand how this came to be, it is necessary to set the stage with a brief overview of democracy promotion's place within foreign policy and the multibillion dollar industry known as democracy assistance.

Democracy Promotion and the Origins of Democracy Assistance

Few aspects of foreign policy have been as hotly contested in the post-9/11 era as that of democracy promotion. By its proponents, democracy promotion is lauded as "the right thing to do" (Fukuyama and McFaul 2007: 4), "vital" to Western interests (Roberts 2009: 18), and the product of "compelling . . . ideals" (Craner and Wollock 2008: 10). Skeptics, by contrast, have dismissed the effort as no more than "a convenient tool used by different players for their own selfish reasons" (Houngnikpo 2003: 197) or, as Noam Chomsky puts it, the promotion of "rule by the rich and the powerful."[2]

The controversy stems, in part, from the frequency with which the promotion of democracy has been used to rationalize major foreign policy decisions throughout the twentieth and twenty-first centuries. Democracy's promotion is here defined as any effort undertaken by a government, an international institution, a nongovernmental organization, or an individual, with the stated ambition of supporting the emergence or the deepening, or both, of democracy abroad. It has been used by the United States and Western European states to legitimize a wide array of foreign policy interventions, including but not limited to, the 2003 intervention in Iraq, the economic and political sanctions imposed on Burma, and the diplomatic isolation of Belarus.

The tools through which democracy is promoted are thus varied. Among the most prominent are diplomatic engagement or nonengagement, military intervention, economic assistance or sanctions, democracy assistance, or the acceptance or denial of membership into a coveted club. Such tools may be used individually to compel a state to embrace democracy or they may be used in concert—as was the case in Serbia. The relationship of each of these tools to democracy is very much uncertain. Until recently, however, among that most shrouded in mystery was democracy assistance.

Democracy assistance refers to "aid programs explicitly designed to bolster democratic institutions, processes, and principles" in foreign countries (Carothers 1999: vii). Today democracy assistance is provided to organizations and institutions in more than a hundred countries. In both authoritarian states and new democracies, it is geared toward influencing democratic outcomes in a large number of areas and institutions, including media outlets, nongovernmental organizations, trade unions, elections, political parties, police departments, legislatures, and local governments.

Ironically, the roots of democracy assistance can be traced not to aid invested in any political institutions but rather to aid directed toward economic growth. In the 1960s, fueled by the economic studies of Seymour Martin Lipset, which linked socioeconomic development with democracy, U.S. foreign policy makers widely believed that the key to building democracy in developing states lay in wealth creation and, in particular, in the development of a vibrant middle class. Support for economic development abroad, American policy makers believed, would simultaneously support the promotion of democracy abroad as well. The founding of the U.S. Agency for International Development (USAID) in 1961 by John F. Kennedy was designed to streamline U.S. efforts to support economic development abroad, particularly in Latin America. American aid to sympathetic governments, it was hoped, would provide a counterweight to Soviet influence and the rising prowess of Cuba's new government, led by Fidel Castro.

U.S. assistance did eventually kick-start economic growth, but a contemporaneous outgrowth of democracy was not forthcoming. Instead, military dictatorships sprang up across Latin America. Eager to stem the tide of Communism along its southern border, U.S. agencies turned a blind eye to governments' democratic aspirations for the region and instead covertly and overtly funneled assistance to military dictatorships (Carothers 1999; Powers 1979; Ranelagh 1986).

It was not until the 1980s that U.S. democracy assistance, as we know it today, emerged. Once again fueled by the looming threat of Communism, U.S. foreign policy makers sought to contrast the ideology of Communism with that of democracy. A critical part of that was President Ronald Reagan's founding of the National Endowment for Democracy (NED)—a nonprofit, nonpartisan, government-funded aid initiative dedicated to providing foreign assistance explicitly geared toward the support of democratic institutions abroad.

The inspiration for NED stemmed from the apparent success of West

Germany's efforts to support democracy abroad. The German party foundations—the Friedrich-Ebert-Stiftung (FES) and Konrad-Adenauer-Stiftung (KAS)—both received funding from the German government to support projects dedicated to "socio-political education" and "social structures" abroad (Pinto-Duschinsky 1991: 34). Their activities in Spain and Portugal in the 1970s were thought to have helped facilitate these countries' transitions from dictatorship to democracy. In fact, FES's assistance—by and large covert—was seen as "decisive" in helping Spanish political émigrés reconstruct political parties after the death of General Francisco Franco in 1975 (Dakowska 2005: 154).

NED's founding gave rise to the birth of democracy assistance across Latin America, Asia, and—to a far more limited extent—the Soviet Union. But it was not until the fall of Communism that democracy assistance truly took off. In 1989, President George H.W. Bush and the U.S. Congress established the Support for East European Democracy (SEED) program. Over the course of several years, the United States invested more than a billion dollars in economic, social, and political aid designed to support democracy in postcommunist Europe. Aid to other parts of the world gradually increased as well so that by 2012 USAID alone spent more than $1.5 billion on democracy-related projects around the world.[3]

Most democracy assistance targets civil society organizations, elections, constitutions, judiciaries, police, legislatures, local governments, militaries, trade unions, media organizations, and political parties. These forms of democracy assistance fall into specific subsets, the largest of which are rule-of-law assistance, governance assistance, civil society assistance, and electoral and political party assistance, henceforth referred to as political party aid. By far the most controversial has been aid geared toward political parties.

The controversy regarding political party aid stems from two major concerns. The first is widespread skepticism about the integrity of political parties. Across the globe, political parties are perceived as corrupt, self-serving, polarizing, and at fault for paralyzing the political process. Aid providers are thus understandably reticent to be associated too closely with these reviled institutions. They are particularly wary of being seen *supporting* the very actors whom the public blames for their countries' gravest democratic ills.

But aid providers' reticence has other causes as well. One stems from the direct role political parties play in democracy. It is, after all, political parties—rather than civil society organizations, unions, or the media—that drive the electoral process. They not only compete in elections, but they select and place candidates into the highest echelons of power. Democracy's very viability thus depends on the notion that these parties compete on a level political playing field. Foreign assistance to political parties, however, risks skewing that playing field by awarding actors external to the democratic process outsized influence. As Ohman et al. (2005: 12) explains, "There is considerable risk" that external aid to political parties "in partner countries is perceived as prejudiced and, hence, unfair support for certain parties." By selectively targeting political parties, foreign contributions have the potential to leave some parties better equipped than others, thereby putting them at an electoral advantage. According to Bussey (2000: 75), these interventions, however well intended, risk undermining the free market of ideas and giving individuals external to the democratic process too much influence over voters' electoral preferences.

For this reason, almost half of all democracies boast some form of legislation banning foreigners or foreign entities, or both, from donating to domestic political parties.[4] This is also why allegations of foreign interference in American electoral campaigns—like those witnessed in 1996, when Chinese authorities were accused of covertly financing the Democratic National Committee, or in 2012, when foreign-connected political action committees raised more than $5 million for Republican and Democratic presidential candidates—generate public uproar. Indeed, although polities generally welcome foreign investments in domestic infrastructure, industry, business, health care, education, or debt, they are enormously suspicious of similar contributions made to their political parties because—more than any other actor or organization—it is political parties that lie at the heart of the modern democratic process.

The Inevitability of Political Parties

Political parties are defined here as any political group or institution that competes in elections and seeks to place candidates in public office (Sartori 1976: 57). The definition of political parties thus derives from their functions, and the same is true of their perceived significance. Indeed, the importance of political parties is most often explained by the functions political parties perform, not only in linking citizens to the democratic process but also in organizing political life and managing governmental affairs.

Political parties link citizens to government (Diamond 1997; Linz and

Stepan 1996; Randall and Svåsand 2002). At their best, political parties serve as a conduit for citizens to influence their government and the policies they put forth. Parties achieve this feat by representing citizens' interests, aggregating those interests into easily identifiable political platforms, and articulating those interests on their constituents' behalf.

Parties also play a critical role in organizing political life. They recruit and train individuals capable of running for public office, and they help to structure electoral competition and mold political landscapes by crafting collective political identities. Finally, parties help shape the governing process by, among other things, setting their nations' policy-making agendas and helping to develop policy alternatives. When in government, parties devise and pass laws and procedures and, in some instances, even craft constitutions. For each of the reasons laid out in Table 1, scholars see parties as critical for democracy.

Political parties may also be critical for nondemocracies. Throughout the twentieth century, parties served a wide variety of purposes not only in democratic contexts but in authoritarian ones as well. Totalitarian regimes like those of the Soviet Union, Nazi Germany, and Benito Mussolini's Italy, for

Table 1. How Parties Help Democracy

Function 1: Link Citizens to Government

Represent the public's demands and interests.
Aggregate interests into political platforms.
Articulate interests and demands.
Integrate voters into political life.

Function 2: Organize Political Life

Nominate candidates.
Recruit and train political representatives.
Organize political opposition.
Organize electoral competition.
Mobilize supporters.

Function 3: Link Government to Citizens

Make government accountable to citizens.
Set policy-making agenda.
Develop policy alternatives.
Devise and pass laws.

Source: Adapted from Randall and Svåsand 2002.

example, relied on political parties to consolidate their power bases, build loyalties, and eliminate opponents. One-party states were the hallmark of totalitarianism leading to and following World War II. But nondemocratic regimes have also relied on *multiple* political parties—including ostensible opposition parties—to maintain their authority. Geddes (2008: 2) estimates that as many as two-thirds of authoritarian regimes make at least some use of political parties. That political parties persist where democracy does not has much to do with the functions that parties serve within these nondemocratic contexts.

Among these functions, political parties provide a vehicle through which authoritarian leaders can consolidate their rule, most notably by assuaging potential rivals and managing inter-elite conflict. Much like they do in democratic regimes, political parties in nondemocratic regimes help organize political life. They provide the structure through which to recruit and train political figures, as well as to build loyalty to the regime and the nation. China's one-party state, for example, relies on the Communist Party to groom candidates for public office. Party congresses provide the stepping-stones for China's ambitious politicians to work their way up the political ladder. The assignments awarded by China's one-party state enable politicians to accrue decades' worth of knowledge and managerial experience and ultimately inculcate a high degree of loyalty to the regime.

Political parties also provide authoritarian regimes with a veneer of legitimacy. In one-party states, large political parties offer the semblance of a transparent political process in which one can rise through the ranks of politics and perform public service. In authoritarian states that allow for multiple political parties, these organizations offer a symbol of political choice and competition. Although in many instances this "choice" is more pretense than substance, the very appearance of multiple political parties lends credence to dictators' claims to democratic legitimacy.

Political parties can serve as an indispensable tool for authoritarian regimes that institute an electoral process. In Russia, for example, political parties offer a structured network through which ruling authorities can mobilize supporters and secure victory at the ballot box. In Russia and other countries where parties of the regime enjoy unparalleled access to state infrastructure and national resources, political parties provide an ideal means through which to rally further support around their rule.

Of course, political parties do not only sustain dictators. They can also help bring them down. Perhaps the greatest indicator of political parties' role in the onset of democracy is found within the expanding literature on "electoral revolutions" (see Bunce and Wolchik 2006; Howard and Roessler 2006; Kuzio 2006; McFaul 2005; Petrova 2010; Schedler 2002; Wahman 2011). Starting in Bulgaria and Romania in 1996, moving on to Slovakia in 1998, Croatia and Serbia in 2000, Georgia in 2003, and then finally Ukraine and Kyrgyzstan in 2005, political parties and independent NGOs forged anti-regime coalitions that led to mass public protests and the eventual unseating of dictators.

Among the handful of elements deemed critical for these instances of regime change stood the unity of opposition political parties.[5] Political parties' ability to forge united coalitions and, in some cases, to back a common candidate for presidential elections, was thought to be critically important for the ousting of a dictator—thus suggesting that parties' "heroic moment" may in fact precede the actual onset of democracy (O'Donnell and Schmitter 1986: 57). As Table 2 explains, there are several ways in which parties may contribute to transitions to democracy.

The first of these is by helping foster liberal outcomes. In this initial phase

Table 2. How Parties Help the Transition to Democracy

Function 1: Fostering Liberal Outcomes
Develop pro-democratic platforms.
Advocate pro-democratic policies.
Organize mass protests.

Function 2: Enabling Regime Change

Make pacts and negotiate transition.
Support unity of opposition during key electoral moments.
Mobilize citizenry.

Function 3: Deepening Democratic Gains

Mediate conflicting interests.
Bind social groups.
Educate public on "rules of the game."
Instill democratic attitudes and expectations.
Provide stability and legitimacy.
Organize nation's first free and fair elections.
Institute democratic rules of the game.
Oversee processes of lustration.
Channel energy of civil society into official institutions.

of democratization, (opposition) political parties can help to spur fledgling processes of liberalization within otherwise nondemocratic regimes through the development of progressive pro-democratic platforms and the advocacy of pro-democratic policies. They can also help to encourage authoritarian leaders to redefine and extend rights and civil liberties. Similarly, by organizing mass protests in the wake of regime-sponsored brutality, political parties can undermine the legitimacy of the regime and levy pressure for substantive policy changes capable of protecting individuals and social groups from state-backed oppression. Political parties can also play an active role in inciting the birth of democratic rule in those settings where pluralism predates democracy.

Linz and Stepan (1996), for example, argue that negotiations and pacts drawn between key elites—the leaders of opposition political parties among them—and regime officials facilitate democratic transition. Using case studies drawn from Latin America and Southern Europe, the authors argue that agreements between state authorities and rival parties enabled the emergence of democracy in these regions throughout the mid-twentieth century. Authors such as Scheddler (2002), McFaul (2005), Bunce and Wolchik (2006), and Howard and Roessler (2006) have since argued that confrontation, rather than agreement, between state authorities and rival political forces may lead to electoral revolution. In semi-authoritarian regimes, including Vladimir Mečiar's Slovakia and Milošević's Serbia, these authors argue that political parties helped pave the way toward regime change by forming inclusive anti-regime electoral coalitions, as well as by mobilizing citizens in the aftermath of electoral fraud.

But political parties' bearing on democratization processes need not end there. In the aftermath of regime change, political parties can help to deepen and consolidate democratic gains by, among other things, organizing their nations' first free and fair elections and helping to channel popular democratic sentiment into official institution. They can also oversee policies of lustration. Where necessary, they can support societal cohesion and socialize the electorate on the rights and responsibilities associated with democracy. Authors such as Tordoff (2002), Burnell (2006), and de Zeeuw (2008) have shown that, particularly in divided, post-conflict societies, political parties can play a vital role in mediating conflict through the aggregation of interests and the articulation of political preferences.

Political parties can also contribute to stability and legitimacy in newly democratic systems by respecting electoral laws and playing by the rules of the democratic game (Huntington 1968, Mainwaring and Scully 1995; Van Biezen 2003). They help instill attitudes and expectations in the public about the norms and routines of democratic practice, thereby contributing to the institutionalization and consolidation of democracy (Randall 2007: 638). According to Van Biezen (2003: 4), though their role in democratic transitions may be "relatively undervalued, the positive contribution of political parties to the consolidation of democracy is more generally acknowledged. In fact, parties are seen to make a relevant, if not crucial, contribution to the consolidation of a newly established democratic polity."

But if parties' import for democracy and democratization is potentially great, their impact in practice is often far more circumscribed. As political parties have mushroomed across the globe, their rise has been met not only by democratic aspirations but also by a "dark underside" (Carothers 2006a: 4). Almost universally, political parties are lambasted as ineffectual and self-serving, corrupt and power-hungry.[6] Their failure to fulfill citizens' expectations risk rendering parties an impediment to—rather than a promoter of—democratization processes in the polities that arguably need them most: new democracies and those on the cusp of democratic breakthrough.

The Trouble with Parties

Political parties in authoritarian and newly democratic regimes commonly suffer from a host of ailments that leave them ill equipped to forge the path to democracy. One such ailment is that they are too personalistic. At their best, they are well intentioned but thinly institutionalized and leader-centric. At their worst, they serve as vehicles for the self-aggrandizement of power-hungry party leaders. Even nominally pro-democratic parties in such regimes often lack clear ideological grounding: their identity is wrapped in their leader's persona, not in a coherent party program.

This can have potentially devastating consequences, especially in non-democratic settings. Parties in such regimes frequently engage in cross-party rivalry, lack internal transparency, and participate in political infighting. As a result, when they seek to unseat a sitting regime collectively, they often struggle to forge coalitions and maintain a united front. Parties' contribution to regime change through pact-making and coalition unity is therefore often limited. Their contribution is further curtailed by their miniscule financial resources and paltry physical infrastructure, which rarely extends beyond the state capital. Chronic underfunding frequently forces opposition parties to rely on external sources of wealth—most notably, tycoons and even foreign governments—which state authorities exploit to undermine their opponents' credibility in the eyes of the public, thus making it difficult for parties to win the public support needed to mobilize citizens against the regime.

The troubles that plague parties and party systems in authoritarian contexts often continue in the aftermath of regime change. In most cases, parties in new democracies are unresponsive to citizens' needs and desires, playing only a marginal role outside of the electoral arena. In the postcommunist context, "They often seem to lack strong organizational structures and to have weak electoral and partisan links with society" (Spirova 2005: 602). As a result, they commonly suffer from what Carothers (2006a: 3–2) has called a "standard lament," according to which they are perceived as corrupt, self-serving, ideologically indistinct, and leader-centric.

It is thus not surprising that political parties are often the institution least trusted in new democracies—a fact that Van Biezen (2003: 38) says "discourages the creation of stable linkages between parties and society." Indeed, in many newly democratic contexts, multiple new parties flow into and out of power during any given election cycle. They frequently suffer from low levels of institutionalization, high polarization, extreme fragmentation, and weak ideological patterning. The consequences of such weaknesses extend beyond parties and party systems. According to Enyedi (2006: 229), "The lack of members and loyal supporters makes it difficult for parties to articulate and aggregate preferences" in new democracies. Similarly, Tóka (1997) maintains that high rates of volatility undermine the accountability and responsiveness of parties in power, while Mainwaring (1998) argues that low levels of institutionalization impede democratic consolidation.

Precisely because weak parties and party systems are believed to impede democratization processes, both the United States and European Union (EU) member states provide millions of dollars in foreign assistance to political parties abroad.

Aiding Parties Abroad

Like democracy assistance, political party assistance first materialized in the early 1970s, in concert with the unfolding of democracy's Third Wave, when the German *Stiftungen* channeled support to political parties in Southern

Europe. It was not until the collapse of the Soviet Union, however, that party aid became a hallmark of the democracy promotion agenda. The emergence of multiparty life throughout Europe's central and eastern quarters presented the world's democracy promoters with newly fertile terrain. A strong ideological and organizational resemblance to, as well as geographic proximately with, Western Europe, made Central and Eastern Europe (CEE) and the Baltics a natural first destination for party aid. Throughout the next twenty years, party aid would proliferate across the globe, emerging into what is now a multi-million dollar enterprise.

Political party assistance is designed to foster democratic processes in new democracies and in nondemocracies by enabling political parties to better carry out their representative functions. As a form of foreign aid, party assistance roots itself in the (highly contested) premise that external actors can and do make a difference in propelling countries' democratic trajectories. Even more controversially, it rests on the assumption that external actors can influence political parties' internal workings—for the better.

Today political party assistance is the prerogative of several dozen organizations based primarily—though not exclusively—in Western Europe and the United States. Foremost among these are the two American party institutes—NDI and IRI—and the six German *Stiftungen*—FES, KAS, the Friedrich-Naumann-Stiftung (FNS), the Hanns-Seidel-Stiftung (HSS), the Heinrich-Böll-Stiftung (HBS), and the Rosa-Luxemburg-Stiftung (RLS). In recent years, other established European democracies have followed suit, including Sweden, the United Kingdom, the Netherlands, France, and Spain, each of which has established organizations such as the Olof Palme International Center, the Westminster Foundation for Democracy (WFD), the Netherlands Institute for Multiparty Democracy (NIMD), Fondation Jean-Jaurès, and the Fundación Pablo Iglesias, respectively. A handful of young postcommunist democracies—themselves former recipients of democracy assistance—have also undertaken efforts to distribute political party assistance, as have several multilateral organizations such as the Organization for Security and Co-operation in Europe (OSCE) and the United Nations Development Program (UNDP). Others, like the Institute for Democracy and Electoral Assistance (IDEA), have opted to serve as knowledge banks on political party development and party aid.

Of direct implementers, American and German party aid organizations are not only the oldest but also the largest, working in more than eighty countries across the globe. Their combined annual budgets exceed $550 million.[7]

Table 3. Party Aid Implementers

Organization	Country of Origin	Ideology
Alfred Mozer Stichting	The Netherlands	Social Democracy
Konstantine Karamanlis Institute for Democracy	Greece	Conservative
Fondation Jean-Jaurès	France	Social Democracy
Fundación Pablo Iglesias	Spain	Social Democracy
Robert Schumann Foundation	France	Christian Democracy
Friedrich-Ebert-Stiftung	Germany	Social Democracy
Friedrich-Naumann-Stiftung	Germany	Liberal Democracy
Hanns-Seidel-Stiftung	Germany	Christian Democracy
Heinrich-Böll-Stiftung	Germany	Green Party
International Republican Institute	United States	Republican Party
Konrad-Adenauer-Stiftung	Germany	Christian Democracy
National Democratic Institute	United States	Democratic Party
Netherlands Institute for Multiparty Democracy	The Netherlands	None
Olof Palme International Center	Sweden	Social Democracy
Renner Institute	Austria	Social Democracy
Rosa-Luxemburg-Stiftung	Germany	Social Democracy
Westminster Foundation for Democracy	United Kingdom	None

By contrast, the budgets of Europe's smaller party aid providers run from just under $1 million to $4 million. Many work in only a small number of countries, devoting their limited resources to specific geographic regions. Table 3 provides an overview of the main organizations currently providing democracy assistance to political parties abroad.

Just as party aid providers offer assistance and sometimes grants to aid recipients, so too do aid providers act as grant seekers. Among the donors funding the budgets of party aid providers are primarily foreign ministries and government aid agencies. Nongovernmental organizations, such as the National Endowment for Democracy, provide modest assistance to the aforementioned organizations. Most of the assistance comes from government sources. In the case of the German *Stiftungen*, for example, as much as 95 percent of their budgets come from the Federal Ministry for Economic Cooperation and Development (Dakowska 2005: 2). Table 4 provides an overview of party aid donors.

Table 4. Donors of Party Aid

Donor	Origin	Aid Type	Implementer
National Endowment for Democracy	United States	NGO	NDI and IRI
Federal Ministry for Economic Cooperation and Development	Germany	Government	FES, KAS, FNS, HSS, HBS, RLS
Foreign Ministry	Germany	Government	FES, KAS, FNS, HSS, HBS, RLS
Swedish International Development Cooperation Agency	Sweden	Government	Olof Palme International Center[a]
Foreign and Commonwealth Office	United Kingdom	Government	WFD[b]
Department for International Development	United Kingdom	Government	WFD
Netherlands Ministry of Foreign Affairs	The Netherlands	Government	NIMD
U.S. Agency for International Development	United States	Government	NDI and IRI

[a] The Olof Palme International Center also receives modest funding from the Swedish Labour Movement's International Solidarity Fund and returns on its assets. However, as the center itself acknowledges, "We are highly dependent on SIDA for our financing" (Olof Palme 2010: 19).
[b] The WFD receives the bulk of its support from the Foreign and Commonwealth Office. A small amount of support also comes from the Department for International Development and the British Council.

Each of these party aid providers works with political parties with the goal of making them more representative, transparent, accountable, and effective. Party aid providers thus say that they strive to make parties internally democratic, media and technologically savvy, responsive to the electorate, in touch with their grassroots supporters, financially transparent, ideologically defined, and gender balanced. Table 5 provides an overview of the stated goals of political party aid.

Aid providers work to realize such goals through a combination of skills-building training, educational seminars and workshops, study tours, public opinion polls, and financial and material assistance. As Table 6 explains, such activities are often channeled through one of five types of party aid: campaign assistance, organizational assistance, program and ideology assistance, legislative assistance, and party system assistance.

Table 5. Stated Goals of Party Aid

Strong central party organizations
Internal democracy
Well-defined party platforms
Clear ideological identity, avoiding ideological extremes
Transparent, broad-based, and adequate funding
Effective campaigns with strong grassroots components
Effective governance capacity
Geographic diversity
Clear membership base
Close relations with civil society organizations
Strong role for women
Strong youth programs

Source: Adapted from Carothers 2006a (98).

As the most prominent form of party aid, campaign assistance targets everything from the recruitment of party candidates to platform and message development. This includes helping parties to select and train potential candidates and developing strategic plans, as well as assisting in fundraising, message development, and the training of staff and party volunteers. Campaign aid also focuses on campaigning itself, including door-to-door outreach, GOTV campaigns, political advertisements, and media relations. On election day, campaign assistance will even help enable parties to monitor polling stations (Carothers 2006a).

Between election cycles, party aid often manifests itself as organizational assistance. Such aid aims, on the one hand, to improve the organizational capacities of parties—helping parties to establish clearly defined lines of authority, hone management skills, and establish effective internal communication (Kumar 2005). On the other hand, it seeks to encourage parties to engage in nationwide outreach—helping parties to expand their membership, build a stable base of supporters, and learn new fundraising techniques (Carothers 2006a). Often central to organizational assistance is an emphasis on internal democracy and inclusiveness. Party aid providers frequently encourage their partners to adopt internal party elections (that is, primaries), as well as to establish youth and women's wings equipped with meaningful prerogatives (see Carothers 2006a; Scarrow 2005).

Program or ideology aid, by contrast, aims to strengthen the substantive ambitions of parties: helping them to promote clear and cohesive programmatic

Table 6. Types of Party Aid

Aid Type	Objective
Campaign Aid	Expand party membership.
	Recruit party candidates.
	Modernize campaign practices.
	Encourage grassroots networks.
	Increase use of public opinion polls.
	Enable election monitoring.
Organizational Aid	Establish organizational coherence.
	Establish good administration and clear lines of authority.
	Encourage strategic planning.
	Establish effective internal communication.
	Support internally democratic rules and procedures.
	Create effective outreach.
	Establish strong youth and women's wings.
Program and Ideology Aid	Create ideologically coherent party programs.
	Encourage the use of public opinion polls.
	Situate parties along a clear left-right spectrum.
	Incorporate parties within a European party family.
	Encourage long-term fraternal relationships.
	Encourage the socialization of democratic norms.
	Encourage the acceptance of basic democratic values.
Legislative Aid	Work effectively with parliamentary colleagues.
	Establish centers for citizen outreach.
	Fulfill electoral promises.
	Communicate legislative successes with the electorate.
Party System Aid	Encourage cooperative inter-party dialogue.
	Reduce political polarization.
	Establish transparent channels of party financing.
	Establish a clear legal framework for multiparty politics.

agendas that cater to specific sets of interests and cleavages (which, for better or worse, are not always present in newly democratic and nondemocratic regimes). Such assistance will thus include educational initiatives seeking to teach partner parties the basic attributes of political ideologies, whether social democracy, conservatism, or liberalism. It will also encourage parties to stay tuned to their electorates' wishes by relying on public opinion data to inform platform development. Ultimately, the stated hope of party aid providers—

particularly European aid providers—is to encourage a party system in which parties are neatly aligned along a left-right spectrum and are thus able to offer their electorate clearly distinguishable policy preferences. German aid providers also have an added goal of forging close fraternal bonds between aid recipients and *Stiftungen* mother parties (Dakowska 2005; Erdmann 2006; Weissenbach 2010)

Particularly in new democracies, party aid will also take the form of legislative assistance. As opposition parties assume the reins of power, such aid seeks to enhance parties' parliamentary capacities: helping them to form and manage party caucuses, assisting in their analysis and drafting of legislation, encouraging them to form national ombudsmen, and helping them promote their policy achievements to the electorate (Carothers 2006a). Such aid aims, above all, to help parties realize the goals they set during the campaign season.

Finally, an increasingly prominent form of party assistance is that of party system aid. Rather than target specific parties one by one, party system assistance seeks "to foster changes in all the parties in a country at once" by altering parties' relations with one another and amending the legal and financial structure in which party life is embedded (Carothers 2006a: 190). Party system aid will thus focus on supporting multiparty collaboration and interparty linkages by, among other things, pressing for grand coalitions, supporting joint events, and encouraging multiparty collaboration on policy proposals (Kumar 2005: 510–11). In newly democratic settings, party system aid will often focus on promoting legal and regulatory reform: creating state laws that clearly specify what a political party is, the activities parties may engage in, and the behaviors that are permissible (Carothers 2006a: 190).

Of course, political party assistance does not exist in a vacuum and neither do the political parties that aid seeks to influence. Consequently, in addition to targeting political parties directly through the forms of assistance laid out in this chapter, practitioners also work to influence them indirectly.

Assistance given to advocacy groups, for example, is used to encourage political parties to alter their political programs or to favor certain policies. Similarly, aid targeted at civil society groups engaged in Get-Out-the-Vote campaigns can swing the electoral tide in some parties' favor. Likewise, support for electoral monitoring groups can add credibility to political parties' claims that an election has been rigged or is in fact truly free and fair. Particularly in nondemocratic regimes—like that of Milošević in Serbia—these indirect forms of assistance have the potential to play a major role in determining the effectiveness of political party assistance.

Moving Beyond Aid's Stated Goal

For all the growing attention devoted to political party aid, its overarching utility and the motivations underpinning it remain clouded in controversy. Although analysts and practitioners broadly agree that most party aid is modest in impact,[8] they also submit that in certain cases it has the potential to be far more than that. At the forefront of those cases is Serbia, where political party aid is thought to have played a major role in unseating a dictator.

Indeed, the publicly stated goals of party aid rarely, if ever, include regime change. But in rare instances (like that of Serbia), rather than concentrate on achieving financial transparency or internal party democracy, aid providers may stray from their standard ambitions and work to achieve something far more controversial: regime change.

By empowering anti-regime parties with specific skills and material resources, democracy assistance to political parties occasionally works to combat authoritarianism and even to bring down a dictator. Yet such goals are often left inexplicit or, at the very least, not put into print. It is precisely because party aid practitioners are presumed to work in ways that extend beyond their official mandates and stated goals that party aid has sparked controversy the world over—causing some regimes to ban their work altogether. This controversy is also one reason that the subject—and the case of Serbia in particular—has piqued the curiosity of scholars and the media.

CHAPTER TWO

The Absence of Aid in Milošević's
Serbia, 1990–1996

In the winter of 1990 Serbia staged its first postcommunist multiparty elections. Like its counterparts in Central and Eastern Europe, Serbia looked set to emerge from the ashes of one-party rule as a pluralist, if not an entirely liberal, democracy (Gagnon 1994; Pavlović and Antonić 2007; Ramet 1991). Yet as they had in Croatia and Slovenia before it, Serbia's electoral results hailed not democracy's onset but a rather more ominous turn of events: the forthcoming dissolution of the multi-ethnic Socialist Federal Republic of Yugoslavia. The outbreak of war and the atrocities that followed in the footsteps of Yugoslavia's first multiparty elections are by now well known (see Cohen 1993; Little and Silber 1995; Woodward 1995). But while the world stood aghast as Slobodan Milošević quashed Kosovo's autonomy, aided and abetted Bosnia's breakaway Serbs, and fueled ethnic conflict in Croatia, far less attention was paid to the Serbian leader's steady assault on his own republic's nascent democratic institutions. As civil war raged at Serbia's doorstep, a political war was being waged within Serbia proper, one that effectively drew Serbia into a political "gray zone" of regime hybridity, where it was caught between outright dictatorship and a basic electoral democracy.

It seems obvious, in retrospect, that Milošević wished to monopolize Serbia's nascent pluralist institutions. Yet, in the spring of 1984, when Milošević assumed the position of president of the City Committee of the League of Communists of Belgrade, few inside or outside of Yugoslavia found reason to be alarmed. Professing support for Communism and free market economics, Yugoslav unity and Serbian claims to Kosovo, an admiration for American democracy but a preference for one-party rule, Slobodan Milošević was the proverbial Janus face, offering all things to all people but fully embodying none.

Within less than a decade, however, Milošević would fall into both domestic and international disrepute. His instrumental role in the wars of the former Yugoslavia and his steady encroachment on the political and civil liberties of his people would earn the Yugoslav leader infamy as "the Butcher of the Balkans" and "Europe's Last Dictator."[1] Milošević's authoritarian leanings and his penchant for state-sponsored violence would have a tremendous impact not only on the political parties and party system that emerged throughout his tenure but also on the forms of foreign aid that would—and would not—be forthcoming. Understanding how Milošević built and maintained his rule despite what some authors have labeled a "substantive" and "talented" anti-Milošević opposition (Dodder and Branson 1999) is vital to understanding why aid emerged only in the late 1990s—long after Serbia's democratic opposition first requested it.

As shall be seen, the unique dynamics of competitive authoritarianism presented prospective aid providers with both adversity and opportunity. Daunting though the challenges proved to be, there were several occasions lasting weeks and sometimes months during which a democratic breakthrough appeared to be within reach. Time and again, Serbia's democratic opposition pleaded with Western governments and aid agencies for their support. Time and again their efforts were rebuffed. Thanks to cultural misconceptions and strategic miscalculations, Western governments made the conscious decision *not* to support domestic alternatives to Milošević throughout most of the 1990s—even when these alternatives were avowedly antiwar and pro-democratic. In doing so, they allowed a committed, albeit imperfect, anti-Milošević opposition to go unaided and mistakenly justified a policy of inaction.

Milošević's Serbia

The story of Slobodan Milošević's rise to power is not one of fabled lineage[2]. Rather, it is one of a deeply ambitious, unscrupulous man who exploited friends, colleagues, and budding nationalist sentiments to work his way into the highest echelons of Yugoslav power. Just three years into Milošević's political career, the young communist apparatchik successfully tapped into a burgeoning wave of nationalist sentiment. By the eve of Serbia's first postcommunist elections, Milošević's popularity went unrivaled. Winning 65 percent of the Serbian vote—more than four times the total won by his nearest competitor, Vuk Drašković—Milošević became Serbia's first freely elected postcommunist president in December 1990. In that same month, his party—the Socialist Party of Serbia (SPS)—won 77 percent of the seats in Serbia's 250-seat parliament.

Yet for all of his success in Serbia's landmark elections, Milošević's widespread popular appeal proved ephemeral. Just months after securing his electoral victory, domestic opposition to his rule reached a boiling point. In March 1991, scores of demonstrators took to the streets of Belgrade protesting the regime's refusal to abide by the principles of free and independent media. For ten days, tens of thousands of Serbian citizens protested in the Yugoslav capital, occupying Belgrade's central square even as state tanks descended on them. Though ultimately unable to force Milošević's resignation, the events of March 1991 marked the first of what would become a frequent and protracted series of antigovernment, pro-democratic protests that would become a hallmark of Milošević's Serbia and form "the lifeblood of opposition political life" throughout Serbia (Kesić 2005: 101).

Milošević succeeded in maintaining his rule despite this domestic opposition. He accomplished this dubious feat not by banning political parties or blatantly stealing elections but by steadily monopolizing three key instruments of power: Serbia's once independent media, its nascent political institutions, and its powerful security services and police. He began with Serbia's media.

Upon taking office as the republic's first postcommunist president, Milošević wasted little time securing his hold over a media industry once ranked among the richest, most diverse, and freest in the communist world (Thompson 1999). He did so through three key tactics: by appointing regime loyalists to key positions within the state-run media, censoring media content, and denying the independence of non-state owned media outlets. Among Milošević's first targets were Serbia's leading news outlets: Radio Television Serbia (RTS), the newspaper *Politika*, and the daily tabloid *Politika ekspres*. By the late 1990s, most Serbian media outlets were in Milošević's pocket. Through the media, Milošević was assured not only that he would have the undivided attention of the electorate but also that his political adversaries would be denied the same. Serbia's state-run media consistently provided a sunny portrait of a country undivided and wholly dedicated to Milošević's cause. This media stranglehold would have a profound impact on the viability of the then still embryonic political opposition to Milošević.

With his hold on the media secure, Milošević tightened his grip on Serbia's political institutions. This was initially accomplished through legal maneuvering, most notably the repeated alteration of Serbia's electoral laws, which govern how parliamentarian seats are distributed in a multiparty system. Thanks to Milošević's finagling, from December 1990 to September 1997, Serbia boasted three different electoral systems: a two-round majoritarian electoral system, a proportional electoral system with nine large electoral units, and a proportional electoral system comprising twenty-nine electoral units of varying sizes. In each instance, alterations were made with an eye on consolidating Milošević's parliamentary majority. Thus, when crafting Serbia's first post-communist electoral system, Milošević's supporters opted for a majoritarian system known to harshly penalize small parties by inflating the proportion of seats dedicated to the nation's largest party—thereby allowing Milošević to transform his party's 1990 electoral winnings, turning 46.1 percent of the popular vote into 77.6 percent of seats in parliament, thus creating a manufactured majority.

Milošević's hold over parliament had several consequences. First and most importantly, it enabled him to command Serbia's government through the appointment of Serbia's prime minister. It also awarded Milošević control of the republic's judiciary. Because Serbia's parliament, not president, had the power to appoint and dismiss republican judges, power in parliament soon translated into the coercion of Serbia's "independent" judiciary.

In addition to political institutions, Milošević closed in on the police, army, and secret services. By placing allies in positions of authority, Milošević was able to root out even the most nascent of rivals. From 1991 to 1992 Milošević launched a purge on the army, personally discharging 130 generals and other high-ranking officers. Milošević loyalists were rewarded with prestigious promotions. In 1995, Serbia's parliament passed a law awarding Serbia's president the exclusive right to promote police officers and commanders. In an act of special decree, Serbia's president also assigned himself full control of Serbia's secret services, including the State Security Service (SDB).

The politicization of Serbia's police and secret services had a profound impact on Serbian politics in general and on Milošević's political opponents in particular. The Serbian leader relied on the police to disperse mass demonstrations, to badger and beat members of the opposition, as well as to covertly monitor his rivals. Through a nationwide eavesdropping system, the SDB could tap into the phone lines of the regime's political foes, tracking thousands of conversations per minute. Throughout the 1990s, police were regularly employed to stamp out demonstrations, intimidate the opposition, and even spawn rivalries among party leaders. Much later in his rule—as his popularity waned and that of his opponents soared—Milošević would use his stranglehold over the SDB to threaten, kidnap, and even assassinate his rivals.

The cumulative effect of Milošević's three foundations of power was the birth of a political system that was neither fully authoritarian nor wholly democratic but, instead, one that straddled the line between the two. From 1990 through 1996, Milošević relied on his unparalleled access to the republic's media, political institutions, and armed forces to consolidate the political capital he had amassed in the run-up to Communism's collapse. But however eager he was to disadvantage his political foes, he never went so far as to ensure that his hold on power would go uncontested. In this respect, allusions to Milošević "the dictator" have been overstated.

Yet, if the Serbia that emerged after Milošević's election in December 1990 was not a dictatorship, neither was it merely a flawed democracy. Rather, Milošević's Serbia embodied a specific breed of hybrid regime; Levitsky and Way (2002; 2010) have dubbed it "competitive authoritarianism." As a competitive authoritarian regime, Milošević's Serbia combined the procedures of democracy with the practice of authoritarianism. Unlike other hybrid regimes, it permitted more than the mere semblance of political competition. It not only allowed rival political parties to exist and staged regular multiparty elections, but its elections were genuinely competitive inasmuch as the outcome was not predetermined. As a result, Serbia's parliament was politically diverse, with critics of the regime at times comprising as much as 50 percent of parliament. Still, such critics were forced to compete on an unlevel playing field that was heavily skewed in Milošević's favor. The nature of such inequality would have a profound impact on both the dynamics of political competition and the types of political parties born within Serbia's confines.

Political Party Development

In Serbia's first postcommunist elections, held in December 1990, voters were asked to choose among more than fifty registered parties of various political stripes and shades. By any standard, Serbs had at their command a plethora of electoral options: communists and anti-communists; parties of the rural and urban tradition; nationalists and anti-nationalists; self-declared liberals, socialists, and monarchists. Yet the magnitude of political diversity masked the paucity of meaningful choice. Lacking membership, financial and material resources, and clearly defined political programs, the majority of Serbia's newly minted parties failed to enter parliament. Of the few that did, none succeeded in capturing the imagination of the Serbian electorate quite like Milošević's SPS. By election's end, Milošević had won the Serbian presidency and his party had captured 77 percent of Serbia's parliamentary seats. Its nearest opponent, Vuk Drašković's Serbian Renewal Movement (SPO), garnered just 8 percent of the seats in parliament.

That the SPS should have won so large a plurality of the votes cast in Serbia's first postcommunist elections was in some respects surprising. After all, throughout much of Eastern and Central Europe, communist-successor parties fared poorly in their nations' first free elections. Yet with Milošević at its helm, Serbia's Communist Party—the League of Communists of Serbia — successfully reinvented itself as the Socialist Party of Serbia in the summer of 1990. By capitalizing on its predecessor's unrivaled membership and republic-wide infrastructure, the SPS amassed more than 450,000 registered members—more than that of all other parties combined—and dozens of party offices scattered throughout the republic even before coming to office. During its decade in power, not once would the SPS win the majority of votes cast in Serbia's parliamentary elections. Still, its privileged position as the sole successor of Serbia's Communist Party and its willingness to form coalitions with parties from across the aisle—including members of the opposition—would award the SPS a privileged status in Serbia's political system, enabling Milošević to institutionalize, perpetuate, and consolidate his rule.

Yet if Serbia's party system centered on the unquestionable supremacy of one party (the SPS), it was *not* a one-party system. In each of the three parliamentary elections held between 1990 and 1996, the SPS competed against an array of political parties of which the Serbian Renewal Movement, the Serbian Radical Party, and the Democratic Party (DS) were the most formidable. In addition, several smaller parties also proved to be a mainstay of Serbian political life throughout the early and mid-1990s, among them the Civic Alliance of Serbia (GSS) and the Democratic Party of Serbia (DSS). With few exceptions, these parties fell into one of two camps: allies and opponents of the Milošević regime.

Allies of the Regime

Nearly all of Serbia's political parties considered allying with the regime at one time or another. For most, cooperation with the SPS proved fleeting—a temporary flirtation that ended in recrimination. For some, however, cooperation was a long-term enterprise that promised mutual benefits and only marginal conflict. Mira Marković's Yugoslav Left Party (JUL)[3] and Željko "Arkan" Ražnatović's Party of Serbian Unity (SSJ) were two such parties, but by far the largest and most significant was that of Vojislav Šešelj, the Serbian Radical Party (SRS).

Founded in February 1991, the SRS promoted an ultra-nationalist brand of politics that was extremist even by SPS standards. It was in fact Šešelj, the party's president, who infamously set Serbian sights on the Karlobag-Karlovac-Virovitica line, a term synonymous with the Greater Serbia project. Shortly after its formation, the SRS became an icon of Serbian nationalist sentiment and the party of choice for Serbia's far-right voters. In the elections of December 1992, it won an impressive 23 percent of the vote, thanks in part to having won Milošević's favor.

The SRS embraced a symbiotic relationship with the regime, offering what Pavlović (2001) calls "fake opposition" to the SPS. For much of the 1990s the two parties worked in tandem. The SRS provided support for the regime and its policies in return for positive media coverage, lucrative ministerial positions, and the regime's vocal stamp of approval.

For the regime, this marriage of convenience proved advantageous both inside and outside of Serbia. On the regional front, the SRS's paramilitary units executed the regime's dirty work in a war-ridden Bosnia; looting, raping, and killing with what is widely believed to have been the tacit approval of the SPS.[4] To the international community, Milošević could feign ignorance of atrocities committed in Serbia's name while portraying himself as a voice of moderation. Domestically, the SRS served both as a coalition partner as well as a "striking fist" to be used against the opposition.[5]

Yet, like much of Serbian politics, the SRS's support for the regime could not be taken for granted. When in 1993 the SPS placed its support behind the Vance-Owen Peace Plan—an act that Šešelj equated with the abandonment of Bosnia's Serbian minority—the relationship soured. Though fences between the SRS and SPS would eventually be mended, the parties' falling-out pointed to the complexity of the Serbian party system. Throughout the 1990s, parties' relationships to the regime were in constant flux, with parties shifting unpredictably from foe to (potential) ally.

Opponents of the Regime

Consistent and uncompromised opposition proved exceedingly difficult in Milošević's Serbia. Opposition parties were confronted with a barrage of regime-sponsored enticements aimed at luring its rivals into acquiescence. Though not always indifferent to the regime's menu of manipulation, several parties offered staunch and explicit opposition to the regime and its policies.

By far the most prominent of Serbia's opposition parties was the SPO. Formed in March 1990, the SPO was the brainchild of Vuk Drašković, Serbia's "King of the Streets." A novelist by profession, Drašković began his venture into public life as a staunch nationalist—writing such controversial works as *The Knife*, which personified the victimization of Serbs at the hands of Croat fascists and Muslims. As Drašković moved toward politics, he exploited his populist credentials and flamboyant persona to launch his party, the SPO. He was soon at the forefront of the anti-regime movement, winning 15.8 percent of the vote in Serbia's first postcommunist elections.

Throughout most of the 1990s, the SPO was a fervent critic of the Milošević regime, frequently calling for the Serbian president's resignation and the reconstitution of Serbian politics along democratic lines. The SPO launched Serbia's first massive demonstrations in Belgrade aimed at unseating Milošević. In return, Drašković received the brunt of the regime's aggression. In addition to being labeled "enemy of the state," he was harassed, arrested, and beaten by state authorities.

During one particularly protracted period of Drašković's detention, Serbia's second-largest opposition party—the DS—came into its own. Founded in February 1990 by thirteen of Serbia's most prolific intellectuals, the DS was in many respects the antithesis of Drašković's SPO. Where the SPO was forged on one man's magnetic personality, the DS attempted to bridge a disparate array of competing ideologies under a single roof. Where the SPO drove to the fringes of Serbian politics, the DS sought the middle ground. What the two parties shared was a deep-seated disdain of Milošević's politics. Like the SPO, the DS embarked on a campaign aimed at unseating the Milošević regime. Though initially confined to a subsidiary role within Serbia's opposition, the DS soon became a political force in its own right. By 1993, the DS had won almost 12 percent of the vote in Serbian parliamentary elections and was spearheading anti-Milošević rallies.

Although the DS and SPO lay at the forefront of the Serbian opposition, several smaller parties took on an equally active, if less prominent, role during the immediate postcommunist period. These included parties like Vojislav Koštunica's DSS and Vesna Pešić's GSS. Of these, only the DSS succeeded in entering parliament on its own, having received 5 percent of the vote in the parliamentary elections of December 1993. The rest, given their paltry membership base and meager public support, were forced to rely on electoral coalitions to win seats in parliament.

Polarized Party Politics

The polarization of Serbia's political scene—divided as it was by those for and against Milošević—ensured that the country's politics were deeply divisive for most of the 1990s. Far from embodying a unified Serbian electorate, Milošević oversaw a Serbia that was awash in protest and opposition. Mass rallies frequently brought tens of thousands of protesters to the streets of Serbia's capital. Opposition political parties and their leaders frequently claimed a vocal role within such protests—whether it was by calling for people to take to the streets or by joining protesters' calls for peace and democracy.

The first major protest emerged in the winter of 1991. In February, Milošević's increasingly blatant encroachment on free and independent media led Drašković to call for a protest rally. On 9 March, tens of thousands took to the streets demanding the liberalization of Serbia's media and the resignations of the head of Radio-Television Belgrade and the sitting minister of Interior. The peaceful protests were met by extreme force. An attack by the riot police left two dead; when this did not suffice in quelling the protest, the Yugoslav National Army finished the job by arresting Drašković and putting tanks on the streets.

In the days that followed, some 500,000 people, including high-ranking members of the DS, gathered in Belgrade's central square to voice their discontent. Cities and towns across Serbia came out in support of the protestors' efforts. But when only days later Milošević agreed to a series of moderate concessions, the first major opportunity to topple Milošević came and went.

The second large-scale protest took place in the spring of 1992, when tens of thousands of protestors took to the streets of Serbia's capital. Protestors called not only for an end to the war in Bosnia but also for the immediate cessation of Milošević's anti-democratic rule. At the helm of these protests was Drašković, who was joined by leading members of the DS and Serbian Liberal Party (SLS). All three parties complained of the speed with which the country's new constitution had been adopted and the regime's monopoly of the media. But it was Drašković who stole the show, calling on protesters to "liberate Serbia" from the stranglehold of Milošević's rule. "Serbia's enemies," he said, "are not in London, New York, Paris, or Moscow" but "right here in Belgrade."[6] In the days following the protests, the *New York Times* reported that the city was "awash with rumors" of Milošević's imminent resignation.[7]

The third large-scale protest took place in the aftermath of a violent assault on an opposition member of parliament. On 1 June 1993, Mihailo Marković, a representative of the SPO, was beaten unconscious in the halls of the Yugoslav parliament by a member of the SRS. SPO supporters responded with a peaceful protest that took a violent turn with the arrival of the regime's special police forces. Drašković and his wife were arrested and beaten. With Drašković in prison, opposition parties, including the GSS and SLS, organized protests calling for Drašković's release, which Milošević finally conceded to on 9 July.

The fourth—and most impressive—display of anti-regime protests was that spawned by Zajedno,[8] an alliance led by three of Serbia's leading democratic parties: the SPO, DS, and GSS. After having their municipal-level electoral victories overturned by the Milošević regime in November 1996, Zajedno oversaw the largest wave of anti-regime protests in Serbian history. For three months, Zajedno's three major opposition parties spearheaded mass demonstrations in cities across Serbia.

Zajedno's protests were not the first to bring together a wide array of opposition parties intent on unseating the regime and securing democracy. From 1990 through 1996, opposition parties formed or attempted to form a total of seven pro-democratic coalitions and electoral alliances (Table 7). This included the Associated Opposition of Serbia (AOS), whose goal it was to secure multiparty elections, a new democratic constitution, and an extended campaign period in the run-up to Serbia's first postcommunist elections. It also included the Democratic Movement of Serbia (DEPOS), a union of five opposition parties small and large that spoke out against the regime's electoral abuses and anti-democratic policies. Most significant, it included Zajedno, an alliance that brought all of Serbia's main opposition parties together for the first time.

An Imperfect Opposition

Despite their numerous efforts to upend Serbian politics, parties' opposition to Milošević was often superseded by interparty strife and rivalries, as well as

Table 7. Coalitions Attempted in Serbia from 1990 Through 1996

Coalition[a]	Year Formed	Duration	Members[b]
AOS	1990	6 months	DS, SPO, NRP, DF, LP, SSP
USDO	1991	3 months	SPO, SLS, ND–MS, DF
DEPOS	1992	18 months	SPO, SLS, ND–MS, SSS, DSS
DEKO	1992	a few days	SPO, SLS, ND–MS, SSS, DSS, DS, GSS, SD
DEPOS II	1993	3 months	SPO, ND, GSS
DA	1995	4 months	DS, DSS, SLS, SNS
Zajedno	1996	5 months	SPO, DS, GSS

Source: Adapted from Spoerri 2008: 75.
[a] Associated Opposition of Serbia (AOS), Democratic Alternative (DA), Democratic Coalition (DEKO), Democratic Movement of Serbia (DEPOS), Democratic Opposition of Serbia (DOS), United Serbian Democratic Opposition (USO), Zajedno (Together).
[b] Civic Alliance of Serbia (GSS), Democratic Forum (DF), Democratic Party (DS), Democratic Party of Serbia (DSS), Liberal Party (LP), National Radical Party (NRP), New Democracy (ND), New Democracy–Movement for Serbia (ND–MS), Serbian Congressional Party (SNS), Serbian Renewal Movement (SPO), Serbian St. Sava Party (SSP), Serbian Peasant's Party (SSS).

direct efforts on the part of the regime to co-opt and de-legitimize opposition forces. As a result, political analysts have long been wary of ascribing too much importance to Serbia's troubled opposition. Pavlović (2001: 1), for example, calls Serbia's opposition in the 1990s "the worst in Europe." Similarly, Goati (2001: 52) laments that "Serbia's opposition acted in a disunited manner, expending more energy in mutual conflicts than in the struggle against the SPS and the ruling order."

The foremost reason parties were susceptible to such conflicts lay in the personalized nature of Serbian politics. When Serbia's party system came to fruition in 1990, many parties distinguished themselves not by their programmatic profiles but by the personalities of their leaders. Charisma and personal ambition often took precedence over policy and substance. Serbia's parties were also institutionally weak—low on active members as well as loyal voters. While the SPS boasted a republic-wide infrastructure, the opposition's reach was overwhelmingly confined to Serbia's capital and major city centers.[9] Parties' institutional and organizational underdevelopment further reinforced their dependence on their leaders, who determined everything from the formation of electoral alliances to positions on Serbia's national question and attitudes toward the Milošević regime.

One of the most damaging repercussions of Serbia's personalized politics was parties' inability to develop and hone their own party cadre. Rather than capitalize on building talent within the party, "leaders used and discarded individuals based almost exclusively on loyalty to themselves" (Kesić 2005: 101). This offered ambitious party members one of two options: to oust a sitting leader by way of an intraparty coup or to start their own parties. Because the former was exceedingly difficult,[10] almost all of Serbia's opposition parties fractured during the period from 1990 to 1996 (Table 8).

Personalized politics affected more than parties' internal makeup, however. It also influenced their ability to form and maintain a united front against the regime. All too often, vanity, rather than substance, lay at the heart of interparty strife. Personal jealousies, vendettas, and rivalry often made cooperation among the various opposition parties unattainable or tenuous, which invariably worked to Milošević's advantage. Though Milošević's Machiavellian maneuverings no doubt contributed to parties' infighting,[11] party leaders' own inability to overcome their personal differences left parties unable to mount a credible threat to the SPS and reflected poorly on the alternative they offered voters. The state-run media had merely to draw attention to party leaders' own divisive and derogatory statements to expose the perils of an opposition-led government.

Infighting among Serbia's fledgling opposition benefited the regime in more ways than one. Whereas in other postcommunist countries such ills

Table 8. Political Party Fragmentation 1990–1996

Party	Offshoot	Year	Leader
DS	Serbian Liberal Party (SLS)	1990	N. Milošević
	Democratic Party of Serbia (DSS)	1992	V. Koštunica
	Democratic Center (DC)	1994[a]	D. Mićunović
SPO	Serbian People's Party	1994	S. Ratikić
SRS	Radical Party of Nikola Pasic	1995	J. Glamočanin
GSS	Serbian Democratic Union (SDU)	1996	Z. Korać

Source: Adapted from Orlović 2008: 452.
[a] Although the DC was not officially founded until 1996, Mićunović and his supporters left the party in 1994.

were taken to legitimate—indeed, necessitate—foreign aid, in Serbia they gave license to aid's absence. Indeed, the plight of Serbia's opposition was exploited not as evidence of aid's necessity but as a rallying cry for those in the United States and Europe who advocated doing nothing for Serbia's democrats.

The Absence of Aid

The story of foreign aid to Serbia begins in the run-up to what Carothers (1999: 40) calls the "mushrooming" of democracy assistance across the globe. It was during the months immediately preceding Communism's collapse that NED and other donor organizations first familiarized themselves with Vuk Drašković.[12] Relying on contacts forged in Western Europe and North America, prospective donors met with the region's future opinion makers: civic activists, academics, cultural icons, and up-and-coming politicians. Thus, when in 1990 Yugoslavia's six constituent republics called for foundational elections, donors explored their options. With NED funding, the American party institutes, NDI and IRI, monitored the region's first elections held in Croatia and Slovenia in the spring of 1990.[13] During their stay, they also met with political party members, including those in Serbia. What they found did not bode well for the future of Yugoslavia's union.

Internally divided and fluent in nationalist rhetoric, the future party leaders with whom donors met seemed more concerned with the ills of the Yugoslav Federation and the wrongs of Communism than in forming substantive political parties that spoke to Yugoslavs' concerns. Wary of the impending dissolution of the multiethnic state, NDI focused its efforts on lowering the tensions between opinion makers throughout the federation. In October 1990, the institute organized a conference in Cavtat, Croatia, titled "Democratic Governance in Multi-Ethnic States."[14] In what organizers now label as a "naïve" effort, the conference assembled fifty political party members,[15] academics, and civic activists from across Yugoslavia to engage in discussions with foreign experts boasting firsthand experience in multiethnic governance. It would be the last time Yugoslav officials would share the same table.

IRI representatives, by contrast, planned to develop a full-fledged democratic assistance program like those then being crafted in Romania and Bulgaria. The program officer charged with IRI's Yugoslav programs at the time launched a series of trainings with party members throughout the country, including Serbia. She and other party trainers traveled to and from Yugoslavia offering technical assistance, advice, and party training manuals. On several occasions, IRI even brought Yugoslav party members abroad to receive additional training. According to the IRI program officer for Serbia, "If the program had developed, it could have moved to the form where we were printing posters to offering cars and office equipment."[16] IRI might even "have sent in a campaign staff force that would have advised on strategy and offered day-to-day tactical advice."[17] But it did not. By the spring of 1992, the escalation of violence in Bosnia and Serbia's increasingly pernicious role in it prompted the United States and its European allies to break ties with Milošević's Serbia. Serbia's fledgling democrats would not be spared.

On 30 May 1992, the United Nations Security Council adopted Resolution 757, imposing comprehensive sanctions—economic, financial, diplomatic, and cultural—on Serbia and its Yugoslav counterpart, Montenegro, for the escalating violence in Bosnia. Governments in North America and Western Europe chose to interpret the sanctions in their strictest sense. In the weeks leading to the UN's pronouncement, American and European ambassadors and diplomatic staff were recalled, as was the European Commission's mission to Belgrade. At the same time, countries' import and export relations with the Federal Republic of Yugoslavia ended and financial sanctions were imposed. Even relations of a seemingly innocuous nature were restricted: Yugoslav athletes were banned from competing in the 1992 Olympics and the Yugoslav soccer team was denied its place in the European football championships.

Countries chose to make a similar decision regarding democracy assistance. As a political officer then working for the Dutch Embassy in Serbia explained, "It wasn't clear at the time whether the sanctions permitted the provision of support to [opposition] groups within Serbia."[18] What was clear, however, was that countries in both Western Europe and North America would opt to interpret international sanctions in a very restrictive way. Initially, at least, this meant that Western democracy aid—including political party aid—drew to a halt (Figure 1).

In early 1992, governments closed whatever aid agencies were operating in Belgrade. The few NGOs providing support to democratic actors in Serbia responded similarly. Thus, despite aid providers' belief that aid could be helpful for Serbian democrats, stringent regulations were imposed on where IRI and NDI could and could not spend money. In 1992, the U.S. party institutes froze their Serbia programs, opting to work only in Slovenia and Croatia. And so, just as Milošević was ratcheting up pressure inside and outside of Serbia, the United States and the European Union turned their backs on the domestic

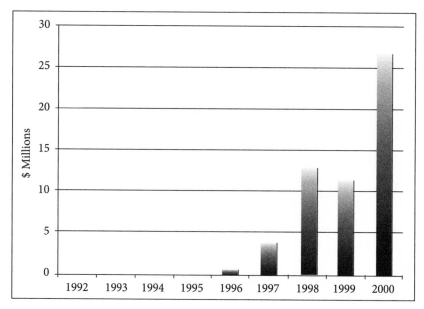

Figure 1. U.S. Assistance to the Federal Republic of Yugoslavia
Note: SEED aid includes humanitarian, democracy, and economic assistance. These figures apply to aid provided to the FRY, which included both Serbia and Montenegro throughout this period.
Source: SEED reports, 1992–2000.

opposition to Milošević. In the process, they chose to eliminate aid precisely when party assistance could have made its greatest impact in Serbia by helping to level Serbia's political playing field in the middle of Serbia's transition to authoritarianism.

Perhaps the first to suffer as a consequence of the international "freeze" was Milan Panić, a Serbian-born American whose ventures into the pharmaceutical industry had earned him millions. In 1992, Panić was appointed to the position of Yugoslav prime minister. As prime minister, Panić became a vocal opponent of the wars then ongoing in Bosnia and Croatia. During his inaugural address, he called not only for peace in Bosnia but also for the departure of all military and paramilitary units from neighboring lands. During his brief stint as prime minister, he even became Serbia's first postcommunist official to meet with Albanian leaders in Kosovo. But perhaps his most spectacular moment came at a London peace conference in 1992, when he famously "elbowed Milošević aside" to introduce his own twelve-point plan to end the Balkan wars—a plan that included explicit reference to Serbia's recognition of Bosnian and Croatian independence (Hockenos 2003: 159). In fact, an article in the *New York Times* lauded Panić for having "consistently attacked Mr. Milošević and other militant Serbian nationalists" with his calls "for peace and compromise solutions to the war in Bosnia and the greater Yugoslav crisis."[19]

As an increasingly vocal regime critic, Panić was also a major proponent of democracy assistance. In late 1992, he approached international decision makers pleading for an exemption of UN sanctions to allow for democracy assistance—and, in particular, political party assistance. He was left "bitterly disappointed."[20] Panić's request that U.S. and European authorities "provide all of Yugoslavia's political parties with a television capability equal to that of Serbia's ruling regime" fell on deaf ears.[21] At the time, British authorities in particular were averse to any notion of supporting Serbia's nascent democratic opposition. According to Douglas Schoen, Panić's pollster who would go on to work for President Bill Clinton, "The supine response of the West would emerge as a major obstacle to our effort to bring about regime change" (Schoen 2007: 110). Indeed, the intense media blockade on Panić's candidacy and his vilification by Milošević loyalists ensured that Panić won 32 percent of the vote in presidential elections held later that year—a decent showing but far from the 53 percent brought in by Milošević.

The decision to deny Panić such assistance was not without controversy. In the United States, a small band of senators, spearheaded by Republican Senator Richard Lugar of Indiana, were alarmed by the administration's refusal to assist Serbian democrats and they mounted a collective appeal for democracy aid. For Lugar in particular, Panić's defeat was a rebuke of the Clinton administration's approach to the Serbian opposition. In October 1993, Lugar underscored such doubts in a letter to then Secretary of State Warren Christopher[22] in which he implored the United States to "interpret UN sanctions on Serbia in ways that will promote more equitable participation in the Serbian elections by pro-democratic candidates and parties," and "exempt from international sanctions those U.S.-origin proposals intended to promote democracy in that beleaguered country."[23] Lugar's sentiments were shared by members of the U.S. Foreign Relations Committee. In 1993, the Committee voted *unanimously* to exempt democratic assistance to Serbia from UN sanctions.

Despite the support of the Foreign Relations Committee, however, aid was not forthcoming. For most working in the aid industry and Western governments, the thought of assisting opposition groups—even those opposed to Milošević—was simply unpalatable. According to Robert Benjamin, director of NDI's Central and Eastern Europe programs, NDI assistance to Serbian parties simply wasn't seen to be a possibility in the mid-1990s; in fact, there was no discussion about Serbia's democracy whatsoever.[24]

Still, some individuals did want to help. One such individual was Paul McCarthy, a senior program officer for NED. As one of the few supporters of democracy aid to Serbia, McCarthy says he was both a donor and an advocate. He "believed that unless you looked at the internal situation in Serbia, the whole region would be lost."[25] But, as he himself admits, that was not a popular position to take in the early and mid-1990s. To the contrary, as the decade unfolded, the attention of the United States and Western Europe increasingly came to rest on neighboring Bosnia—where reports of rape camps and genocide were being called the worst atrocities since the Holocaust.

One unfortunate consequence of the international community's (belated) concern for the Bosnian war was that it came at the expense of Serbia's domestic democratic opposition. Thus when in early 1996 voices in USAID began suggesting that the American aid agency start focusing on Serbia, it quickly became apparent that not everyone wanted to touch Serbia at the time.[26] To the contrary, no one in the State Department was willing to give the green light for providing democracy aid to Serbia—the perceived aggressor in the Bosnian conflict. Yet for those advocating aid to Serbia, this refusal was "disturbing," not simply because of what it meant for Serbian democracy, but "because the problems in Bosnia were being driven from Serbia."[27] Senator Lugar shared such concerns.

In a 1996 opinion piece published in the *Washington Times*, Lugar chastened U.S. policy makers for refusing to "provide material support to moderate and pro-democratic forces in Serbia," opting instead "for timidity and distance."[28] In yet another letter sent to then Secretary of State Warren Christopher in March 1996, Lugar urged the administration "to take an immediate, vigorous and concerted initiative to support the independent sector in the Federal Republic of Yugoslavia, particularly in Serbia."[29] He complained that his government had "deferred to the international sanctions regime by rejecting or delaying proposals for democratic programs of the National Endowment for Democracy (NED) and other pro-democracy organizations proposing to work with indigenous groups striving for an open society."[30] This was all the more pressing because "the leaders of the independent sector in Serbia and Montenegro have made know[n] their strong desire for U.S.

support and have been greatly discouraged and disappointed by repeated U.S. refusals to assist them. They cannot understand why we continue to deny them vital support."[31]

Lugar's efforts were to little avail. Foreign diplomats and special envoys ultimately opted *not* to engage Serbia's opposition parties and politicians, preferring instead to deal exclusively with Milošević.

Engaging Milošević, at the Opposition's Expense

Throughout the 1990s, high-level officials—including Secretary of State Madeleine Albright and President Bill Clinton—met directly with Milošević, whether to negotiate a peace in Bosnia or, later, to thwart the impending NATO bombing of Serbia. Unlike Milošević, however, leaders from major opposition parties like the SPO or DS were refused contact with senior government officials. In his memoirs, the late U.S. diplomat Richard Holbrooke (1999: 358) acknowledged that neither the United States sent no senior officials to Belgrade to bolster the opposition's profile. In his words, "Washington missed a change to affect events; except for one ineffectual trip to Washington, Zajedno had no contact with senior American government officials" (Holbrooke 1999: 345). But Washington was not alone. Neither the United States nor the EU did anything to bolster the prospects of opposition victories in the aftermath of the 1996 local-level elections, and the EU in particular took steps that ultimately worked against the opposition's interests.

In the winter of 1996–1997, Serbia's opposition staged a stunning electoral upset in local elections across the country. Having banded together under the unified mantel of Zajedno, Serbia's opposition shocked Milošević and the world, by staging municipal victories in cities and towns across Serbia—including Belgrade, Niš, and Novi Sad. When state authorities subsequently annulled the opposition's victories and demanded that elections be reheld, students and disaffected citizens took the streets, demanding that the original electoral results be reinstated. For weeks, protestors endured freezing temperatures to insist that democratic electoral results be respected. Yet rather than support Serbia's democrats in realizing their lawfully won electoral mandate, the international community left them in the cold.

Particularly disturbing, from the perspective of the opposition, was the EU's decision on 22 November 1996 to release a statement echoing Milošević's calls for a third round of local elections—despite Zajedno's claims to have won

major victories. While the European Council's presidency urged Serbia's authorities to investigate the opposition's complaints of electoral irregularities,
it seemed to side with the regime by requesting electoral re-runs, which the
opposition opposed. The statement won a furious reply from the Zajedno
leadership.[32] Nor was Zajedno amused when on what was the twenty-third
day of Zajedno's mass protests, Italy's foreign minister Lamberto Dini publicly
dismissed the opposition's demand for the reinstatement of Zajedno victories,
arguing that such a result was simply "not in the cards."[33] In fact, the *Los Angeles Times* reported that Serbian opposition leaders "were coming under increasing pressure from Western mediators to accept new elections, which
would mean abandoning their principal goal—recognition of the victories
they already obtained."[34] Though European officials would ultimately back
away from such positions, their seeming indifference caused considerable resentment among leading members of the Zajedno coalition.[35] Goran Svilanović, a minister of foreign affairs in post-Milošević Yugoslavia, dubs it "a
cold shower."[36]

Such actions would feed into the prevailing narrative among members of
Serbia's democratic opposition that Western powers were not in fact interested in working for the best interests of Serbian democracy. Indeed in a 2001
article, Svetozar Stojanović (2001), a longtime dissident and staunch Milošević
critic, opined that "The West long helped Milošević to remain in power." The
sentiment was shared by many in Serbia. For years, Serbian politicians and
opinion makers lambasted the United States and the EU for supporting Milošević. Politicians, including Vesna Pešić and Goran Svilanović, argue that
until the very late 1990s, the United States and the EU legitimized Milošević's
rule while undermining theirs.

Understanding Aid's Absence

There were several reasons why the major powers for so long refused to lend
their support to Serbia's political opposition. The first has already been hinted
at. When war broke out in Bosnia in the summer of 1992, it sparked a humanitarian disaster the likes of which Europe had not witnessed since World War
II. As news of atrocities surfaced, the international aid community's attention
came to lie on Bosnia, often at the expense of Serbia. As USAID's Europe and
Eurasia Bureau Director explains, USAID "didn't do too much in Serbia in the
early 1990s because the big issue of course was Bosnia."[37] Aid organizations,

he says, "didn't pay too much attention to Serbia" because the major issue for them "was what they [the Serbs] were doing in Bosnia rather than what they were doing at home."[38] Yet, as another former USAID employee notes, "If you had followed the region, you couldn't help but see that Serbia was there too. No one was paying attention to Serbia."[39]

This oversight was compounded when one took the rest of postcommunist Europe into consideration. According to the last U.S. ambassador to Yugoslavia, Warren Zimmermann (1996: 46), "U.S. policy in Eastern Europe was heavily focused on Poland and Hungary, countries that were moving on the reform path faster than Yugoslavia and without the baggage of divisive nationalism. Yugoslavia would be seen as a poor risk and therefore a low priority." Indeed, the aid community had its hands full dealing not only with Bosnia but also with the newly democratic countries of Central and Eastern Europe. Explains a USAID employee working on the Balkans at the time, after the fall of the Berlin Wall, "We were so overwhelmed with work. A new country was popping up every few months . . . [USAID] needed to move into all these new places, it was hard enough to move contracts and money, let alone hiring, offices, and getting on the ground." In the early 1990s, USAID had only a handful of employees working in its newly founded democracy office. Serbia, she says, just "wasn't a priority. There was so much to do for all the other countries . . . no one had the energy."

Nor did they have the will. As news spread of ethnic cleansing, concentration camps, mass rapes, and genocide, the United States and its European allies grew increasingly wary of Serbia. By the early 1990s, Serbia had become a pariah state. The thought of aiding forces within Serbia—however well intentioned those forces may have been—was viewed as distasteful. A former representative of NDI explained, "Serbia had this terrible reputation. The perception was that it was like going into Apartheid South Africa: as long as that regime existed, they wouldn't go into it."[40] Those promoting aid to Serbia faced an uphill battle. As one former democracy promoter recalls, "Most people in Washington wanted to build a wall around Serbia and let them rot, to tell you the truth. People who were outraged by perceived war crimes . . . hated the idea of cultivating Serbia."[41] Indeed, as early advocates of foreign aid soon came to learn, it was not a given that people wanted to support change in Serbia.

It was also not a given that they believed that change was possible. David Owen (1997: 1-3), coauthor of the failed Vance-Owen Peace Plan, begins his tellingly entitled memoir, *Balkan Odyssey*, with the following words: "Nothing is simple in the Balkans. . . . History points to a tradition in the Balkans of a readiness to solve disputes by the taking up of arms and acceptance of the forceful or even negotiated movement of people as the consequence of war." With these words, Owen gave voice to a perspective then shared by many policy makers as they set their sights on the looming crisis in the former Yugoslavia. When in 1991 the multiethnic federation erupted in violence, policy makers justified a course of inaction on Serbia—and the Balkans more generally—through reference to irresolvable ancient hatreds.

The ancient-hatreds theory had important implications for democracy aid. Aid, after all, could bear little fruit in a region where good and bad knew no distinction and violence was a normal way of life. The people of the Western Balkans were thus best left to their own devices. This perception was particularly prominent in France and the United Kingdom, where policy makers opposed even the most modest forms of intervention. But it was also prevalent in the United States, where Robert D. Kaplan's book *Balkan Ghosts: A Journey Through History*—which preceded Owen's memoir and lay the foundations for the ancient-hatreds thesis—shaped popular opinion, including that of President Clinton.[42]

The vision of the Balkans as a primordial and an exotic terrain applied not only to the outbreak of conflict but also to the peoples of the former Yugoslavia, many of whom, Owen (1997: 1) maintained, "were literally strangers to the truth." Many believed that the Balkans was simply not ready for democracy. As Owen (1997: 2) lamented, leaders of the Balkans "had no experience in democracy." Their opinions, he wrote, had been formed in a society "where truth was valued far, far less than in the Western democracies" (Owen 1997: 2). The patronizing attitudes of many foreign policy makers made democracy assistance to Serbia a moot topic.

Many donors also questioned whether parties wished to receive foreign aid. IRI's efforts were repeatedly thwarted during its early ventures into Yugoslavia, in part because of the rising tide of authoritarianism but mostly because of parties' fear of being unduly stigmatized by their associations with the United States. A former IRI program officer explains, "The fear coupled with the difficult circumstances of the Serbian opposition across the board made our work very difficult. It made it such that they didn't feel themselves in a position to accept our assistance."[43] Indeed, some donors believed parties themselves were unwilling to accept foreign support for fear of being branded traitors and lackeys. Gerald Hyman, the former director of USAID's Democracy and Governance Office, for example, believes support from the United States and Europe "would have been the kiss of death" for Serbia's opposition.[44]

Yet perhaps the chief reason aid to Serbia's democratic opposition was not forthcoming lay in the West's reticence to fully discredit Milošević. Throughout much of the 1990s, foreign policy makers viewed Milošević as a stable—if unsavory—interlocutor. Most important, he was the only figure deemed capable of following through on his political commitments, particularly as concerned Serbia's Bosnian Serb neighbors. As the CIA explained, there was "no good and politically viable alternative" to Milošević—whatever his faults, he was "the only Serb leader the West can deal with and the only one capable of delivering a comprehensive solution."[45] Richard Holbrooke—the celebrated diplomat lauded for having ended the war in Bosnia—believed Milošević was "key" to achieving regional stability, and he brazenly upheld "a strategy of dealing solely with Milošević."[46]

For the leaders of Serbia's democratic opposition, such sentiments meant not only that foreign officials had little confidence in the opposition's ability to mount a meaningful challenge to Milošević, but also that they saw little advantage in supporting opposition parties' efforts to achieve such a victory. To the contrary, regime change would likely have led to greater uncertainty— something the international community was keen to avoid.

Matters were considerably complicated by the troubled state of Serbia's democratic opposition. Riddled with ego-driven leaders and extravagant personalities, Serbian parties were not only unnerving but also downright scary. In interviews with U.S. and European policy makers and aid providers, Vuk Drašković—the leader of Serbia's democratic opposition—was invariably ridiculed as "spooky," "nuts," "erratic," and a "prima donna." Foreign critics of Serbia's opposition parties tended to fall into one of two camps: According to one view, Milošević's foes were more "rabidly nationalistic" than Milošević himself and thus posed a far greater threat to Yugoslav security.[47] The second view held that Serbian parties were incompetent and thus ultimately unreliable. A Dutch diplomat says, "The consensus at the time was that the opposition was weak and divided. They didn't know what they wanted."[48] Indeed, for much of the 1990s the world was convinced of the ineptitude and even danger of the Serbian opposition. The consequence of such sentiments was that aid to Serbian parties remained a moot topic. As a result, Serbia's opposition went unaided, and Milošević's power structure unhindered. Not only were the results of this policy disastrous but so was the logic behind it.

A Troubled Rationale for Inaction

Many reasons accounted for party aid's absence in Milošević's Serbia. Each was as tragic as it was misinformed. Ultimately, however, the decision not to use democracy aid to the benefit of Serbian democrats was dictated not by the best interests of Serbian democracy but by larger foreign policy goals. For most of the 1990s, those goals did not coincide with Milošević's ouster.

Among the most ludicrous of the reasons legitimizing inaction was the ancient-hatreds thesis. As early as 1989, the CIA located the source of Yugoslavia's rupture not in ancient animosities or cultural deficits but in the inability of Yugoslav leaders to stem growing nationalism, political divisions, and economic deterioration.[49] For aid providers, too, it was clear that Serbia (and for that matter, the region) was not uniquely ill equipped for democratic rule. Despite the tremendous ferment in the region, aid providers insist that Serbia "was not a totally barren environment. Some types of pluralism were developing." Many practitioners with firsthand experience in Serbia believed democracy aid could have a real future in the country. After all, if ancient hatreds had not stood in the way of democracy's development throughout the nation-states of Western Europe, there was little reason to assume they would in Eastern Europe.

Equally unsound was the notion that the aid community could not afford to support Serbian parties amid the burgeoning landscape of needy recipients in postcommunist Europe. Though attention may well have lain elsewhere, it is difficult to argue that a modest aid effort could not have been forthcoming, in which party aid may have played a small role. Certainly, it could not have been for lack of funds. Indeed, though it is true that the fall of Communism was met by an increase in demand for democracy assistance, it is also true that such demand was met by an increase in supply. In 1989, the United States established the Support for East European Democracy (SEED) program, which devoted approximately $300 million a year to U.S. efforts aimed at furthering democracy in postcommunist Europe. Carothers (1999: 41) estimates that the United States spent close to $1 billion on democracy-related projects in Central and Eastern Europe and the former Soviet Union throughout this same period. That year also marked the emergence of a host of new European democracy foundations, with cumulative expenditures roughly mirroring those of their American counterparts. Given such sizeable funds, it is hard to imagine that even modest resources could not have been reserved for Serbia's parties.

Nor is it likely that Serbia's opposition would have spurned foreign efforts to provide democracy assistance. In a 1996 letter to U.S. Secretary of State Warren Christopher, Senator Richard Lugar of Indiana noted that anti-Milošević groups had repeatedly come forward, urging American policy makers to provide them with aid. Indeed, in their early forays to Serbia, aid providers found Serbian parties to be very willing to receive foreign support. According to one NDI senior program officer, though they lacked "a well thought through idea of what they needed," parties offered "fairly positive reactions" when discussing the prospect of assistance.[50] NED program officers who traveled to the region reached a similar conclusion.[51] Although Serbian politicians were more reticent to walk into a relationship than were individuals in the other Yugoslav republics, they were clearly willing to engage in substantive discussions regarding the forms of assistance that might be provided.

Certainly, this is the sentiment offered by most Serbian party leaders. Drašković, for example, says he "demanded support from Western states and from right-wing oriented parties."[52] He insists he was not afraid of the regime's attempts to discredit him as a foreign-funded lackey and repeatedly sought out foreign assistance. Evidence lends credence to Drašković's claims. In a public statement made on a trip to London in 1993, Drašković could not have been clearer, stating, "I want concrete support." His party, he said, was "the biggest opposition group in Serbia, and the only property we have is one car. If we could under such circumstances get—as we got in the last election—1.2 million votes, only 100,000 less than Milošević's party who have faxes and control the television, then we must be the eighth wonder of the world."[53] The same was true for presidential candidate Milan Panić. When in late 1992 Panić requested that foreign policy makers support the opposition's efforts to create an open media, he was left "bitterly disappointed."[54] Kesić (2005: 99) writes that "the complete absence of support from the United States and the relative indifference shown by the international community crushed the spirit of Serbia's opposition movement." The notion that Serbia's opposition would have rebuffed foreign efforts to provide aid is thus untenable.

Also untenable is the notion of Milošević's presumed indispensability for Yugoslav peace. Foreign policy makers' decision to sidestep Serbia's opposition and to communicate solely with Milošević did little to raise the profile of the Serbian opposition in the eyes of the Serbian public. Ironically, it may have helped garner domestic support for Milošević within Serbia, given that it bolstered his international prestige. According to Mihailo Marković of the SPO, foreign policy makers simply "never understood that the man who set Yugo-slavia on fire will never put the fire out, that the lifeblood of the Serbian gov-ernment is war" (as quoted in Thomas 1999: 159). Daniel Serwer of the United States Institute of Peace (USIP) agrees. He believes that the mastermind of U.S. policy toward Serbia at the time—Richard Holbrooke—"never under-stood the degree to which his meetings with Milošević helped to give Mi-lošević legitimacy" within Serbia.[55] Such opinions are shared by many in Serbia. As Pešić laments, "The U.S. was more on the strong side."[56]

Also problematic were concerns regarding the nationalism and ineptitude of Serbia's opposition. Though many parties may have espoused greater na-tionalism than their postcommunist colleagues in Central and Eastern Eu-rope, several explicitly denounced nationalist rhetoric and made pro-peace policies the centerpieces of their platforms.[57] None of these parties, however, received assistance from the democracy aid community. And although it is true that anti-Milošević parties suffered numerous faults, their ills were largely reminiscent of those witnessed elsewhere in the postcommunist space. Parties with shallow membership, poor organizational development, weak partisan identities, and personality-based profiles were (and remain) the norm throughout Central and Eastern Europe. Unlike in Serbia, however, these qualms failed to deter aid providers. In fact, it was their very presence that justified aid's onset throughout the region—after all, had such parties not suf-fered from flaws, they would not have required aid.

Moreover, many of the ills afflicting political party life in Serbia were caused as much by party leaders' failures as they were by Milošević's duplicity. Milošević "proved highly adept at splitting his opposition forces and using individual opposition leaders for his own political purposes" (Cohen 2001: 111). Through Machiavellian incentives and backdoor deal making, Milošević repeatedly succeeded in sowing intraparty strife and driving a wedge between competing opposition forces (Antonić 2002: 169). Although aid may not have fully redressed such issues, it may well have helped parties provide more co-herent opposition against the Serbian president. The failure to foresee aid's potential benefits would be something the aid community would soon come to regret.

A Legacy of Missed Opportunities

This chapter has argued that there were several major opportunities that the international community could have exploited to support democratic alternatives to Milošević throughout the early and mid-1990s. These opportunities presented a real chance for the Western aid providers to support political parties and candidates committed to a peaceful, democratic future for their country. Ultimately, however, they went unexploited.

The first such opportunity was witnessed in March 1991, when Milošević forces killed two protesters and sent army tanks into the streets of Belgrade . In the days that followed, demonstrations sprang up across Serbia, as students, politicians, and disgruntled citizens rose up to protest the declining standard of living in Serbia and Milošević's increasingly monopolization of state media. Rather than reach out to these groups, however, and support nascent forms of resistance, aid providers chose to keep their distance, dismissing Serbia's opposition as unpalatable and nationalistic.

The second opportunity came in 1992, in the run-up to the presidential elections featuring Milan Panić. By no means a perfect candidate, Panić was avowedly pro-peace and a strong proponent of a more democratic Serbia.[58] Moreover, he had much of the Serbian opposition united behind his candidacy. Yet despite his repeated appeals to U.S. foreign policy makers for further aid to Serbia's independent media and to civil and political society, his efforts were rebuffed. Panić ultimately lost the elections of 1992. It would be another eight years before Milošević himself would reappear on an electoral ballot.

The third major opportunity to support democracy in Serbia came in late 1996, with the roll-out of protests across Serbia, inspired by Milošević's brazen electoral theft of local-level victories staged by the Zajedno alliance. For months, Milošević's opponents braved winter-weather conditions to come to the streets and demand that their votes be respected. Yet Zajedno received no support from Western donors and was initially at least, even encouraged to back off from its allegations of electoral theft.

In the absence of foreign assistance, Serbia's nascent democratic opposition was forced to contend with Milošević's authoritarianism on its own. Without external resources, his opponents were outspent and out-strategized by the regime and its allies. This unlevel playing field greatly diminished the odds of unseating Milošević through democratic means—an unfortunate outcome that was not lost on everyone in the international community.

CHAPTER THREE

Preparing for Regime Change, 1997–2000

For years after Milošević's ascent to power, foreign leaders refused to intervene in Serbia on democracy's behalf—opting instead to allow Serbia's anti-Milošević opposition to go unaided. Opposition parties were seen as too nationalistic and too flawed to warrant support, and Milošević was seen as too strong and too crucial for regional peace. Such excuses ceased to convince in the aftermath of the Kosovo war. Exploiting Milošević's electoral gamble to hold early presidential elections in September 2000, the transatlantic community undertook a multipronged effort to help Serbia's democratic forces unseat Milošević.

With foreign assistance, Serbia's opposition ran a "grueling" campaign, knocking on doors, giving speeches, and inundating public spaces with their promotional materials (ICG 2000a). On 24 September 2000, Serbia's opposition achieved a stunning breakthrough, winning 51.7 percent of the federal vote—enough to avoid a second-round run-off, which would have pitted Milošević against the opposition-backed Vojislav Koštunica. When Milošević cronies denied the scope of Koštunica's victory, a wave of nonviolent resistance swept across Serbia. A general strike featuring Serbia's coal miners—once steadfast Milošević loyalists—was soon followed by mass public protests, during which citizens in cities and towns small and large took to the streets (Bujošević and Radovanović 2001).[1] On 5 October 2000, half a million protesters flocked to the steps of the Yugoslav parliament, united in their demand for Milošević's resignation. Twenty-four hours later, Milošević had conceded defeat.

The ouster of Milošević represented a new direction for democracy aid. For the first time in history, aid would be used in concert with high-level diplomacy, targeted sanctions, and covert operations to oust a sitting head of state. In their effort to promote regime change, foreign governments would look to democracy assistance to achieve their goal. In the process, they would help secure a democratic opening in Serbia that would build a path toward eventual EU membership. But the entanglement of democracy aid with the promotion of regime change would also set into motion a controversial legacy that would later be used to legitimize the persecution of democracy aid and aid providers in other authoritarian states.

This chapter shines a light on the supportive role aid to political parties played in contributing to Milošević's ouster. As shall be seen, external assistance helped pay for opposition parties' office rentals, cell phones, fax machines, computers, tour buses, and promotional materials, including billboards and commercials featuring the opposition and its supporters. Through creative funding mechanisms, innovative training programs, and the help of Serbia's neighbors, aid providers channeled funds from neighboring states, diplomatic missions, and even airline offices. Top-of-the-line pollsters helped Serbia's opposition test its campaign rhetoric and fine-tune its public messages. Foreign-funded trainers taught party members to knock on doors, target potential voters, and identify electoral fraud. All of this contributed to the opposition's victory in October 2000.

Yet for all of its importance, the impact of foreign assistance on Milošević's ouster has often been overstated. The following pages make the case for a more modest appraisal of aid's success, one that recognizes its strengths as well as its weaknesses. As shall be seen, donors made several savvy moves that helped support Serbia's democratic opposition. Material assistance helped parties and civil society organizations launch professional, nationwide campaigns. Foreign-funded election monitors helped ensure that opposition leaders had tangible proof of Milošević's electoral fraud. And the backing of Koštunica by the United States and the EU helped propel into the presidency the only candidate capable of defeating Milošević.

Yet foreign initiatives also left much to be desired. A costly endeavor to build a regional network of independent media towers aimed at providing alternative information to Serbian citizens in hard-to-reach areas largely foundered. Numerous attempts to unite Serbia's opposition—a cornerstone of the aid effort—failed to entice Serbia's most vaunted opposition politician—Vuk Drašković—to come onboard. High-profile initiatives designed to raise the profile of the opposition often backfired—discrediting opposition candidates in the eyes of many Serbs. So too did a poorly orchestrated sanctions regime and a controversial multi-million-dollar campaign aimed at maintaining the financial solvency of Montenegro's prime minister. Despite foreign aid's utility in facilitating regime change, it was not unambiguously helpful, nor was it determinative.

Ultimately, aid worked because it was no longer counteracted by the strategy that had dictated the agenda on Serbia for most of the decade—that of engaging Milošević and ignoring his opponents. Indeed, it was only when U.S. and EU authorities stopped undermining the legitimacy of Serbia's democratic opposition that aid could begin to make its mark.

Creeping Authoritarianism

In the winter of 1996, a strange thing happened in Serbia: Opposition parties won elections. As Chapter 2 explained, after having formed a united front under the banner of Zajedno, Serbia's opposition parties for the first time succeeded in undermining Milošević's power base, winning mayoral positions in all of Serbia's major cities. In early 1997, the opposition won an even more surprising victory: the Milošević regime reinstated their victories, meaning opposition candidates could assume power in cities and towns across the republic.

The surprising electoral victories won by Serbia's democratic opposition could very well have ushered in a period of democratic liberalization. Instead, the years that followed Zajedno's victory were marked by two conflicting trends: While the ascendance of democratic forces to positions of power in cities and towns across Serbia was testament to a democratic opening; a regime-led crackdown on independent media, universities, and political opponents spoke to the hardening of the regime's authoritarian character. Until October 2000, it was the latter trend that looked to be prevailing. By then, Milošević's Serbia had descended into something approaching, albeit never fully embodying, all-out authoritarianism.

In ramping up the pressure on the opposition, the regime began as it had in the past—by reining in Serbia's independent press.[2] By 1997, all of Serbia's television stations were (in some cases, only temporarily) under the command of Milošević loyalists and only a handful of several hundred radio stations throughout Serbia were not. Yet even the remnants of Serbia's independent press caused Milošević consternation and so in October 1998 Serbia's SPS-led parliament passed the Law on Public Information,[3] which awarded authorities the power to restrict coverage deemed "anti-patriotic" or "anti-government." Domestic media found to be in violation of the law received fines upward of several hundred thousand dollars, sums that effectively shut down Serbia's independent press.[4] By late 2000, Serbia's media was among the most oppressed in the world.

The regime's crackdown on political alternatives did not cease with the media. In June 1998, the regime enacted a new Law on Universities, awarding the Milošević-backed minister of education final say on all university appointments—including the right to appoint and dismiss staff and to draft faculty policy. According to one analyst, the law "stripped the University system of any autonomy it once had."[5]

Shortly after Zajedno's local-level victories, Serbia's parliament also adopted a new law on municipalities, limiting the powers of local-level officials. In addition to reducing the funds available to local governments, it allowed Serbian ministers to overrule decentralized decision-making processes and denied local governments control over local media. The law further centralized Serbian power and eliminated the two-round majoritarian electoral system that had served Zajedno so well, imposing in its place a first-past-the-post system in all local elections—meaning that whatever party received the most votes in the first round of elections, won the elections outright. The development, analysts warned, would effectively "allow the ruling regime, familiar with electoral manipulation, to secure victory for its candidates more easily" (NYU Law Review 1999).

The manipulation of electoral system laws and even electoral results themselves were integral to the regime's growing arsenal of authoritarianism. Confronted with Zajedno's unexpected victory, Milošević adopted two tactics: annulling electoral results in those areas where the opposition achieved victories and misappropriating opposition mandates in areas where the alliance won only a slim majority. In the Serbian city of Niš, for example, an electoral commission deprived Zajedno of eleven mandates, awarding them instead to the SPS.

The most telling sign of authoritarian entrenchment was Milošević's increasing reliance on the secret services. In the years immediately preceding his fall from power, Milošević increasingly deployed the secret services to eliminate critics and opponents. In April 1999, Slavko Ćuruvija, a journalist and an independent publisher critical of the regime, was murdered;[6] in August 2000, so too was Ivan Stambolić, a former Milošević ally turned vocal critic and potential presidential rival. Nor was Vuk Drašković spared. In the two years before Milošević's fall, the fabled leader of Serbia's opposition narrowly escaped death from regime-orchestrated assassination attempts, not once but twice. The increasingly authoritarian tone of Milošević's politics had important implications both for Serbia's democratic opposition and for the provision of party assistance in Serbia.

Party Politics in the Run-Up to Revolution

In the months that preceded Milošević's ouster, a group of eighteen parties formed a united front: the Democratic Opposition of Serbia (DOS). In addition to jointly backing a single presidential candidate in the run-up to September 2000's elections, DOS members avidly campaigned on that candidate's behalf—knocking on doors, giving speeches, and issuing public praise. In doing so, Serbia's opposition seemingly transformed from a wayward, ego-driven bunch into a dedicated, electoral machine aimed at achieving regime change. Yet the transformation of Serbia's party politics should not be overstated.

The same parties, the same politicians, and the same cleavages dominated Serbian party life from 1990 through 2000. In fact, not a single significant party in Serbia experienced a change in its leadership in the latter half of the 1990s, with the exception of the GSS—a small party of just several thousand members.[7] The persistence of Serbia's party leadership accounted for the endurance of personal rivalries, animosities, and jealousy, which continued to wreak havoc on Serbia's politics well into 2000.

As in the first half of the decade, Serbia's opposition leaders continued to be seen as petty and weak. They struggled to maintain alliances and frequently engaged in public recrimination, lambasting one another for their perceived deficiencies. As late as June 2000, the independent weekly *Vreme* denounced the opposition as indecisive, inactive, and disunited—attributes that had "weakened the credibility of the opposition in the public's eye."[8]

Also similar throughout the early and late 1990s were political cleavages. As they had in the past, Serbia's parties continued to differentiate themselves with respect to their position on Serbia's "national question" and their attitude toward the "rules of the game." The signing in 1995 of the Dayton Peace Accords effectively moved the SPS to the center of mainstream politics, allowing the party to brand itself as a voice of peace and moderation. Many in the opposition—including Zoran Đinđić's DS—responded by moving further toward the right. But the initiation of hostilities in Kosovo, where Serbian forces responded with ever greater severity to Kosovar Albanian acts of separatism, brought the SPS firmly back to the right and further inflamed the already heightened nationalism of Serbia's party scene.

The second fault line of Serbian politics—the regime's anti-democratic character—was similarly augmented by the late 1990s. The Serbian government's authoritarian tone and frequent use of violence galvanized segments of the opposition into action. By 1998, many were convinced that Serbia faced a "to be or not to be" moment, which accounted for the formation of Serbia's largest and longest-lasting coalition to date: the Democratic Opposition of Serbia.

One area where party life did seem to change, however, was with respect to the decline of the SPO. During the NATO bombing of Serbia, Drašković accepted Milošević's invitation to join a federal coalition with the SPS in return for being appointed deputy prime minister of the Federal Republic of Yugoslavia. The transition from opposition figurehead to regime-cohabitant cost Drašković dearly. Despite his decision to leave the position just several months later, his reputation as leader of the opposition was irreparably tarnished. SPO's relative decline in the aftermath of Drašković's decision would explain the peripheral role his party would play in the run-up to Milošević's ouster and the formation of DOS, and its predecessor, the Alliance for Change.

A United Opposition, Almost

Drawing on the lessons of Zajedno's success two years earlier, in July 1998 the leaders of six opposition parties—Zoran Đinđić of the DS, Vesna Pešić of the GSS, Velimir Ilić of the New Serbia (NS), Nebojša Čović of the Democratic Alternative (DA), Vuk Obradović of the Social Democracy (SD), and Vladan Batić of the Christian Democratic Party of Serbia (DHSS)—as well as two former politicians—Milan Panić and Dragoslav Avramović—founded the Alliance for Change.[9] By December 1998, this rapidly expanding anti-Milošević coalition encompassed fourteen parties and associations, making the Alliance for Change Serbia's largest coalition to date.

Despite its breadth, however, the alliance suffered from several shortcomings. Most notably, it did not include either the SPO or the DSS—two of Serbia's most significant opposition parties. Drašković, in particular, was unconvinced by the Alliance's revolutionary pretensions. A self-proclaimed "king of the streets," Drašković believed he knew "better than anyone else in the world what could be the best moment for demonstrations to bring down Milošević."[10] According to Drašković, this was not the time.

Drašković's absence was not the Alliance's sole dilemma. Despite having developed a draft program, its leaders found little common purpose. Without the promise of elections, there was no real goal behind which the Alliance could unite. Party leaders were also still unable to put aside their personal ambitions for the coalition's larger well-being. As the *New York Times* reported of an Alliance rally held in the city of Kraljevo, "The leaders sat around like at a funeral, and they competed with each other over who will make the first speech and the last."[11] Rather than agree on joint speaking points, each party leader delved into competing topics tangentially. As a result, the Alliance's numerous rallies failed to inspire and by the fall of 1999 its efforts had largely petered out.

The gradual loss of faith in the Alliance for Change did not, however, put an end to the opposition's pursuit of unity. On 7 September 1999, Dragoljub Mićunović—the former head of DS and the founder and president of the small pro-democratic opposition party DC—invited the leaders of more than twenty opposition parties to participate in a series of discussions aimed at forging a common stand against Milošević. Mićunović hoped "to reawaken the hopes of citizens, to show that political agreement and compromise is possible."[12] On 30 September, these aspirations looked to be realized when the representatives of seventeen parties, as well as Avramović, met for a private roundtable discussion. Participants included leaders of the SPO, Alliance for Change, and DSS, among others.

Parties to the roundtable agreed to three primary goals—the resignation or replacement of Serbia's authoritarian regime, an early round of elections, and free and fair electoral conditions. In addition, they promised to continue meeting on a weekly basis in an effort to further define their internal relations and external position toward the regime. Yet as the frequency of the meetings increased, the presence of high-level officials dwindled. Though the Alliance for Change and the SPO would eventually agree on the conditions of electoral participation, they failed to find consensus on the true nature of their alliance. Cohen (2001: 326) explains, "Real progress in achieving unity proved extremely difficult."

It therefore came as a surprise when on 10 January 2000 Drašković hosted a six-hour meeting between the representatives of more than a dozen parties and alliances at SPO headquarters. According to participants, the meeting represented a newfound chance at unity: "This time," party leaders predicted, "the opposition will stay together."[13]

At the heart of this conviction lay the newly proactive role taken on by

Drašković. The failure of the Alliance was thought to demonstrate that without the SPO—Serbia's largest opposition party—no coalition would stand much chance against Milošević's SPS. The 10 January assembly was thus promoted as a "historic meeting" that would revolutionize Serbian opposition politics (Drašković 2007: 377).

The fruits of the meeting did indeed look promising. In addition to issuing a joint call for early general elections, the parties pledged to initiate a series of joint protest rallies in the likely event that the regime did not heed their calls. Moreover, participants vowed not to cooperate with the regime but instead to abide by respectful and fair relations with their opposition counterparts. In an act of goodwill, Drašković announced that Studio B—the sole TV station in SPO hands—would award each member of the opposition one full hour of coverage. With other such meetings promised, the prospect of a truly grand opposition coalition looked hopeful.

Yet as the International Crisis Group (2000: 14) subsequently reported, the 10 January agreement "did not overcome the mistrust between the opposition parties, reconcile personal animosities between some of the party leaders, nor create a common platform or a common strategy." In the weeks that followed, opposition parties quarreled over everything from the timing of their protests to the order of their speeches to the nature of their alliance. By early spring, they could no longer agree on whether to protest at all. When in May 2000 Milošević allies closed in on Studio B, tensions within the opposition came to a head.

Members of the Alliance for Change advocated dramatic acts of civil disobedience, including a hunger strike, but the SPO sought a more modest course of action based on the application of foreign (namely, Russian) pressure. Drašković's reticent prescriptions raised questions regarding the nature of his relationship with the regime. The incessant bickering over opposing strategies further "weakened the credibility of the opposition in the public's eye."[14]

Over the next several weeks, divisions between Drašković and the Alliance deepened further. When in June 2000 Drašković narrowly survived a second assassination attempt in Budva, party leaders were slow to rally around him. To the contrary, many publicly aired their skepticism regarding his claims, hinting that Drašković himself may have staged the attack in an effort to steal the limelight. According to Drašković, his colleagues' indifference was too much to bear: "I couldn't survive in my soul the fact that not one leader of [the opposition] even phoned me."[15] For Drašković, the assassination

attempt had underscored his pivotal role as leader of the Serbian opposition[16]—
if his colleagues were unwilling to recognize this, then he would have to pursue his battle with the regime on his own.

By mid-July 2000, relations between Drašković and the Alliance had
reached an impasse and Đinđić pronounced reconciliation as "unrealistic."[17]
When on 27 July Milošević unexpectedly announced that presidential elections would be held that September, Drašković decided to go it alone. On 4
August 2000 he nominated SPO candidate, Vojislav Mihailović, for the position of Yugoslav president. The nomination of Mihailović—a candidate unknown to the broader public and the grandson of the vaunted Chetnik duke,
Dragoljub "Draža" Mihailović—was an act of spite against the Alliance's intentions to unite behind a single opposition candidate.

Most important, Mihailović's nomination dashed any hopes of true opposition unity. Writing of Drašković's decision, the *New York Times* reported,
"The split in the always fractious opposition virtually assures that Mr. Milošević . . . will win another four years in power in September."[18] Three days
later, Vojislav Koštunica confirmed the division by accepting the nomination
of a large swath of opposition parties, which now included members of the
Alliance for Change; the three-party coalition formed by the Democratic
Center (DC), New Democracy (ND), and DA; the Vojvodina coalition; and
others. Within days of Koštunica's announcement, these parties were rigor-
ously campaigning under the banner of a united opposition: the Democratic
Opposition of Serbia.

DOS Defeats Milošević

Members of the eighteen-party DOS alliance traveled through cities and towns
across Serbia, making as many as six stops a day. On their arrival, party leaders
gave speeches, shook hands, kissed babies, posed for photos, and shared candy
with their fellow citizens—who often gathered in droves of hundreds and thousands along city squares. DOS rallies were star-studded affairs, with popular
musicians, actors, and public intellectuals regularly promoting the opposition
and speaking positively on Koštunica's behalf. In addition to these high-profile
efforts were tens of thousands of civil society activists and party members who,
working from small offices in cities as diverse as Leskovac and Zrenjanin, distributed leaflets, hung posters, and sang Koštunica's praises.

The public efforts of DOS to secure the electoral victory of Koštunica were complemented by a diverse array of covert and overt tactics undertaken by key segments of the Serbian opposition to prepare for the event of electoral fraud.

A nationwide electoral monitoring campaign was assembled in the weeks before the September 2000 election. For the first time in Serbian history, opposition-party monitors would be present at every polling station in Serbia, with the exception of Kosovo.

Čedomir Jovanović, a young member of the DS, helped to organize the national onslaught of thousands of individuals who descended on Belgrade from small towns throughout Serbia on 5 October 2000.[19] Nebojša Čović, a former SPS official, and several members of the DHSS helped to negotiate a strike by the Kolubara coal miners. The efforts of Čović, in particular, ensured that the police would abstain from using violence against these former Milošević loyalists (Bujošević and Radovanović 2001: 34).

Yet it was the behind-the-scenes interventions by Zoran Đinđić, the DS president, that were perhaps most critical to Milošević's subsequent resignation. In the days before Milošević's ouster, Đinđić is believed to have negotiated a truce with Milorad "Legija" Ulemek, the leader of Serbia's infamous Red Berets—the Special Operations Unit (JSO) accused and convicted of carrying out some of the regime's worst crimes in the region and domestically.[20] It is widely believed that Ulemak agreed *not* to fire on protestors on 5 October in exchange for Đinđić's assurances that the JSO would not come under assault by Milošević's opponents and potential successors—thus ensuring that Serbia's democratic revolution would remain nonviolent (see, for example, Andreas 2005; Bujošević and Radovanović 2001).[21]

Ultimately, the multifaceted arsenal of overt and covert operations led by Serbia's political elite and civil society groups succeeded. On 24 September 2000 DOS presidential candidate, Vojislav Koštunica, won 51.7 percent of the federal vote. When Milošević cronies denied the scope of Koštunica's victory—demanding a repeat of the elections—a wave of nonviolent resistance swept across Serbia. A nationwide strike organized by Serbia's anti-Milošević opposition was followed by mass public protests, during which citizens in cities and towns small and large took to the streets. The protests reached a climax on 5 October 2000, when half a million protestors flocked to the steps of the Yugoslav parliament, united in their demand for Milošević's resignation. Protesters young and old descended on Serbia's capital from all across Serbia. Some came in cars, others on foot, and still others in tractors. From the early morning onward, they sang songs, mocked Milošević, and demanded that he step down and recognize the electoral victory won by Koštunica. Just twenty-four hours later, Slobodan Milošević conceded defeat and the last revolution of the twentieth century was born.

Within hours of Koštunica's assumption of power, analysts got to work explaining Milošević's defeat. High on their list were the United States and the EU, whose assistance, it was said, helped account for Koštunica's surprising electoral victory and the mass peaceful protests that followed.

Aid Begins

The decision to support democratic parties in Serbia was born not in the months before Milošević's fall, but several years before: In early 1997, as mass public protests supported by Zajedno were reaching their zenith.[22] In February, U.S. government officials announced that they would dedicate $2 million to democracy aid—with some of it going to political party work. That same year, the EU launched the first of its democracy aid programs targeting Serbian media groups.

With democrats in public office across Serbia, foreign governments at last believed they had a domestic partner capable of effecting change within Serbia. Over the next several weeks, Britain, Germany, the Netherlands, Sweden, and the United States rolled out modest bilateral aid programs from diplomatic missions based in Belgrade. Awarding small grants of $5,000 to $10,000, these missions supported the work of fledgling media outlets, human rights groups, and student organizations. For some donors, however, Zajedno's municipal victories spoke to the need for a more encompassing aid effort, within which party aid was to prove an integral part.

The first and only party aid provider to set up shop in Serbia *before* Zajedno's formation was the German party institute, the Friedrich-Ebert-Stiftung (FES). More than a year in the making,[23] FES operations were modest, consisting of little more than a single local Serbian representative, a table, a computer, a phone, and a small office shared by a local NGO. This changed with the formation of Zajedno, however. With "whistles in hand," FES's representative participated in Zajedno's daily protests and, according to her own pronouncements, FES "became a part of Serbia's fight for freedom and democracy."[24] Deeming the prospects for democratic change to be widening, in the autumn of 1996 FES expanded its staff and assumed a larger office space with the intention of undertaking more ambitious projects.

Just as FES was ramping up its effort, a second *Stiftung* established a presence in Serbia: the German conservative party's Konrad-Adenauer-Stiftung (KAS). With fewer resources than its FES counterpart, KAS's Serbia office consisted of just one officer, who worked out of her Belgrade apartment.

Compared to their German counterparts, the American party institutes made a late start in Serbia. It was only in August 1997 that NDI established its office, and it was several weeks later that IRI followed suit. Plans to launch a set of American party aid programs had crystallized in February 1997. With the promise of a significant boost in Serbia-related funds following Zajedno's victories, USAID issued an exploratory mission to Belgrade, which was soon followed by similar ventures by NDI and IRI. Initially hoping to assemble local offices that would work to support the Zajedno coalition, the American party institutes soon found that the funds at their disposal—offered first by the National Endowment for Democracy (NED)—were insufficient to embark on the ambitious programs they desired.

Unlike the German *Stiftungen*, IRI and NDI planned to establish operations in Serbia, mirroring their programs in the rest of postcommunist Europe. They thus intended to hire American staff members, foreign trainers, and a fully resourced office presence, all of which demanded a budget significantly higher than what the *Stiftungen* envisioned or what U.S. funders such as NED were willing to provide. To establish the presence they wanted, NDI and IRI would have to wait for USAID grants. Always more tardy and stringent (though ultimately more generous) in its grant-giving procedure, USAID would not deliver its funding until the summer of 1997—a full six months after the Zajedno street protests had drawn to a close and several months after Zajedno's alliance had collapsed.

Even then, the American party institutes were slow to get their programs up and running. Having opted to hire non-Serb directors, the institutes had to contend with an increasingly hostile Serbian government that monitored their every move, tapped their phone lines, denied them access to domestic bank accounts, and issued visas only sparingly. The refusal of Serbian authorities to award long-term residence to foreigners—granting only one- to three-month, single-entry stays—adversely affected the American party institutes' programs, forcing resident representatives to devote considerable time to applying for visa extensions.

The root of the problem lay in the Serbian government's conscious efforts to destabilize the institutes' work. For example, IRI's Serbia director was awarded only one-month, single-entry visas throughout her stay in Serbia, forcing her to spend much of her time planning projects and writing reports from nearby cities in Hungary and Montenegro. At one point, she was even asked to stand trial because of her de facto residence in the absence of a long-term visa. The time and effort it took to win even a short-term stay in Serbia made it virtually impossible for the institutes to employ international trainers. Instead, resident directors conducted most party-building training sessions themselves.

The party institutes were not the only aid providers whose work was inhibited by the regime's authoritarianism. When in December 1997 Dušan Gamser assumed the role of the FNS local representative, he kept a much lower profile than had his colleagues from the institutes. He calls his activities from this period "semi-clandestine," admitting that he rarely spoke of the FNS, even among close colleagues within his party, the GSS. In fact, he believes that few in Serbia even knew of his affiliation with the German foundation—a relationship that Gamser was eager to downplay given the strong anti-German sentiment then abounding in Serbia.

KAS's Gordana Pilipović adopted a similar approach. Like Gamser, she worked from her home and endured "great personal risk" doing even that (KAS 2006: 1). Because Pilipović's German supervisor could not enter Serbia, she made numerous trips to border cities in neighboring areas like Republika Srpska or Budva, where she would report on the progress of KAS activities to her superiors. The situation was more dire still for FES's resident director, Jelena Volić Hellbusch, who in 2000 was declared persona non grata and forced to flee the country (FES 2006).

The amount of energy the regime expended on destabilizing party aid providers' earliest efforts is somewhat puzzling, considering the modest scale and scope of donors' initial ambitions. Party foundations did not just have a menial presence in Serbia—the largest, NDI, had only four employees, but the foundations themselves had entirely benign objectives. During their first year and a half in Serbia, party aid practitioners concentrated on promoting a pluralistic process and consolidating Zajedno's recent gains, rather than actively pursuing regime change. Many also initially sought out the SPS—offering to lend their assistance to Milošević's party. Far from seeking to undermine Milošević's rule, Ulrich Storck, FES's regional director at the time, maintains that his *Stiftung's* primary goal was to help "create a space for dialogue with democratic forces in Serbia" (FES 2006: 16, translated from the Serbian). By contrast, IRI sought to support the development of multiparty systems, while Ray Jennings, who helped establish the USAID Office of Transition Initiatives

(OTI) in Belgrade shortly after NDI set up shop, says his office focused on "opening the political space" and "leveling the playing field."[25]

Donors' modest objectives were complemented by humble activities. Much time was spent getting to know Serbia's political environment, fraternizing with members of the opposition, and keeping their respective headquarters up to date on Serbian current affairs. FES's Marc Meinardus fondly recalls his days spent drinking Turkish coffee and *rakija* (a domestic brandy) while smoking "many cigarettes in smoky restaurant and hotel lobbies with [his] friends from the democratic opposition" (FES 2006).

Throughout this early period, the provision of political party aid accounted for but a portion of donors' work and, in the case of the German *Stiftungen*, a small portion at that. In fact, the bulk of the aid FES, KAS, and FNS provided went not to parties but to civil society organizations striving toward interethnic reconciliation. FES, for its part, worked closely with Serbian unions, strengthening their organizational structures and easing their integration into international unions.

Nor were the American party institutes solely concerned with party development. Given its considerable experience with election monitoring, NDI decided to complement party work with support for the Center for Free Elections and Democracy (CeSID), a nonpartisan civic organization whose primary mandate was the observation of elections. IRI, by contrast, concentrated its nonparty work on youth and student organizations, an effort that ultimately matured into a close relationship with the anti-Milošević youth movement, Otpor.

During the first few years of their engagement in Serbia, party aid providers organized seminars, summer schools, meetings, opinion polls, and training for local party branches. In February 1997, FES invited newly elected politicians representing the Zajedno coalition to participate in its annual Academy for Local Politics in Freiburg, Germany. That summer, it also helped DS organize its first school for party officials in the small southwestern Serbian city of Kušići. From 1998 onward, FES would organize annual multiparty educational training for dozens of Serbian party members. FES would also help support the activities of the Center for Modern Skills, an educational wing of the DS that trained young party members in the how-to of modern politics.[26]

Unlike the *Stiftungen*, the bulk of NDI and IRI's energy during their early years in Serbia was devoted to increasing the capacities of local party branches. Dividing their attention geographically—with IRI focusing on offices located in the north and east of Serbia, NDI focusing on central and southern Serbia, and both sharing Belgrade—the institutes set out to train party branches. In practical terms, this meant helping party branches strengthen their organizational development, improve their methods of public communication, and hone their leadership skills.

In January 1998, NDI began by targeting the local branches of the DS, GSS, and SPO in the cities of Čačak, Kraljevo, Niš, Valjevo, Vranje, and Užice.[27] IRI followed suit in April, working with local party branches throughout the Vojvodina region. Both institutes started with small groups of five to fifteen participants, often including a local branch president, a few of his (and in far fewer cases, her) close associates, and several party activists. Training sessions lasted anywhere from two to three hours and were invariably held in smoke-filled offices that were as miserably equipped as they were poorly ventilated. Having initiated these first training sessions on the heels of Serbian presidential elections, the institutes opted to focus not directly on campaigning techniques but on strengthening the basic infrastructure of local party branches. According to IRI, its long-term aim was to persuade local leaders to be more responsive to local input. Training thus explored the utility of political canvassing, voter databases, intraparty communication, fundraising, and more. For those individuals who proved most responsive, NDI sought to forge yet closer ties.

After an initial round of training, NDI identified several dozen activists that it divided into working groups of six to ten people. Over the next six months, it worked intensively with these individuals until finally, in September 1998, a dozen were chosen to embark on a campaign observation mission to Poland. The twelve participants watched Polish party members in action, observing their grassroots campaigning style and door-to-door canvassing. Although they represented three different parties—the DS, GSS, and SPO—the group came away with a common experience that would prove to be key in the activities NDI later conducted in the run-up to Milošević's ouster. Indeed, six of the twelve participants would go on to form the core of NDI's Regional Trainer program, which would be launched in late 2000.

A second area in which the American party institutes specialized was that of opinion polling. Already in October 1997, IRI contacted several Belgrade-based polling firms before finally settling on Strategic Marketing Research. A combination of polling data and focus groups, it was thought, would serve as a "fundamental building block in an overall effort to direct political parties toward more issues-based political activity by more clearly illustrating the issues on the minds of 'swing' voters in a scientific, methodological fashion" (IRI 1997).

The institutes would continue such efforts for well over a decade. Despite this, however, European and American authorities remained reluctant to get too deeply involved in Serbia's internal affairs. This had direct consequences for the extent of democracy assistance foreign governments would devote to the Serbian cause—sums that paled in comparison to those dedicated to similar efforts elsewhere in the region.

Aid Confronts Diplomacy

In the months before the NATO bombing of Serbia, a severe degree of skepticism dominated the democracy promotion community. Most donors simply did not believe that anything could be done to help the Serbian opposition. For proponents of greater foreign engagement in Serbia, it was an uphill battle to increase the funds dedicated to democracy.

And so, in November 1998 Senator Richard Lugar reissued his calls for greater engagement with Serbia's democratic opposition. "The allies," he claimed, "have underestimated the potential influence of a concerted program to promote democratic change in Serbia."[28] In a letter to President Bill Clinton written the following month, Lugar and seven other members of Congress reiterated this position, calling on the administration to "help facilitate a transition to a democratic government committed to the rule of law."[29] Serbia's democrats, they wrote, "need a clear signal that the United States favors the replacement of the Milošević regime with a democratic government and is taking steps to encourage that outcome." The letter fell on deaf ears. Until the Kosovo war of 1999, neither the United States nor the EU was prepared to side with Serbia's democrats for fear of destabilizing Milošević and, with him, the only perceived chance for regional stability.

By 1998, violence had abated in Bosnia and Croatia, but it was brewing in full force in the Serbian province of Kosovo. The province's ethnic Albanian majority desperately wanted independence. For years, the Albanian community had organized (primarily nonviolently) to protest Serbia's encroachment on their province's autonomy and make the case for independence. Frustrated both by the lack of progress in attaining independence through nonviolence and by the upsurge in state-sponsored repression in Kosovo, Kosovars' calls for independence became increasingly militarized. Throughout the 1990s, facets

of the Kosovar community began launching armed campaigns to free themselves from Serbia, eventually forming the Kosovo Liberation Army (KLA).

The KLA was immediately denounced as a terrorist organization by Milošević, and blamed for carrying out attacks on Serbian police officers. When
the KLA supported an armed insurrection following a state-sponsored attack
in Drenica in February 1998 that left dozens dead, Serb forces sprang into
action. What began as sporadic violence quickly descended into an all-out
war that U.S. Secretary of State Madeleine Albright warned had international
implications.

Yet when war first began in Kosovo, much of the foreign policy-making
community still believed that the key to peace in Kosovo lay not in Milošević's
rivals but in Milošević himself. Here, the recipe for peace in Bosnia—the
highly vaunted Dayton Peace Accords—was thought to be instructive. The
cessation of violence in Bosnia had been forged on the basis of Milošević's
grasp of realpolitik. Many foreign policy makers familiar with the Balkans
thus believed that if properly convinced through the threat of force, Milošević
would abandon the Serbs of Kosovo, reject his ethnocentric crusade, and ultimately submit to foreign pressure—much as he had in Dayton. Richard Holbrooke, the celebrated mastermind of Dayton, was thus employed to rework
his magic, this time in Kosovo.

The key to Holbrooke's strategy lay in one-on-one meetings. Direct negotiations with Milošević meant staging high-level meetings with the Yugoslav
president—speaking to him and of him both behind closed doors and in public and, in that way, conferring upon Milošević a level of legitimacy few others
in the Balkans enjoyed.

For Serbia's struggling democratic opposition, Holbrooke's tactics signaled
a stinging rebuke of their efforts to unseat Milošević. Indeed, Holbrooke repeatedly sidestepped Serbia's democratic opposition in his quest to bring
peace to Kosovo. As a political counselor for the U.S. Embassy in Belgrade at
the time admits, the notion of engaging Serbia's democratic opposition in a
high-level way "just didn't loom large in that period."[30] As a consequence, the
modest forms of democracy aid that were provided in 1997 and 1998 were
awarded amid a policy vacuum, divorced from complementary diplomatic
initiatives and other forms of high-level politics that could otherwise have
reinforced Western support for Serbia's democratic opposition.

But not everyone agreed with Holbrooke's policy choices. For a long time,
his colleagues in the political section of the U.S. mission to Belgrade argued
against engagement with Milošević for fear of adding further clout to his

domestic prestige.[31] In his testimony before the U.S. Congress, Milan Panić, the former prime minister of Serbia and an early Milošević foe, made a similar case. He argued that it was "high time" the world cut ties with the Serbian strongman: "If international leaders no longer parade to Belgrade to meet with him, his public image as the internationally recognized leader and protector of the Serbian nation will quickly fade, and it will become apparent to an overwhelming majority of Serbs that his regime no longer enjoys international legitimacy."[32] At least some of Panić's audience agreed. Christopher Smith, a Republican member of the House, warned that many of his congressional colleagues were "disgusted by the fact that the international community, led by the United States, had worked through Slobodan Milošević to end the very conflicts in the Balkans which he instigated as a means to maintain and enhance his power."[33]

Nor was disagreement with Holbrooke confined to American policy makers. To the contrary, when violence in Kosovo first erupted, both the British and German governments were early proponents of a strong reply. They advocated the reinstatement of harsh economic sanctions, guided by the conviction that Holbrooke's efforts would prove fruitless. As the *New York Times* reported in June 1998, "The Europeans . . . felt that Mr. Milošević had manipulated the Americans, promising to open a dialogue but not promising it would lead to any results."[34]

The confusion over when and how to respond to the Kosovo crisis created an incoherent policy in which democracy aid floated free of—and, in some respects, was even undermined by—diplomacy. But when in early 1999 it became apparent that Milošević was calling Holbrooke's bluff, the beginning of a transatlantic consensus emerged.

From Military Intervention to Regime Change

In the fall of 1998, NATO members embarked on what would be the first step aimed at preparing Milošević for war. From the beginning, it was clear that quelling violence in Kosovo would take precedence over efforts aimed at bolstering Serbia's democrats or explicitly seeking Milošević's ouster. At least initially, the mere threat of bombing was presumed to be sufficient to avert NATO intervention. Thus, when aid providers were evacuated in March 1999, they assumed they would be back in a matter of weeks.[35]

Few expected the outbreak of NATO bombing, let alone the protracted duration of that mission. Yet on 24 March 1999, NATO fighter jets flew over Serbian skies, marking the start of the Kosovo war. The bombing would continue for seventy-eight days. Midway into the bombing, on 27 May 1999, the International Criminal Tribunal for the former Yugoslavia (ICTY) announced that it was indicting Slobodan Milošević and four other senior FRY officials for murder, persecution, and deportation in Kosovo.

NATO intervention created several uncertainties for party aid providers. On the one hand, with bombs falling, it was clear that operating programs from within Serbia was no longer a palatable option even for the bravest of aid providers.[36] On the other hand, given that NATO member states—many of which were funders of democracy aid—were responsible for the bombardment, even if the operation of such programs were logistically possible, it was no longer clear whether domestic partners would accept it. After all, the bombing campaign—which left an estimated 500 casualties throughout Serbia and Kosovo—was deeply unpopular within Serbia and galvanized resentment against the West. Despite such concerns, however, party aid providers were reluctant to close shop. Said one former NDI officer: "It was our position that we should wait until the bombing was over . . . and see if people that had worked with us still wanted to work with us [after the bombing]. We had a moral obligation to work with them if at all possible, since they'd stuck their necks out working with us for the previous year and a half."[37]

And so, the German *Stiftungen* and American party institutes continued their work. Although FES, KAS, and FNS maintained their Belgrade residences, NDI set up shop in neighboring Hungary, while IRI alternated between Croatia and Macedonia. Like their domestic partners, aid providers spent their days sleeping and nights working. With training and polling on hold, they devoted their time to keeping tabs on their friends and colleagues, e-mailing, calling, gathering information, but most of all simply waiting for the bombing to end.

Then, on 10 June, Milošević agreed to withdraw Serbian troops from Kosovo. After close to three months of airstrikes, the Kosovo war had ended. As NATO troops moved to occupy the province, a new consensus emerged in Western Europe and North America. Its name was regime change.

Aiding Regime Change

Few leaders were more explicit about the need for regime change than Tony Blair, the British prime minister, who argued publicly that regional stability remained in doubt so long as "Milošević remains in power."[38] Blair's French counterpart, President Jacques Chirac, publicly labeled Milošević a "big obstacle to reconstruction," acknowledging that the quicker Milošević was removed from office, "the better for everyone."[39]

U.S. officials were no less reticent in sharing their wishes. James Dobbins, the U.S. special envoy for Kosovo and a chief adviser to the U.S. president and secretary of state on the Balkans, says that by the time the NATO bombing had ended, "getting rid of Milošević was the principle objective."[40] In July 1999, U.S. officials, for the first time, explicitly underscored their desire to see Milošević removed from office. Regime change was now foremost on the international agenda. Said one U.S. official, "We want to see Milošević gone, we want to see a new leadership in Serbia, we want to help the opposition to that end."[41]

After almost a decade of Milošević's rule—a decade that saw Serbia digress into bloodshed, authoritarianism, and poverty—Western leaders finally set their sights on regime change.[42] At long last, supporting nascent democratic forces was identified as critical to achieving that goal. Democracy would thus ultimately help deliver what the NATO bombing did not: rid the Balkans of Milošević. Robert Thomas, a Serbia expert and an aid practitioner with the Conservative Party of the Westminster Foundation for Democracy, explains, "After the bombing . . . the general environment became more sympathetic to the idea that democratization work should be done with the Serbian opposition." In his words, "Democratization was the strategy for regime change in Serbia."[43]

Overt democracy assistance would thus be used by foreign governments not simply to support democratic development in a nondemocratic regime but to oust Milošević—Yugoslavia's sitting head of state. Speaking at a congressional meeting held in the summer of 1999, Robert Gelbard, Clinton's special representative for the Balkans, went so far as to call democracy assistance a "key aspect" of U.S. policy on Serbia.[44] As one former coordinator of U.S. aid to Serbia would later remark, democracy assistance proved to be "a cheap way to bring about regime change."[45] It is difficult to overstate the manifold repercussions this would have, not only for the aid initiative in Serbia but also for aid's perceived legitimacy in other authoritarian contexts. From Serbia onward, democracy aid would have to grapple with the reputation of an enterprise bent on fomenting regime change.

Not surprising, the new focus on regime change was not lost on Milošević. Following the NATO bombing, he forbade the core member states of NATO—Britain, France, Germany, and the United States—from reestablishing diplomatic missions in Belgrade. Their aid providers were barred from reentering the country. FES's resident director, a Serbian national, was declared persona non grata and forced to take refuge abroad. Those who remained in Serbia—like Freedom House's resident director, Michael Staresinic—faced a harrowing security environment, in which regime-sponsored threats and monitoring were a constant part of daily life.

Despite the atmosphere of fear, democracy assistance poured into Serbia at a fast pace. An estimated $80 million was spent by the U.S. and European governments and NGOs on overt democracy assistance initiatives from 1999 through 2000. Using these funds, governments throughout Western Europe and North America revamped their aid to Serbia, reducing the bureaucratic hurdles that previously impeded financial transactions and expanding the sums that were available for domestic opposition forces. New actors—including diplomatic missions based in Belgrade—also took part in the party aid effort. These initiatives produced a multipronged strategy that strove to bolster the democratic opposition; support a free, fair, and highly participatory electoral process; and isolate Milošević.

Bolstering the Democratic Opposition

Support for Serbia's democratic opposition was a cornerstone of the effort to oust Milošević. Several facets of this strategy would later be replicated in other authoritarian regimes, and much of the democracy aid toolkit used during this period to bolster Serbia's democratic opposition would come to form part of the standard democracy aid arsenal used in other nondemocratic regimes. As innocuous as much of this arsenal was, however, some of it was quite controversial. In the months leading to Milošević's ouster, the lines between standard democracy aid and covert assistance were often crossed, and the standard rules of practice governing democracy aid were frequently abandoned—by necessity if not always by choice.

Training the Opposition

Perhaps the least controversial—but by no means least significant—facet of the aid agenda was what might be considered the core of the democracy assistance arsenal: training for democratic activists, party members, and poll watchers. Because of the many obstacles imposed by the Milošević regime, training sessions were held in one of two ways: (1) hosted in neighboring capitals and (2) conducted through training-of-trainers programs that would enable Serbian party members to transfer skills to colleagues within opposition coalitions without raising the suspicions of the regime. Both methods became critical components of democracy assistance in Serbia and elsewhere.

Most party training and meetings were held not in Serbia but in neighboring states, including Hungary and Montenegro. The cities of Szeged, Budapest, and Budva proved to be convenient destinations that did not require cumbersome visa applications for Serbian nationals and raised few questions among Serbian customs officers. Once abroad, Serbs could receive training and advice, as well as strategize with fellow opposition leaders without fear of infiltration by Milošević cronies. For party leaders, such meetings included in-depth discussions of polling results, the need for opposition unity, and possible presidential candidates. For parties' rank and file, by contrast, the opportunity to travel abroad brought intensive training that often lasted several days. Party members were taught how to engage in grassroots activism, attract volunteers and recruit new members, plan rural campaigns, and speak to the media.

In November 1999, NDI added a second component to the training mix: an innovative training-of-trainers program dubbed Regional Trainer. NDI's Regional Trainer program was developed "in response to requests from political parties as a follow-up to training that had previously been conducted by NDI program directors and other trainers inside Serbia but was no longer possible due to travel restrictions of expatriates" (NDI 2001: 2). Working first with six of the young party members that had traveled to Poland on an NDI-funded election-monitoring visit in September 1998, NDI taught regional trainers how to train fellow coalition members from the Alliance for Change. For a few hundred dollars a month, these trainers effectively became NDI employees, conducting training on NDI's behalf.[46] The NDI director trained these fledgling trainers in message development, public speaking, leaflet writing, door-to-door campaigning, teamwork, and event planning. After returning to Serbia, NDI's regional trainers would impart such lessons to other rank-and-file members of the Alliance for Change, often working in groups of ten to twenty-five participants, with trainings lasting for about two hours. By the summer of 2000, NDI added six more regional trainers and trained upward of 5,000 party members.

Equipping the Opposition

As donors devised strategies toward helping Serbia's democratic opposition, the dearth of oppositional party resources grew increasingly difficult to ignore. As James Hooper, the director of the Balkans Action Council, explained to the U.S. Congress in June 1999, Serbia's opposition parties "need money . . . faxes, computers, phones, vehicles, gasoline, and other essential tools of political campaigning."[47] Yet, even in the summer of 1999 after the Kosovo war, it was still a taboo subject to support the Serbian opposition directly. Indeed, in its quarterly report for June through September 1999, IRI resident directors complained that their previous agreements with USAID "did not provide for material items given directly to Serbian organizations," despite the fact that this "was a great necessity for them" (IRI 1999).

This changed in late 1999. Normally reticent to provide direct funding to political parties, the U.S. government and NED made an exception for Serbia's opposition when it created the Alliance for Change.[48] Thus, in August 1999, IRI and NDI received the go-ahead to provide material assistance to Serbian parties. In IRI's case, it received a $74,276 grant to pay for the Alliance's office rentals and utilities; furniture and supplies; several mobile phones, desktop computers, laser printers, fax machine, photocopiers and scanners; and promotional materials, including flags, posters, and leaflets. The grant also covered bus rentals to transport Alliance supporters to rallies across the country.

By contrast, NDI was awarded $38,414 to "provide material assistance to Serbia's Alliance for Change that would facilitate and improve coverage of Alliance activities by domestic independent media" (NED 1999). This assistance included the rental of a media van, broadcast fees for Alliance commercials, advertising fees for newspapers, sound and light rentals at Alliance rallies, laptops and printers, a power generator and portable fax machine, one satellite phone and five mobile phones, as well as an array of campaign paraphernalia, including buttons, whistles, and bullhorns. Though modest, NED grants jumpstarted a larger effort by USAID.[49] That October, IRI received a new USAID program grant for Serbia, which included a substantial material support component. That same month, NDI was also awarded a new wave of material support, enabling it to pay for everything from printers and lighting to bus tours and speaking engagements for Alliance leaders.

Like the American Institutes, European party foundations and diplomatic missions also provided material and financial assistance. Thanks to their location within Serbia, KAS and FES were ideally situated to channel German funding to Serbian parties. KAS, for example, funded parts of DOS's electoral campaign and paid for office equipment and rentals. Although only small sums were distributed, they were in several instances large enough to support high-cost items like cars. The Dutch mission in Belgrade, too, provided parties with cash, helping them pay for promotional leaflets, fliers, buttons, and public opinion polls. Although the Dutch did their best to provide such support through intermediaries—most notably, the NGO branches affiliated with the top party brass—they did so with the intent of directly supporting parties. As one Dutch diplomat explains, "Officially it's pretty difficult—even prohibited— to fund political parties per se, but most of these [Serbian] politicians had their own NGOs that were clearly working for their political parties and we would support them . . . We would openly discuss this with politicians, so it was obvious they were closely linked."[50] Indeed, just as organizational affiliates would later enable Serbian tycoons to bankroll political parties without a clear paper trail, these same NGOs created a clever way for foreign funders to bypass their government's official sanctioning of funding parties.

Other creative funding mechanisms soon ensued. These allowed cash and material assistance to enter Serbia—a country that, because of severe international sanctions, lacked a transparent banking system. For the Dutch mission in Belgrade, for example, the Dutch air carrier, KLM, provided a surprising solution. KLM's Belgrade office was sitting on substantial liquid assets— money it could not get out of the country because of the sanctions. The Dutch mission helped KLM unload its funds—using a car to transfer cash from KLM's Belgrade office to the diplomat mission. The Dutch Ministry of Foreign Affairs would, in turn, compensate KLM back in the Netherlands, while the embassy provided small grants to oppositional organizations, like Otpor.[51]

Other countries and agencies pursued different options. The CIA and the State Department, for example, established their own mechanisms for cash dispersal—with covert encounters in hotel rooms, where cash would trade hands and eventually find its way to members of the opposition. Other countries chose to store funds in the private bank accounts of Serbian citizens, who would provide this money to their political counterparts. NDI, for example, relied on trusted Serbian staff members to transfer cash from Hungary to Serbia. In several instances, diplomatic missions themselves became a meeting point for the swapping of funds. For instance, party leaders seeking Dutch assistance would contact embassy staff members and receive financial support on the spot.

Of the material assistance to Serbian parties, much of it was provided in cash. Though an expeditious transaction method, this did not provide for stellar bookkeeping. Indeed, according to OTI, "Record keeping was irregular and was shielded to minimize opportunities for regime harassment" (Cook and Spalatin 2002: 6). Whatever the cause, coffers full of cash were a staple of a foreign aid effort to oust Milošević.

Supporting Opposition Unity

Another part of the democracy aid effort focused on achieving opposition unity. From late 1999 onward, foreign policy makers and donors on either side of the Atlantic made the attainment of unity a prime objective in their efforts to oust Milošević. The initiatives rested on two strategies: persuasion and coercion. Where the former centered largely on the powers of polling data, private pleas, and high-profile meetings, the latter revolved around the interplay between conditionality and visa bans.

From late 1999 through early 2000, EU and U.S. policy makers, including U.S. Secretary of State Madeleine Albright and German Foreign Minister Joschka Fischer, met repeatedly with members of Serbia's opposition. Speaking at an international conference held in Berlin, Germany, in December 1999, Albright clarified the meaning of opposition unity, insisting Serbian politicians put aside their personal differences. The United States, she explained, was "not interested in supporting one politician in preference of another, but rather, wished to support all those who opposed "the forces of repression that have been dragging Serbia down and holding it back."[52] Behind closed doors, Fischer, Albright, and party aid practitioners used such opportunities to extol the virtues of opposition unity. They did so through public opinion polls.

Public opinion polling had long been the prerogative of the American party institutes and, in Serbia's case, of NDI in particular. In the fall of 1999, NDI commissioned Clinton's chief pollsters, Mark Penn and Doug Schoen (the very same Schoen who in 1992 advised Milošević's presidential adversary, Milan Panić) of Penn Schoen Berland, to conduct a "Serbia Issues Poll." Their findings indicated that support for the Alliance for Change was strong and that it enjoyed high name recognition and higher favorability ratings than the other major parties. More important, the pollsters found that voters would be more inclined to vote if they believed Milošević and the SPS could actually be defeated—a result deemed likely only if the opposition achieved unity. The lesson was clear: Unless Serbia's opposition united, voters would not come out to support them. This message formed the mantra of U.S. aid providers leading into the elections in September 2000.

In October 1999, NDI hosted a meeting in Budapest with twenty high-ranking members of the Alliance for Change. During the conference, Schoen and NDI extolled the virtues of opposition unity. The Budapest meeting marked the first meeting of many in which polls would be shared with the opposition for the purpose of galvanizing joint action.

Polling was not the only tool at Western policy makers' disposal, however. The United States and the EU also sought to lure the opposition into unity through coercion. For example, the provision of direct assistance was made contingent on opposition unity. Funds for office rentals, computers, and fax machines were provided not to individual parties but to coalitions like the Alliance for Change and, later, DOS. Parties had to demonstrate an organizational commitment to unity in order to receive the funds and materials for which they were most eager. To qualify for aid, they had to unite.

Backing a Common Candidate

Closely connected to the desire for a united opposition, was the desire for a single leader to lead the coalition against Milošević on an opposition-sponsored presidential ticket. Party aid providers therefore buttressed their research into opposition unity with assessments of politicians' electoral competitiveness.

Initially, it was Dragoslav Avramović, the beloved and iconic former World Bank economist who famously stabilized the Yugoslav economy in the 1990s, who appeared best suited to lead DOS. As the *New York Times* reported shortly after the NATO bombing, the Clinton administration was pushing for Avramović to take the reins of the coalition. Yet Avramović was an unlikely candidate. Well into his eighties, Avramović suffered from health concerns and by his own admission lacked the energy for what was likely to prove a hard-fought campaign.[53] The Alliance and Western donors thus sought an alternative.

Vojislav Koštunica was their answer. An avowed patriot known for the steadfastness of his convictions and his refutation of international meddling, the DSS president boasted low negatives within Serbian public opinion.[54] Koštunica's name emerged from the sidelines as a person that DOS could agree on. A long list of other positives followed: Having strayed from the limelight, Koštunica was unaffected by the allegations of corruption that for so long had haunted members of the opposition and even Milošević himself. An ardent anticommunist, Koštunica had proven himself uncompromising in his attitudes toward the previous regime. An unrepentant nationalist, he could not be accused of anti-Serb pretensions or cowardice. With no direct ties to foreign assistance, he was impossible to label a traitor or foreign mercenary. More than any other candidate, barring Avramović, Koštunica was the individual best poised to defeat Milošević.

Party aid providers and foreign governments were keenly aware of this. At high-profile meetings from Berlin to Washington, U.S. and EU officials repeatedly underscored the virtues of the DSS leader. In private meetings with DOS officials, they reiterated their backing of a Koštunica candidacy, pressing individuals like Đinđić to suspend their own political ambitions for the sake of a DOS victory. Using NDI's public opinion polls, they heralded the common gains to be won if Koštunica were to receive DOS's backing.

Forging a Common Program

DOS needed more than just a person, however; it needed a program. Speaking before the U.S. Congress in late 1998, NED's Paul McCarthy stated that "the West should help the democratic political opposition develop a concrete program which offers positive alternatives to the restrictive policies of the Milošević regime." Such efforts, he maintained, demanded "immediate attention" (as quoted in CSCE 1999: 29). Yet it would not be until the following year that assistance for program development would be forthcoming.

Key to this program, foreign policy makers believed, was an emphasis on liberal economic reforms. In late 1999, the Center for International Private Enterprise (CIPE)—one of NED's four core American grantees—received USAID funding to provide technical assistance and policy support to Serbia's opposition for the realization of a comprehensive economic reform program. According to Andrew Wilson, CIPE's senior program officer for Eastern Europe, the debate on democracy assistance had long been dominated by media and civil society support. As a result, aid for economic development had been shortchanged. CIPE believed this was problematic, not least because although voters wanted economic growth they questioned the opposition's ability to achieve this. CIPE thus sought to bolster DOS's economic credentials by help-ing the opposition develop a positive legislative agenda that offered concrete proposals for economic reform. Working closely with the G17—a group of Serbia's leading economists that formed the "policy wing" of DOS—CIPE en-couraged the promotion of liberal market reforms.

Complementing the economic dimensions of program development were party aid providers, who used public opinion polls to determine the extent of public support for programmatic issues. On the basis of these preferences, they helped DOS develop a common program that the coalition published in August 2000. The "Program for a Democratic Serbia" lay the foundation for deep "structural social reforms" (Sekelj 2001: 104). DOS's program vowed to fight corruption, initiate democracy, and renew citizens' faith in the state. Among other things, it also promised to pass a new constitution that would decentralize power in Serbia, repeal repressive laws, and force more transpar-ency on government finances.

Broadcasting Their Message

Along with direct support for Serbia's democratic opposition, foreign aid pro-viders made a "concerted effort before the [September 2000] elections to pro-vide citizens with the information they needed to make up their minds"—in favor of DOS (McClear, McClear, and Graves 2003: 9). Media assistance was an integral part of this and, as the most costly part of the aid effort, indirectly ben-efited Serbia's opposition parties by providing DOS candidates an uncensored platform through which to communicate with the Serbian electorate. Media assistance generally took one of two forms: support for domestic independent media outlets and support for infrastructure through which to broadcast for-eign news sources capable of countering Milošević's propaganda machine.

The media aid effort built on a tradition of media assistance that began in the 1990s, when both the EU and the United States offered modest financial support to independent media outlets such as B92, Studio B, *Vreme*, and Borba.[55] By the late 1990s, such assistance had increased dramatically. From 1990 to 1995, the United States and the EU awarded $600,000 and €1.7 mil-lion, respectively; throughout the next five years, however, such numbers had increased more than tenfold, with the United States dedicating $23 million and the EU €17 million to media aid.

Some of this expenditure was dedicated to domestic media outlets for the

purpose of bolstering professional journalism and teaching the many uses of
the Internet—then a novel technology to which relatively few Serbs had regular access. Such assistance was also devoted to expanding domestic media
outlets' outreach. The International Research & Exchanges Board (IREX), for
example, enabled domestic radio and television stations to buy transmitter
tubes, new antennas, and transmission lines. The ambition was to "ensure that
Serbs received fair election coverage from as many sources as possible" (Mc-
Clear, McClear, and Graves 2003: 9). Using such equipment, Serbia's local
media outlets featured DOS and promoted the notion that Koštunica was
leading in the polls. Ignored in the Milošević-dominated state press, speeches
by Koštunica and Đinđić received ample coverage within the local media.

A second—and considerably more costly—part of the media aid effort
involved the establishment of FM transmitters placed in Bosnia, Kosovo, Croatia, and Romania. The so-called Ring Around Serbia enabled foreign aid
providers to rebroadcast domestic Serbian programming from independent
news outlets such as B92 as well as Serbian-language programming from the
Voice of America, the BBC, Deutsche Welle, and Radio France International
to areas across Serbia that had been cut off from independent media. Such
assistance aimed to break the stranglehold that Milošević had over the air-
waves. The Clinton Presidential Library (2006: 2) is yet more explicit, stating
that the Ring Around Serbia was aimed at "weaning public support away from
Milošević."

BOLSTERING THE OPPOSITION'S PRESTIGE

Another way to corrode public support for Milošević was to bolster DOS's
domestic prestige as an international heavyweight, capable of reintegrating
Serbia into the community of nations. Western policy makers sought to
achieve this by organizing a series of high-profile conferences in foreign capitals. The hope was that Serbia's opposition would thereby claim the mantle of
international legitimacy so long monopolized by Slobodan Milošević.

The first such conference was held in Luxembourg on 11 October 1999.
Organized by the the Council of Europe, the conference sought to underscore
the Council's preparedness to give substantial assistance to a future democratic Serbia. Yet the Council's insistence that Serbia's opposition pledge their
support for the International Criminal Tribunal for the former Yugoslavia—a
highly unpopular and illegitimate institution in the eyes of many Serbs—won
little support within opposition ranks. As a consequence, only a handful of

low-ranking Alliance for Change members showed up, thereby turning the EU's first prominent meeting with the Serbian opposition into what was, by most reports, a fiasco.

The second meeting of a similar scale was held in Budva, Montenegro. The conference marked the constitution of an informal threefold alliance of the EU, the United States, and representatives of Serbia's democratic opposition. Held on 2 December 1999, the Budva meeting set the guidelines for trilateral engagement and produced a joint declarative agreement, stating that "cooperation with democratic forces should focus on immediate assistance, support for democracy in [Serbia] and planning for the post-Milošević era."[56] But Budva's primary purpose was to lay the groundwork for a larger meeting held later that month in Berlin, Germany. On 17 December 1999, this heavily publicized conference brought together leading members of the Serbian opposition, as well as foreign ministers and secretaries of state, including Joschka Fischer and Madeleine Albright.

Heralded as "a turning point in the quest of the people of Serbia and Montenegro to live in freedom and without fear,"[57] the purpose of the Berlin meeting was to generate concrete proposals for enabling a democratic breakthrough in Serbia. The United States pledged to double its democracy aid throughout the following year, and the EU promised to look into further spending on local municipalities run by opposition parties. But the Berlin meeting provided more than a platform on which to trade promises regarding democracy aid. It also served as a photo opportunity, during which Serbia's opposition could be seen mingling with the world's most prestigious politicians—an honor no longer bestowed on Milošević.

Strengthening Local Leaders

In addition to receiving direct support to parties, opposition leaders were very "interested in seeing material assistance that would benefit the people of Serbia and for which they could somehow take credit."[58] In October 1999, under the auspices of the EU, the governments of EU member states began exploring strategies through which to do just that. They began by dedicating €4.4 million worth of heating oil to the local governments of Niš and Pirot, both of which were governed by coalitions of opposition parties that were struggling to meet the needs of their citizens in the face of an increasingly harsh winter. The project—"Energy for Democracy"—was enthusiastically received by members of the Serbian opposition.

One such proponent was Dušan Gamser, who likened the EU's experiment to the Berlin Airlift of 1949. According to Gamser, Energy for Democracy proved "crucial" in helping "local democratic governments to function better than their socialist counterparts."[59] Indeed, the perceived success of these initial ventures ensured that by February 2000 Energy for Democracy had expanded to include the opposition strongholds of Subotica, Novi Sad, Sombor, Kraljevo, and Kragujevac. By the time deliveries were completed that April, some €8.8 million had been spent on 17,513 tons of heating oil, representing 99.54 percent of the total quantities requested by Serbian municipalities. Energy for Democracy had helped heat everything from schools and hospitals to public buildings in opposition-controlled communities.[60]

The government of Norway soon joined the EU's efforts and in early 2000 began a similar initiative under the title "Oil for Democracy," targeting the cities of Užice, Čačak, Trstenik, Arilje, and Požega. As the seasons changed from winter to spring, donors diversified the forms their assistance took, moving from heating oil to equipping local schools, repairing city roads and public transport, and even improving waste collection and disposal.[61] That July, the EU launched its "Schools for a Democratic Serbia" program. The program's €3.8 million was dedicated to repairing and purchasing materials such as furniture for kindergartens, primary schools, and other educational establishments—all with the aim of increasing the capacities of opposition authorities and demonstrating the benefits of a DOS-led government.[62]

Free and Fair Elections, with a High Turnout

Efforts to bolster the electoral prospects of DOS were complemented by civil society-led efforts to bring out the vote on the opposition's behalf. Ensuring a high voter turnout in Yugoslav presidential elections was a critical goal for the foreign aid community, as was preparing for the electoral theft that many believed would inevitably accompany Milošević's defeat.

Getting Out the Vote and Otpor

High voter participation was thought to favor Koštunica by increasing the odds that the DOS candidate would pass the 50-percent threshold needed to claim victory in a single round of voting.[63] Working in tandem with the Open Society Institute, Freedom House, OTI, the British Foreign Office, and the governments of various states in Western Europe, party aid providers supported projects aimed at encouraging broader voter participation. In the final weeks leading to the elections, two mass GOTV campaigns materialized: *Gotov Je* (He's Finished) and *Vreme Je* (It's Time). Both were part of *Izlaz 2000* (Exit 2000), a coordinated effort bringing together some 150 local NGOS working on GOTV-related issues.

Although dozens of NGOs received GOTV assistance, the bulk went to Otpor. A youth movement comprised of a reported 70,000 members spread across Serbia, Otpor was far from an obvious target for foreign assistance. Policy makers first worried that Otpor's members, clad in black and waving the emblem of a clenched fist, tread on the fascistic. The movement's message—that Milošević's time was up—was risqué for a democracy aid community which publicly prided itself on being nonpartisan.

Yet Otpor rapidly became the darling of the aid community, ultimately receiving millions in material assistance, know-how, and even cash. By election day, Otpor was widely considered to be the foremost thorn in Milošević's side, with some going so far as to argue that it had "sparked the popular movement that overthrew Slobodan Milošević in 2000" (Rosenberg 2011b: xvii). By many accounts, Otpor was a "driving force" behind Koštunica's victory and the organization itself would later be credited with exporting Serbia's nonviolent revolutionary model to more than a dozen other countries, including Georgia, Ukraine, and, later, Tunisia and Egypt.

Formed on 27 October 1998 by a group of eleven university students, Otpor was the successor of the highly politicized student movement that emerged during the mid-1990s. For more than five years, university students throughout Serbia had taken a vocal and an organized stance against the Milošević regime. In fact, when in early 1997 the member parties of Zajedno called off their protests, students continued the demonstrations unabated.

Poorly resourced and lacking in funds, Otpor began as little more than a conversation, a revolutionary concept thought up in smoke-filled cafés and student dormitories. But its founders' zeal soon spread through word of mouth and scattered "actions." The first such action took place in November 1998, with several Otpor members covering Belgrade's downtown area with graffiti showing clenched fists, the newly devised symbol of resistance.

Shortly after the Kosovo war was declared over, the leaders of Otpor made their first forays into foreign assistance. In the summer of 1999, two Otpor founders, Nenad Konstantinović and Slobodan Homen, traveled to neighboring Republika Srpska, where they met with members of the U.S. State Department.

Over the next several months, Otpor expanded in size and scope, evolving from an organization targeting only urban-based students to a national movement encompassing young and old in rural and urban communities alike. As Otpor's membership increased, so too did its links to the international aid community. Diplomatic missions based in Belgrade soon became regular fixtures of support for Otpor, delivering small sums of cash—often no more than 10,000 deutsch marks—to Otpor leaders. As one European diplomat acknowledged, although such funds were "relatively minor . . . Otpor could do a lot with that to make themselves known, to distribute stuff on the streets . . . they could do a lot in terms of public exposure and campaigning."[64]

While diplomats were providing financial support to Otpor, both FES and IRI[65] were providing material assistance. In September 1999, a $74,735 grant[66] from NED helped IRI pay for Otpor's new offices in Belgrade, Niš, Novi Sad, and Kragujevac; several computers and print materials; and the $450 a month salary of an office manager (NED 1999b). This was followed in October with a meeting held in Budva, Montenegro, where IRI and Otpor representatives set the foundations for further material assistance to come from a much larger USAID grant.

Over the next several months, IRI worked closely with Otpor to develop and hone a GOTV campaign based in large part on lessons learned from Slovakia's Rock the Vote campaign. By March 2000, Otpor had completed its first GOTV plan. IRI funded the testing of Otpor's promotional materials through focus groups and even helped Otpor settle on a slogan for its campaign. By the time the GOTV plan was finalized, Otpor had received two $200,000 grants from IRI and USAID and another grant worth almost $190,000 directly from NED. These funds were funneled through two Otpor members, a number kept deliberately low to ensure that the regime could not paint Otpor members as foreign mercenaries.[67]

IRI's Daniel Calingaert helped Otpor launch twenty new offices throughout Serbia, establish and equip a separate Belgrade-based office dedicated to GOTV actions, and pay for a substantial media component, including commercials on local television networks, radio spots, print media, and billboards. Building on its training with parties, IRI also launched a series of Otpor training programs with a built-in GOTV component. In cities from Budapest to Budva, Otpor members learned how to target specific voter blocs, how to carry out voter contact efforts like door-to-door campaigns, and how to assemble local campaign plans—all of which was based on getting voters to support DOS.

Preparing for Stolen Elections

Just as donors took steps to facilitate a large voter turnout for DOS, so too did they take precautions to thwart electoral fraud. Donors did so at the hand of a large-scale Parallel Vote Tabulation (PVT) effort that would be used to identify inconsistencies in the regime's official presentation of results. According to Sarah Birch (2002: 503), "It was this grass-roots activity that provided the opposition with the tools to substantiate its claim that the regime was fiddling the results during the tabulation process." Indeed, the PVT made it possible to catch Milošević's electoral theft in action.

Serbia's PVT was led by DOS and the election-monitoring group CeSID. Because independent observers like CeSID and the Organization for Security and Co-operation in Europe (OSCE) were barred from taking part in the electoral count, DOS members were charged with verifying the practices found within polling stations. At least two DOS members were placed at every one of Serbia's polling stations. Following the closure of a polling station, these monitors would collectively count the ballots received and would each sign and receive an official, signed copy of that station's results.

The PVT created a system in which opposition monitors could directly phone in, and hand deliver, officially sanctioned electoral results to DOS municipal headquarters and CeSID, detailing precisely how many votes were received on each candidate's behalf. These headquarters, in turn, transmitted their results to DOS's Belgrade headquarters by way of telephone, the Internet, and even courier, in what Louis Sell (2002: 341) calls a "complicated and redundant system intended to foil police harassment." The headquarters, in turn, shared its officially verified results with Serbia's media.

By the evening of Serbia's presidential elections, independent media stations throughout the country were broadcasting Koštunica victories in polling stations throughout Serbia. By 4:30 the following morning, CeSID had released the cumulative results of more than 1,000 polling stations, declaring Koštunica the new president of Yugoslavia.

From the very beginning, the American party institutes made election monitoring an integral part of their work in Serbia.[68] The first of the institutes to do so was NDI, which in 1997 forged a close relationship with the newly formed CeSID.[69] As early as 1997, NDI was sponsoring training for CeSID activists and volunteers and had hired experts to transfer best practices on election monitoring. Though CeSID was denied official credentials to monitor the electoral process within polling stations, it did succeed in fielding hundreds of volunteers to stake out polling stations on election day, who were able to at least get a sense of voter turnout.

To ensure that the monitors placed inside the election stations could identify fraud, IRI trained thousands of prospective DOS poll watchers, teaching them how to recognize any efforts on the regime's part to steal votes.[70] This training began with a meeting in Hungary on 11 and 12 April 2000, when DOS representatives and election experts selected a train-the-trainers methodology and compiled an election monitors handbook. By early August, IRI began its extensive train-the-trainers program, ultimately training some 350 core trainers in towns throughout neighboring Montenegro and Hungary. These individuals then returned to Serbia where they trained 30,000 to 40,000 polling board members on the how-to's of election monitoring. Training included everything from mock elections to role-playing, as well as lectures highlighting the importance of monitoring and presenting the standard procedures for polling station commissions. On election day, each of these monitors was paid about $10 to monitor a polling station with one or two other DOS representatives. These monitors would be critical to proving electoral fraud.

Isolating Milošević

Efforts to bolster and legitimate Serbia's democratic opposition contrasted sharply with efforts that sought to isolate the Milošević regime. Sanctions, covert operations, pressure on Russia, and cash infusions to neighboring Montenegro all sought to extricate Milošević's support base and make it increasingly difficult for Milošević to maintain critical allegiances, either domestically and internationally.

SANCTIONS

In March 1998, the UN Security Council authorized a set of selective sanctions explicitly targeting the arms trade to encourage the Milošević regime to stop the escalating violence in Kosovo. This was followed in late April 1998 by an agreement among Britain, France, Germany, Italy, Russia, and the United States to freeze Yugoslav assets abroad.

What began as purely "symbolic" penalties designed to coax Milošević into negotiating a peaceful resolution in Kosovo, gradually developed into a more hard-hitting, and ever more targeted, sanctions regime aimed at galvanizing Serbian public opinion against Milošević and sowing the seeds of discord from within. The imposition of UN sanctions in early 1998 was thus followed by joint decisions on the part of the EU and the United States to freeze the foreign assets of the Serbian government. In June, EU member states, in conjunction with Bulgaria, Cyprus, the Czech Republic, Estonia, Hungary, Latvia, Lithuania, Poland, Romania, Slovakia, Slovenia, Iceland, Liechtenstein, and Norway banned export credits to the private sector, European investments in Serbia, as well as any goods and services to the regime. That same month, President Clinton issued Executive Order 13088, blocking all property and property interests of the Serbian government and suspending future American investment in that country. This was followed in September 1998 with an EU-imposed flight ban, forbidding Yugoslav national airline JAT from traveling into EU territory.

When the Milošević regime still proved recalcitrant six months later, the EU banned the export of oil to Serbia.[71] The EU then added a visa ban for Milošević, his family, and several hundred of his associates.[72] Later synchronized with a similar ban imposed by the United States, visa restrictions were tactically used to "sow the seeds of doubt" among Serbian officials, with sanctions administrators randomly moving names on and off the list to foster suspicion among Milošević's allies.[73]

Perhaps the most notable evolution in the imposition of sanctions, however, came in April 2000 with an EU decision to convert the union's former blacklist—composed of Serbian companies barred from doing business with EU member states—into a white list, comprised only of those companies permitted to do business with EU member states. The white list placed the burden on Serbian companies to prove the absence of financial ties to the Milošević regime.

Initially, the purpose of international sanctions was merely to isolate Serbia, and thereby force Milošević to make concessions on Kosovo. As the war in Kosovo drew to a close, however, Western governments became increasingly intent not simply on isolating Serbia but also on dividing Milošević loyalists to undermine his grip on power. Targeted economic and travel sanctions were one part of this. They helped to divide tycoons under Milošević by raising the costs of doing business with the regime.[74]

Maintaining Montenegro

A third part of the effort to isolate Milošević lay in building strong ties with Montenegro—a constituent part of the Federal Republic of Yugoslavia. For policy makers in both Western Europe and the United States, Serbia's sister republic "was the one relatively bright spot in Yugoslavia" (SEED 1998: 122). According to Secretary of State Albright, Montenegro's president, Milo Đukanović, had "earned the world's admiration and respect for his courage in protecting the rights and interests of his people despite threats and harassment from Belgrade."[75] Banking on the declining fortunes of Milošević after the 1996 Zajedno demonstrations, Đukanović positioned himself as a savvy political alternative to Milošević's authoritarianism. He thus opposed the Serbian army's incursion into Kosovo and even provided refuge for Kosovar Albanians forced to flee the growing violence. Following his much-publicized repudiation of the Dayton Peace Accords in 1996, Đukanović had succeeded in differentiating his republic "from Serbia by pursuing a path of political and economic reform and openness to the West."[76]

By the late 1990s, Montenegro was serving as a safe haven and "guiding light for the Serbian opposition."[77] Montenegro was also welcoming to donors and diplomats. It provided them with intelligence regarding the movement of Serbian security services, ensured their safety throughout Montenegrin territory, and hosted their many visits and conferences to the region. Throughout the summer of 2000, IRI and NDI held training sessions for campaign managers during which IRI trainers stimulated discussion on campaign strategy and provided insight into the organization of local campaign headquarters, message development, voter contact, campaign coordination within the party, and training techniques—all from Montenegro.

The intensity of activity being staged in Serbia's neighboring republic, as well as its leader's vocal anti-Milošević stance, made Montenegro a natural target for foreign assistance. Speaking before the U.S. Congress, NED's Paul McCarthy acknowledged, "The victory of anti-Milošević forces in Montenegro has created an unprecedented opportunity for democracy-building activities in the tiny republic" (CSCE 1999: 30). With foreign support, it was hoped that Montenegro could serve as a bulwark against the Milošević regime, providing refuge for Serbian opposition leaders and backing DOS candidates come election day. In doing so, it was expected that Montenegro would "play a constructive role in promoting democratic change in Serbia."[78]

But the aid programs that developed in Montenegro were wholly dissimilar to those used in Serbia. Until the early 2000s, foreign aid to Montenegro sought less to foster domestic democratization processes than it did to keep the Đukanović administration afloat. By the spring of 1999, tens of millions of dollars were being injected into the regime's coffers in an effort to keep the fiscally challenged (and notoriously corrupt) Đukanović regime solvent. From 1999 through 2000, the U.S. and EU member states alike poured more than $100 million into maintaining the Đukanović government, paying for everything from the republic's electric bills to its social welfare programs. In 1999 alone, the United States—then the sole donor providing such aid—delivered a total of $35 million of flexible assistance to the Montenegrin government, 92 percent of which was dedicated for budgetary purposes. In 2000, the United States increased this figure to roughly $70 million, $55 million of which was used to support the government's budgetary requirements. During this same period, the EU invested a total of €20 million in "emergency assistance" to the budget of the Republic of Montenegro. By late 2000, the funds directly channeled to Montenegrin authorities greatly exceeded those awarded to Serbian democrats.[79]

What Helped Bring Down Milošević

On 24 September 2000, presidential elections for the Federal Republic of Yugoslavia resulted in a stunning upset. With close to 55 percent of the federal vote, Vojislav Koštunica won an outright majority of the votes cast. Unwilling to accept the scope of his loss, Milošević refused to concede to his democratic rival. Although acknowledging that Koštunica had received more votes than Milošević, the state-sponsored Electoral Commission cast doubt on the totals trumpeted by CeSID and the DOS poll watchers. Contrary to DOS, the Electoral Commission claimed the opposition candidate had failed to win more than 50 percent of the ballots cast—thereby necessitating a second round of elections, which would pit Koštunica in a head-to-head battle with Milošević. The prospect of a second round of elections—and yet another opportunity for Milošević to steal votes and imperil Koštunica's momentum—did not sit well with DOS leaders. So, rather than cave to the pressures of the Milošević-backed Electoral Commission, Serbia's democratic opposition sprang to action. Within hours of Milošević's electoral thievery, DOS activists and supporters took to the streets, demanding Milošević's resignation. Two weeks later, Slobodan Milošević made an unprecedented concession: tendering his resignation amid a wave of peaceful protests.

Many reasons are said to account for Milošević's ouster, but by far the most controversial has been that of external intervention. More than in perhaps any other case of regime change, analysts have pointed to the instrumental role of democracy assistance in facilitating democracy's advent. Several dimensions of the aid initiative have loomed particularly large. For example, scholars have pointed to the impressive sums U.S. and European donors are said to have dedicated to democracy aid in Serbia. They have also lauded the role of Otpor in rallying voters to the ballot box. For their part, practitioners have credited aid for having encouraged opposition unity and bolstered independent media. Others have touted the ostensibly collaborative nature of the aid effort, with Europeans and Americans working in tandem, and democracy aid coalescing with diplomatic initiatives.

Evidence garnered from the testimonies of party aid recipients, donors, and domestic observers suggests that several forms and strategies of aid were indeed effective in helping Serbia's democratic opposition unseat Milošević. This included direct assistance, efforts to prove electoral fraud, the backing of a nationalist candidate (Koštunica), support for local leaders in Serbia's towns and villages, the outsourcing of party aid to Serb practitioners, and the harmony of foreign policy.

Direct Assistance

Among the most significant aspects of the democracy aid effort in Milošević's Serbia was the provision of direct assistance. According to Thomas Carothers (2001: 6), small grants directly targeted at opposition actors and organizations "gave the campaign greater weight than democracy aid typically has." Evidence indicates that the provision of direct material and financial assistance to opposition parties and NGOs was an important contributor in helping to level the political playing field in the run-up to Milošević's ouster.

As IRI explained in early 1999, one of the central problems Serbia's "cash-strapped" opposition faced throughout the 1990s was "that they have very little money and that they do not have much if any equipment for their offices" (IRI Quarterly Report 1999). This changed in 2000, however. Thanks largely—though by no means exclusively—to foreign aid, DOS acquired a national network of campaign offices, its candidates were featured in billboards and campaign commercials that dotted the political landscape, and its members regularly toured Serbia in campaign-sponsored vehicles.

As USAID explains, "A significant amount of material assistance to opposition coalitions and alliances allowed the democratic opposition to counteract the regime's control of most channels of political communication and sources of logistical support for the election campaign" (SEED 2000). The funds governments and donors provided were often modest—in the range of just several thousand dollars to some $30,000 or $40,000 each. Yet their modest size had several advantages.

First, they made it easy for donors to dole out funds unencumbered by what are often lengthy bureaucratic hurdles. Second, grants were small enough that they did not risk flooding the opposition marketplace with excess capital—a situation that would likely have promoted corruption. Yet the grants were sufficient to ensure that recipients' basic needs were met. Thanks to foreign aid, the DOS campaign was slick and colorful and would reach an unprecedented number of households in the months leading to the presidential elections in September 2000.

Using foreign funds, DOS set up branded coalition offices throughout Serbia. DOS members traveled across the republic on foreign-funded campaign buses and held public events with sound systems paid for by the party institutes. The coalition could also afford to advertise its campaign slogans on local media outlets, including opposition radio and television stations. Though some forms of material assistance proved less useful than others—for example, the often-lauded satellite phones provided to DOS leaders went unused[80]—direct aid as a whole proved enormously useful in helping the coalition realize its potential.

NDI program staff believe their willingness to pay for DOS offices— including covering the cost of rent and office equipment—"was really important" to party leaders—not only because it was something they wanted, but because it underscored just "how much NDI was willing to put on the line for them."[81] NDI's willingness to exceed the bounds of its normal mandate and pay for things like office rentals, helped instill a sense of loyalty and common purpose among aid providers and aid recipients, which ultimately encouraged party leaders to take greater heed of NDI's advice—particularly with respect to public opinion polling. The Serbian NDI employee charged with distributing such funds believes that such assistance—while "not a dramatic amount"— was "definitely very useful" and "very effective" for DOS parties in leveling the political playing field.[82]

Electoral Monitoring

One of the less frequently cited aspects of the foreign aid initiative was that of electoral monitoring. Less provocative than the work of Otpor and less controversial than the provision of material and financial aid, the training of election monitors was a significant facet of the democracy aid initiative and one that worked particularly well in galvanizing public sentiment against the regime. When in October 2000 hundreds of thousands of Serbs took to the streets of their nation's capital, this was in large part because they believed Milošević to have committed electoral fraud. Providing the ability to demonstrate such fraud were tens of thousands of IRI-paid election monitors, the NDI-funded election monitoring organization, CeSID, DOS, and United Nations Mission in Kosovo (UNMIK).[83] Together, these groups proved the extent of Koštunica's victory. According to the former U.S. ambassador to Serbia, William Montgomery (2010: 33), "It is impossible to overestimate the importance of this parallel counting of votes and the presence of physical evidence that could verify this."

Critics have argued otherwise, however. Carothers (2001: 4), for example, points out that public outrage over electoral manipulation predated foreign aid. Indeed, when in late 1996 the regime-backed electoral commission refused to recognize Zajedno's local-level victories, Serbs took to the streets, demanding the regime reinstate the opposition's victories. Although critics are correct to point out that Serbs had successfully overturned the regime's electoral manipulations long before foreign aid got underway, the electoral monitoring supported by Western governments differed from past initiatives in one significant respect: It produced tangible evidence of electoral manipulation.

Because of the nationwide system of parallel vote tabulation—an effort that IRI's Kent Patton regards as "the single most important factor" in aid's success—DOS and CeSID were able to verify the precise number of votes won by Koštunica, polling station by polling station. The presence of foreign-funded election monitors meant that "the opposition was able to prove that the results it announced were accurate because it had collected official copies of protocols from virtually all the polling stations in Serbia"—including Kosovo, where for years the regime was rumored to have grossly exaggerated voter turnout (Calingaert 2006: 149). Indeed, using polling station tallies bearing the signatures of regime officials, DOS, CeSID, and UNMIK clearly demonstrated the scope of Koštunica's victory. By contrast, in 1996, Zajedno was not so lucky. Lacking adequate resources, the coalition was unable to monitor all of Serbia's polling stations. For this reason, it never had the evidence required to quash the regime's allegations of electoral irregularities. Lacking tangible evidence of fraud, it took Zajedno three long months to have its victories reinstated. By contrast, it took DOS less than two weeks.

Another important contributing factor was the presence of UNMIK in Kosovo. In past years, Milošević was able to invent hundreds of thousands of votes, by fictitiously alleging that Kosovar Albanians—whose population of 850,000 overwhelmingly boycotted Serb elections—had in fact voted on his behalf.[84] With no independent monitors present in Kosovo prior to 2000, it was impossible to verify whether such votes had in fact been cast or were merely the creation of Milošević loyalists. In the aftermath of the Kosovo war, however, UNMIK monitors ensured that verifiable evidence detailed precisely how many votes had been cast in Kosovo. On the day of the election, 230 two-man UNMIK teams visited 489 polling stations in Kosovo and determined that a total of 44,167 people voted in the elections.[85] This left Milošević unable to manufacture the tens of thousands of additional votes needed to contend a victory in the September 2000 elections.

Backing a Nationalist Candidate

Among the least discussed factors in enabling foreign aid's success was the West's decision to back Koštunica. A communist dissident widely regarded as an unapologetic Serb nationalist, Koštunica was a staunch critic of both the United States and the EU, having refused to support either the Dayton Accords or NATO's intervention in Kosovo. Yet the importance of Koštunica cannot be overestimated for understanding DOS's popularity. Ironically, it was Koštunica's anti-Western credentials that made him so alluring a candidate to so many Serbs.

Vojislav Koštunica was in many respects an odd choice for foreign backing. Widely respected for his uncompromising convictions, Koštunica made a point of berating the international community for its perceived interventionism. In his words, U.S. and EU interventionism was "the kiss of death for all truly democratic and patriotic forces in Serbia" (ICG 2000a: 3). Not only did Koštunica balk at external interference, he outright rejected aid, which he said was "absolutely useless for the opposition and democratic forces in Serbia."[86] Unlike Đinđić, Avramović, or even Drašković, Koštunica adopted a hostile stance toward the United States and the EU, rejecting their offers of assistance and vocally condemning their intentions. Throughout the presidential campaign, he urged his supporters not only to say "no to White Palace" (Milošević's mansion) but "no to the White House." Koštunica himself was thus never a direct recipient of party assistance prior to October 2000. In fact, as a former adviser to Albright notes, U.S. officials didn't have any contact with Koštunica until *after* the 2000 elections.[87]

Whatever their qualms with Koštunica's anti-Western rhetoric, by early 2000 Koštunica boasted supporters on both sides of the Atlantic. At high-profile meetings from Berlin to Washington, U.S. and EU officials sang the praises of the DSS leader, enumerating his many accomplishments and positing the Serb nationalist as the ideal DOS candidate. In private meetings with DOS leaders, donors, party aid providers, and diplomats reiterated their backing of a Koštunica candidacy, pressing individuals like Đinđić to suspend their own political ambitions for the sake of a DOS victory.

A lower-profile player on the Serbian political scene, Koštunica had not yet amassed the political baggage that weighed so heavily on political heavyweights like Đinđić or Drašković. Having strayed from the limelight, Koštunica was unaffected by the allegations of corruption, which for so long had haunted members of the opposition and even Milošević himself. An ardent anti-communist, Koštunica had proven himself uncompromising in his attitudes toward the previous regime. An unrepentant Serbian nationalist, he could not be accused of anti-Serb pretensions or cowardice. With no direct ties to foreign assistance, Koštunica was impossible to label a "traitor" or "foreign mercenary," unlike his more prominent colleagues from the opposition. Indeed, polls taken in the run-up to Milošević's ouster showed the public's confidence in Koštunica's ability to stand up for Serbia's national interests to rank among his greatest strengths.

For Milošević, the mode of attack was thus limited. Unable to brand Koštunica as an anti-Serb traitor, Milošević stressed such quirks as Koštunica's fondness for cats or his alleged marital infidelities. Ironically, Koštunica proved so difficult for the regime to counter precisely because he had distanced himself from the West and portrayed himself as an unflinching independent. That party aid providers were willing to support Koštunica's candidacy regardless of his anti-Western posturing helped ensure their ultimate success in September 2000.

Supporting Local Leaders

Also critical was the decentralized nature of the aid campaign. Dispersing foreign aid across Serbia—rather than localizing it in Belgrade—was a central part of the foreign aid effort and a strategy that succeeded in sustaining nationwide enthusiasm for Koštunica's candidacy. A central part of this strategy was channeling support to Serbia's local mayors. Local officials would play an important role in organizing citizens to participate in the mass public uprisings against Milošević after the electoral theft on 24 September. Indeed, the massive presence of hundreds of thousands of disgruntled citizens across Serbia's capital was made possible not only by Belgrade-based politicos like Čedomir Jovanović but also by small-time, local leaders from across Serbia, who had organized buses, cars, and walks to descend on Belgrade. It was in fact Velimir Ilić, the outspoken mayor of Čačak, who organized a convoy of 10,000 protesters to break down police-imposed barricades en route to Belgrade on 5 October. His use of a bulldozer to tear through the regime's blockades won Milošević's ouster the title "Bulldozer Revolution." For months, these local leaders and party branches gathered supporters, worked on outreach, and staged opposition protests. Their efforts were supported by the advice and assistance of the foreign aid community.

For years, party aid providers, and the American party institutes in particular, had worked with local party branches in towns and villages across Serbia. It was in fact only in late 1999 that the institutes began working in Belgrade. Likewise, many European aid providers, such as the European Commission, worked closely with Serbia's mayors in cities like Niš and Pirot, whose credibility they sought to bolster with scarce energy supplements. Dušan Gamser of the GSS equates such assistance with the Berlin airlift of 1949.[88] Though the wellspring of popular support for Koštunica cannot exclusively, or even mostly, be attributed to foreign aid's geographically decentralized focus, the latter did help to bolster the competencies—both real and perceived—of local governments and party branches across Serbia.

Letting Serbians Lead

Perhaps the defining characteristic of the democracy aid initiative was the hands-on role played by Serbians themselves. In the aftermath of the NATO bombing of Serbia, many donors were forced to relocate their offices and staff to neighboring states. Lacking direct access to party headquarters, local offices, and the bulk of party enthusiasts, they had little recourse but to rely on individuals from within recipient parties. Serbians themselves were thus charged with dispensing cash and material aid to their party members, visiting local offices throughout the country, identifying party needs and potential opportunities, training fellow DOS members, and keeping their colleagues based abroad informed of the state of affairs within Serbia. The hands-on role Serbs played in the aid effort was a noteworthy departure from traditional aid practices—in which foreign experts and trainers are often blamed for co-opting the aid process—and an important contributor to aid's success.

As Stephanie Lynn of NDI admits, many of party aid's achievements were a testament to the people on the ground in Belgrade working for NDI: It was their back and forth and the relationships between staff that made it even possible to assemble DOS leaders and foster an electoral agreement. Although Serbian staff members were in regular contact with American and European practitioners, it was Serbs who forged the contacts, offered the advice and training, transferred the funds, and made the decisions needed to aid the opposition. As one NDI representative explains, "They did it, not us. They were far more brave than I was ever asked to be." The high reliance on Serbian—rather than expatriate staff—was important in breaking down cultural barriers and relieving aid recipients of any suspicions they might harbor regarding foreign staff members.

In his visits to local towns across Serbia, for example, one former NDI staff member recalls that "the most useful information we would get [was] when all the foreigners walked to the car and I remained for five minutes with those guys and they would say, 'Look, it's really a shame for us to say this in front of the Americans, but this is what really happened.'"[89] Another Serbian NDI employee agrees. Thanks to NDI's reliance on Serbian staff members, he says, there was "much faster, quicker, communication" between recipients and providers. Party leaders, he says, "felt like they can call me any day at any time, and they did it all the time."[90] Whereas party leaders might have resisted calling American staff members at all hours of the night, they had fewer qualms in contacting Serbian colleagues when the need arose.

Foreign Policy Harmony

If aid worked in 2000, it was in large part because other facets of U.S. and European foreign policy worked with it. That was in marked contrast to the 1990s, when U.S. and European foreign policy toward the former Yugoslavia, and Serbia in particular, lacked coherence. Repeatedly throughout the 1990s, diplomatic efforts to engage Milošević unilaterally collided with a nascent democracy aid effort that sought to strengthen his opponents. The contradiction of such policies changed in the aftermath of NATO intervention, however. By late 1999, party aid, democracy assistance, and U.S. and European diplomacy were neatly aligned to achieve a single goal: regime change. In the United States, the State Department worked closely with USAID and OTI to craft a flexible policy bent on bolstering Serbia's democrats and undermining Milošević's grasp on power. The harmonization of foreign policy had a profound impact on democracy aid's effectiveness, helping to eliminate the negative dimensions of previous policies, which many believed buttressed Milošević at the opposition's expense.

It also had a major effect on Serbia's opposition, which for years had criticized Western powers for engaging so exclusively with Milošević. In fact, Vesna Pešić—the pro-democratic leader of the antiwar GSS—says her party boycotted officials like Madeleine Albright because they agreed to meet with Milošević after Dayton.[91] Admits one U.S. diplomat who worked closely on Serbia, "Before the bombing . . . there was sort of desire, particularly with [Special Envoy Richard] Holbrooke, to engage Milošević. The view was that Milošević could solve the problem. What that did, however, was strengthen Milošević." Yet the policy of engaging Milošević changed dramatically in the aftermath of the Kosovo war: "After the war we finally understood the problem, which is that you don't want to be viewed as only engaging Milošević, because that would only strengthen his authority inside of Serbia."[92] By contrast, the exclusive engagement of Serbia's democratic opposition lent new credibility to DOS's competence, and helped further isolate Milošević.

What Did Not Work

Although much of the aid was effective in supporting the Serbian opposition's efforts to unseat Milošević in October 2000, some of it was not. In fact, several of the priciest ventures—such as elaborate media investments, high-profile meetings in foreign capitals, and sanctions—were among the *least* effective in helping defeat Milošević. Of the facets of the aid initiative that had little or even negative impact were the "Ring Around Serbia" media campaign, the repeated attempts to forge opposition unity, public praise for the opposition, untargeted sanctions, and efforts to court the Montenegrin vote.

Ring Around Serbia

Among the most expensive of such ventures was the U.S. investment in Serbia's independent media and the (in)famous "Ring Around Serbia" project. Donors who invested in such efforts have offered emphatically positive assessments of media aid's utility, arguing that initiatives like Ring Around Serbia were among "our most effective political development initiatives"[93] and "played a major role in the eventual downfall of the Serbian dictator."[94] Yet many interviewees privately proclaimed such investments to have been mis- and overspent. Former U.S. Balkan envoy James O'Brien goes so far as to call Ring Around Serbia "a disaster," maintaining that the initiative was "largely ineffective" and "not worth the resources provided."[95] In his memoir, U.S. Ambassador William Montgomery (2010: 28) admits that this "expensive idea sounded wonderful but actually couldn't start until it became completely useless."

Indeed, many of the planned media infrastructure projects—such as radio transmitters and towers in neighboring states—were very high-cost and their construction was time-consuming. Those projects required the support and input of neighboring governments and depended on both overt and covert machinations. As a consequence, many of the transmission towers slated for (re-)construction failed to get off the ground in time for Milošević's ouster. Of those that were built, many of the signals were concentrated to the north of Belgrade—where opposition to Milošević was already high. Thus, although strategic marketing estimates that as many as 250,000 listeners tuned into Ring Around Serbia programming, most of these listeners likely already sided with the opposition (McClear, McClear, and Graves 2003: 8). O'Brien acknowledges that there was simply very little demand for the media product that the U.S. government was providing, "but we were doing it and we were going to do it."[96]

Opposition Unity

Another facet of the aid agenda in which the United States invested heavily to limited effect was opposition unity. Opposition unity has long been a desired goal in revolutionary contexts, and diplomats and aid providers frequently tend to view it as an essential ingredient in the facilitation of regime change. This was true in Serbia, as it has been in a number of other cases stemming from Eduard Shevardnadze's Georgia to Bashar al-Assad's Syria. Not surprising, the supposed unity of Serbia's opposition has frequently been credited for enabling Milošević's ouster.

Writing more than a year after Milošević's electoral defeat, Sarah Birch (2002: 501) noted, "One of the main feats of the traditionally fissiparous Serbian opposition was that it managed to overcome its rivalries and united." Similarly, both Michael McFaul (2005: 9) and Albert Cevallos (2001: 8) wrote that unity had been "crucial" to the opposition's success.

Analysts seem to have missed a major point, however: Serbia's opposition was not fully unified, and the coalition's inability to unify completely was apparent just days prior to Milošević's fall. Indeed, both media coverage and public statements issued in the run-up to Milošević's ouster indicate that DOS's unity—and, hence, foreign aid's success—has been greatly exaggerated. For all their coaxing and cajoling, governments and aid implementers failed to win over the man who had until then ranked as the single greatest opponent of Slobodan Milošević. To the contrary, for all the polling, pleas, and high politics, the notorious "king of the squares," Vuk Drašković, remained unconvinced of unity's utility, electing instead to have his own candidate, Vojislav Mihailović, compete in the presidential elections *against* Koštunica.

In an article released just days before September 2000's seminal elections, *Mother Jones* noted that "opposition parties, as they have done for years in Serbia, seemed to be playing right into Milošević's hands by bickering and fielding multiple candidates to oppose Milošević."[97] Writing of Drašković's decision to exit DOS, the *New York Times* reported, "The split in the always fractious opposition virtually assures that Mr. Milošević . . . will win another four years in power in September."[98] Going into late 2000, analysts lamented the opposition's "inability to maintain a united front," arguing that DOS "rallies do not inspire, its leadership is divided, its support is waning, and its program is nonexistent" (Triantaphyllou 2000: vii). Thus, despite the clear message coming from U.S. pollsters, unity beyond the Alliance was slow to materialize.

Even though Montgomery admits that the "international community was obsessed with . . . opposition unity," he agrees he "failed" in his efforts to unite the coalition.[99] Adds a former IRI resident director, "What didn't work so well was the coalition building work. It was tough to talk to [the parties] about the need to work together. They knew it. We could talk about the process, but it was something that they needed to do on their own."[100]

Ultimately, of course, they could not. Despite numerous meetings with foreign diplomats, foreign ministers, and aid providers, Drašković was unconvinced by the polling data, believing the projected levels of support for Koštunica to be grossly exaggerated. For all their efforts, the United States and the EU failed to convince Drašković to join DOS and their vision of a truly united opposition would go unrealized.

That failure speaks less to the mistaken tactics of the aid community than to a wholly unrealistic objective posed by coalition unity. Unity is a complex and misunderstood issue for much of the aid and diplomatic community, which frequently treats unity as synonymous with democracy. The problem, of course, is that democracy is hardly a forum for consensus. Rather, it is about contestation. In many post-authoritarian contexts, people have struggled for generations to earn the basic right to contest their views. Once a semblance of democracy is at hand—even if it is as basic as the right to form political parties—it is hardly surprising that politicians have a hard time suppressing those differences. This is true in Serbia, as it is in countless other cases. Even in revolutionary circumstances, the ambition to unite all factions, groups, and ideologies under a single, organized political banner is often impossible. Nor is it necessary. As DOS's success indicates, even an opposition that is not fully united or entirely representative can achieve a major goal: winning democratic elections and facilitating a transition to democracy.

The International Spotlight

Another part of the aid effort that did not work was the effort to enhance the legitimacy and credibility of Serbia's opposition through high-profile meetings held across Western Europe. Hosted in foreign capitals like Berlin, such meetings were designed to raise the creditability of opposition leaders on the international stage, while also underscoring the West's support of Serbia's democrats. Though substantive, they also served as prestigious photo opportunities, during which opposition leaders would pose for photos with foreign dignitaries. Though well intentioned, many of these events were simply too high profile and ultimately counterproductive, lending credence to Milošević's claims of a Western-sponsored opposition.[101]

Indeed, the most memorable of the images to stem from such meetings was that of Vuk Drašković kissing the hand of U.S. Secretary of State Madeleine Albright. The manipulation of such images in Serbia proved disastrous. Within days, talk of Drašković and his opposition colleagues colluding with

Western officials—who just months before had orchestrated NATO's bombing of Serbia—dominated the regime-controlled media. The daily *Borba* sardonically complimented the "servile" Drašković for "kissing the hand of the person who organized the bloodshed and destruction of our country, the hand of the woman who emphasizes her responsibility for the murder of children, sick and innocent people as her achievement."[102] The directorate secretary of the Yugoslav Left Party (JUL), Ivan Marković, publicly lambasted the SPO leader for serving "the evil Piglet of the twentieth century, who's bloody front paws he has been kissing."[103]

The intensity of bad press that these high-profile meetings generated boded poorly for Serbia's opposition, which had long struggled to counteract Milošević's accusations of "treason" and "pro-Western sympathies." The League of Social Democrats of Vojvodina's Nenad Čanak, who himself attended one such meeting staged in Berlin, admitted his discomfort in having to "share a table with the people considered to be odious in Serbia."[104] According to Čanak, "If there are no obvious results, those meetings can only be harmful for us." [105] Things got so bad that after the Berlin meeting, representatives of the U.S. mission to Serbia sent an informal cable to Washington recommending that U.S. authorities lower the profile of their engagements with the Serbian opposition. After January 2000, high-profile public appearances of opposition leaders with U.S. leaders ended. The same was true for EU leaders. While neither U.S. nor EU officials abandoned their efforts to engage with Serbia's opposition trilaterally, they did opt to limit themselves to closed-door engagements.

Sanctions

If high-profile meetings did not work, then sanctions outright hurt. Sanctions were among the most controversial component of foreign intervention in Serbia's internal politics. Two forms of sanctions were used in the run-up to Milošević's ouster: untargeted sanctions—aimed at isolating Serbia—and targeted sanctions—aimed at isolating Milošević from the tycoons and state security agents that underpinned his power base. Untargeted sanctions were enormously problematic, helping to fuel a criminal economy that bolstered Milošević and undermined democracy. By contrast, targeted sanctions were quite helpful as a means to divide Milošević loyalists and incentivize the shift of allegiances toward post-Milošević authorities. Ultimately, however, both forms of sanctions would suffer from serious drawbacks that would have negative implications throughout the duration of Milošević's tenure and during the post-Milošević period.

The sanctions began in 1992, with the imposition of untargeted UN sanctions. It is no exaggeration to say that UN sanctions—such as the oil and economic embargo—made life *very* difficult for Serbia's citizens. They fueled the worst hyperinflation witnessed in Europe since Weimar Germany, making everyday goods—like bread, milk, and fuel for cars—harrowingly difficult to come by. As a consequence, sanctions were despised across Serbia. They were also a major boost to the regime, helping not only to lay the foundations of an anti-Western narrative but also to prop up a criminal economy that Milošević would use to remain in power.

In the short-term, sanctions provided Milošević with an easy scapegoat on which to lay the blame for his regime's incompetence. As Knudsen (2008: 89) explains, the SRS and SPS used sanctions "as 'evidence' of the existence of an international conspiracy against the Serbian people." Rather than galvanize public sentiment against Milošević, sanctions helped rally Serbs against the West and the opposition. Ironically, they "strengthened the Milošević regime, on which they were intended to exert pressure" (Knudsen 2008: 14). Indeed, rather than galvanize resentment against Milošević, the public's confidence in Milošević actually *rose* throughout the period of the least-targeted sanctions. A leading member of the Alliance for Change, in October 1999, explained that sanctions made "it a lot easier for Milošević to stay in power."[106] Instead of helping Serbia's democratic actors, sanctions worked against them, by strengthening the popular perception that anti-Milošević parties were "collaborators," "lapdogs of the West," "mercenaries," and "traitors."

It was precisely because untargeted sanctions were deemed so counterproductive that EU and U.S. authorities began to institute a more targeted sanctions regime in the late 1990s. The move toward more targeted sanctions began during the Kosovo war, when the EU introduced tight visa restrictions. That May, the EU carefully selected 800 of Milošević's closest associates and their family members. In June, this list was harmonized with that of the United States (ICG 2000b: 5). In the run-up to October 2000, the names on the list were repeatedly shifted in an effort to "sow the seeds of doubt" within the Milošević administration and to make Milošević suspicious of his own allies.[107] The policy contributed to what one political officer at the U.S. Embassy in Belgrade calls an atmosphere of "disinformation."[108] The targeted visa ban worked not only as a form of punishment but also as an inducement, whereby Milošević loyalists who cooperated with DOS were rewarded by having their names removed from the visa ban. The effect, according to O'Brien, was that it "drove people crazy."[109]

Targeted sanctions were made yet more targeted through the EU's conversion from an economic Black List (that is, a list of Serbian businesses with whom the EU would not do business) to a White List—a list of businesses permitted to do business in the EU. The conversion caused a sea change in the sanctions regime. In July 2000, the European Commission introduced its first list of 190 companies with a proven ability to withhold capital and revenues from the FRY and Serbian governments. The White List made it harder for companies and individuals associated with Milošević to defy the sanctions. The more targeted financial sanctions offered by the White List was a major blow to Milošević, making it more difficult for his allies to move money out of the country, to places like Cyprus, London, or even Moscow. The effect was to compel people to draw away from Milošević.

Still, even as sanctions became more targeted, they were never as precise as policy makers would have liked. In part because of this, by early 2000 EU foreign ministers contemplated a whole scale reversal of their sanctions regiment. In February, EU leaders voted to drop their flight ban on EU carriers traveling to Serbia. By the spring, individual foreign ministers were calling for further concessions, among them an end to the oil embargo. In fact, outrage over the sanctions regime reached such heights that in September 2000 EU foreign ministers held a two-day conference in Evian, France, to assess alternatives. Reporting on the meeting, the BBC noted, "Less than a month before the Serbian general elections, many in the EU believe the measures have proved ineffectual in supporting the democratic opposition."[110] French Foreign Minister Hubert Védrine publicly conveyed "genuine skepticism . . . on the part of a growing number of states" concerning EU sanctions, which, he said, had "not achieved their political objectives."[111] Of particular concern was the oil embargo, which many in the EU believed hurt the Serbian population. Ireland's foreign minister, Brian Cowen, remarked that sanctions were "impacting primarily on the ordinary people of Serbia . . . and it cannot be in our interest to impoverish the country."[112]

Nor would it be in the interest of the EU to fuel a criminal economy that would have Europe-wide (if not global) repercussions. According to Andreas (2005: 227), sanctions accounted for a "much higher level of criminalization than would otherwise have been the case in the absence of sanctions" in

Serbia. Sanctions gave rise to a criminal economy that benefited Milošević as well as a coterie of newly professional smugglers who would make millions by dealing in stolen cars, cigarettes, arms, sex trafficking, and heroin. Milošević's son, Marko, for example, is believed to have profited handsomely from the illegal smuggling of cigarettes by forging lucrative links with foreign criminals.[113] The regime itself made a fortune through embargo busting, the fruits of which would "prop up the regime" and incentivize sanctions profiteers to support Milošević (Naylor 1999: 363). As a consequence, many believe that "sanctions are what cemented Milošević's power."[114]

But sanctions would have consequences that reached beyond Milošević. The criminal economy would forge lasting links between Serbian intelligence operatives and criminal smugglers, ensuring that state security operatives had a stake in Serbia's criminal economy for years to come. According to Andreas (2005: 35), "The most difficult political challenge in post-Milošević Serbia" would be "breaking the close symbiosis between the state and organized crime, which was nurtured by sanctions." Unraveling these networks would cost Zoran Đinđić his life in 2003. Yet not only would they impede Serbia's transition, but they would spawn a criminal enterprise that would spread beyond Serbia, into Montenegro, Croatia, and the whole of the Balkans, and ultimately affect states throughout the EU.

Mismanaging Montenegro

Although sanctions were the most controversial aspect of the foreign aid initiative within the realm of public opinion, efforts to prop up the Đukanović regime in neighboring Montenegro were the most contentious behind closed doors. By the late 1990s, this former Yugoslav Republic had become a hotbed of criminal activity, earning as much as 50 percent of its GDP from cigarette smuggling alone.[115]

Yet in the run-up to Milošević's ouster, tens of millions of dollars were poured into the Đukanović government. According to Montgomery (2010: 30), such aid was devised both to bolster Đukanović's government as an anti-Milošević outpost and "to convince the Montenegrin president to actively engage for the Serbian opposition and to encourage his supporters to vote" in September 2000's Yugoslav presidential elections. Although foreign aid succeeded in achieving the former, it had far less success with the latter. To the contrary, the wellspring of unchecked cash, combined with the deeply criminalized state economy, left a legacy of corruption that would not bode well for Montenegrin democracy and its future efforts to join the EU.

One area in which Western authorities hoped Đukanović would prove particularly useful was with respect to Yugoslavia's presidential elections. Western diplomats did their utmost to ensure that Đukanović vocally supported Koštunica and rallied his supporters on Koštunica's behalf. Montgomery (then U.S. ambassador to Croatia) met with Đukanović, as did Albright and British foreign secretary Robin Cook, to implore him to participate in the 2000 elections. These efforts were unsuccessful, however.

Fearing that electoral participation would undermine his efforts to secure Montenegrin secession, Đukanović refused to back Koštunica. Instead, he advocated that Montenegrins boycott the Yugoslav elections—effectively dealing a major blow to Western efforts to increase Koštunica's electoral prospects. According to O'Brien, there was an ongoing debate within the Clinton administration about how to change Đukanović's mind. "Some wanted to cut off assistance to make him participate."[116] In the end, however, neither the United States nor the EU would cut off such aid, opting to overlook the fact that despite their repeated efforts, Đukanović could not be convinced to overtly back Koštunica.

But if diplomatic appeasement and financial enticements would not compel Đukanović to back DOS, the transfer of tens of millions of dollars into Montenegrin officials' bank accounts would not be without impact. The considerable sums put at Đukanović's disposal left minimal role for oversight, opening the door to rampant corruption. One administrator of U.S. "budgetary" aid to Montenegro goes so far as to call the financial arrangements "bizarre."[117] Congress, he said "would tie our hands with regards to direct assistance to Serbia . . . but at the same time wanted us to shovel tens of millions of dollars to Montenegro on the flimsiest sort of arrangements."[118] The aid may have kept Đukanović afloat, but it is an open question as to how much of that assistance was in the end stolen or misappropriated. The same misgivings could, of course, apply to the EU's administration of budgetary assistance, which the union itself acknowledges to have been "exceptional," given that it was provided in the form of straight grants to the Đukanović government.[119]

But many just did not care whether such funds would be properly accounted for or how they may impact an already criminalized state. As U.S. aid officials admit, there was an overriding interest in seeing that Đukanović remained a viable opponent to Belgrade and to Milošević personally.[120] Indeed, many overlooked the possible question marks that "budgetary assistance" raised. Explains one former aid provider, "We knew [Đukanović's] goals were not absolutely the same as ours, we knew his background was not the cleanest, but at that moment our strategic interests in the region coincided."[121] Unfortunately, it would not be enough to secure Đukanović's backing of Koštunica.

NATO Bombing

The most controversial of the international interventions leading to Milošević's ouster was the NATO bombing of Yugoslavia. NATO's intervention in Serbia ended a full sixteen months before Milošević was ousted and its goal was never to unseat Serbia's dictator or to promote democracy in Serbia. Still, this has not stopped analysts and officials—including former NATO general Wesley Clark; the last ambassador to Yugoslavia, Warren Zimmermann; and former secretary of state Lawrence Eagleburger—from commending the virtues of NATO bombing in contributing to Milošević's ouster.[122] Nor has it stopped many Serbians from lambasting the NATO intervention for strengthening Milošević's hand and undermining attempts to unseat him. The real impact of NATO's intervention on Milošević's ouster and democracy in Serbia likely lies somewhere between those two schools of thought.

As mentioned, the goal of the NATO bombing of Yugoslavia was not to unravel the Milošević dictatorship. Rather, it was to end Serbia's incursion into Kosovo and to force the withdrawal of Yugoslav National Army troops from the Serbian province. But the NATO bombing did have an immediate impact on Serbian public opinion and, by extension, Milošević himself: in the short-term, it served to rally the public behind him.

As Dodder and Branson (1999: 8) write, "The NATO missile strikes and air bombardments were met with Serb defiance. Faced with a foreign assault, the people rallied around Milošević and mocked Western claims that NATO had no quarrel with the Serbian people but only with their leaders." Indeed, patriotic euphoria swept across Serbia, as Milošević successfully cast the NATO intervention as part of an international conspiracy intent on exterminating the Serbian people. Former Otpor activist Vladimir Pavlov explains, "Right after the bombing was the peak of Milošević's power. It was either, you're with him or, if you want to fight against him, you're NATO or a traitor."[123] In the short-term at least, the NATO bombing made opposition to

Milošević exceedingly difficult. It made any criticism of the regime appear
unpatriotic, and it made anyone associated with the NATO alliance appear to
be a mercenary. Reporting on the declining dissent against Milošević throughout the NATO bombardment, the *Washington Post* noted, "The few remaining
sources of opposition to Milošević's twelve-year rule have fallen mostly silent
as the country has rallied in patriotic response to NATO's bombs and mis-
siles. . . . Latent dissatisfaction with the Yugoslav army has been overwhelmed
by the perceived need to defend the country."[124]

Indeed, throughout the bombing, opposition to Milošević ground to a
halt. And even after the NATO bombing, political parties on the receiving end
of U.S. and European assistance had to navigate a difficult position—wanting
aid but not wanting to be seen condoning a military intervention that cost
some five hundred Yugoslav civilians their lives and severely damaged Serbia's
infrastructure and economy.

The period of the NATO bombing and its immediate aftermath also resulted in an increasingly oppressive environment for Serbia's opposition. The
violence used to suppress dissent increased sharply, as Milošević narrowed in
on his remaining opponents. Dušan Gamser, a member of the GSS, noted,
"After the bombing, this was perhaps the worst period because the pressure of
the regime was the strongest. We were very cautious."[125]

The NATO bombing also provided a rare opportunity for Milošević to
rebrand himself in the eyes of an otherwise skeptical nation. On the one hand,
the act of perceived aggression against Serbian territory allowed Milošević to
cast himself as the defender of a nation under siege. During the bombing,
Milošević consistently cast Serbia as the victim of international aggression
and himself as Serbia's lone champion. On the other hand, after the NATO
bombing, the considerable damage done to Serbia's infrastructure allowed
Milošević to brand himself as the rebuilder of the country. In the weeks following the NATO bombing, Milošević called for the mass mobilization of
Serbs to rebuild the decimated national infrastructure.[126] State-sponsored
media focused incessantly on the regime's efforts to fix bridges, buildings, and
hospitals destroyed or damaged during the bombing—a process that allowed
Milošević to further brandish his patriotic credentials.

But if NATO's intervention made the opposition's life harder in the short-
term, it may have strengthened its position in the mid-term, particularly in
the run-up to Milošević's ouster. During that period, DOS candidates were
able to use Milošević's failed war in Kosovo against him. DOS candidates
exploited the loss of Serbia's fourth war in less than a decade to portray

Milošević as a weak and bungling leader, incapable of defending the nation. It seemed to work. Already by the fall of 1999, polls indicated that any budding support for Milošević following the NATO intervention was ephemeral. By October, NDI's polling numbers indicated "Serbian voters are extremely angry at Milošević. They blame him for the failing economy, and believe that removing him from office is the best way to improve the situation."[127]

Thus, as Richard Monroe Miles, the U.S. chief of mission in Serbia and later Georgia, noted, the NATO bombing both contributed to and detracted from the ambition to unseat Milošević and promote democracy in Serbia, in the short- and mid-terms.[128] In the long-term, however, the bombing has had more uniformly negative consequences for Serbian democracy and relations with the West. More than a decade after the NATO bombing of Serbia, resentment toward the bombing and the countries that directed it remains palpable. It has justified hostilities toward Western countries and has been used to legitimize warm relations with Russia. Moreover, it has fueled a narrative of victimization that runs deep across many segments of Serbian society and has made the recognition of Serbia's complicity in war crimes—and thus participation in institutions such as the ICTY—more difficult.

Overstated Aid

The failings of several critical aspects of the foreign aid effort demand a revised assessment of the West's role in Serbian regime change. Yet they allow for only a partial retelling. Also significant are the facets of assistance that have been oversold—their impact exaggerated by current accounts of democracy aid's utility in Milošević's unseating. Although the following aspects of the aid effort cannot be denounced as "failures," their impact was less substantial than scholars and practitioners have since suggested.

The Breadth of Support

One key part of the mythologizing of aid in the run-up to Milošević's unseating has been aid's supposed magnitude. Although estimates vary, the total figures are regarded as having been high. Carothers (2001: 7) estimates that U.S. and European expenditures amounted to a total of roughly $80 million in the year leading to Milošević's ouster.[129] In their review of U.S. assistance,

McClear, McClear, and Graves (2003: xii) offer a drastically lower figure—$1 per Serb or about $7 million. All, however, are convinced that the aid effort was large.

Unfortunately, precise estimates of the entire assistance package are hard to come by. According to SEED, the U.S. government alone spent close to $9 million on democracy aid to Serbia in 1999 and another $17 million in 2000. European governments likely equaled if not surpassed this number. The Norwegian government—the largest of the European funders—spent about $5 million in 2000 on democracy assistance (Norad 2010: 66). Yet the largesse of such funds is easily exaggerated.

To begin with, it is important to put the totals of democracy aid into a regional perspective. As Figure 2 demonstrates, the sums awarded to Serbia's democrats were above average when compared to the funds devoted to the region, but they were not excessive. They were particularly modest if one takes population size into account—in which case, apart from Bulgaria and Romania (which were receiving sizeable funds at the time from the EU), Serbia was receiving nothing out of the ordinary. To the contrary, Kosovo, with a population roughly a quarter that of Serbia, received about half of Serbia's allotment. Montenegro, with a population less than a tenth that of Serbia, received a quarter of its assistance. Bosnia, a country with about half the population of Serbia, received close to what Serbia received. And the remaining countries were given aid roughly in proportion to their population sizes. Nor were the

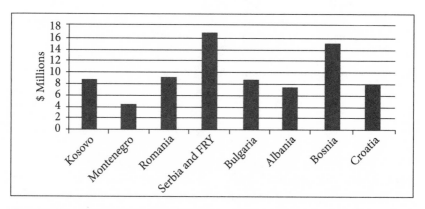

Figure 2. U.S. Democracy Aid to Countries in Central and Eastern Europe in 2000
Source: Adapted from SEED reports, 2001.

sums particularly significant compared to the sums Serbia's democrats would receive in the aftermath of Milošević's departure (see Figure 3). Democracy aid would in fact dramatically increase in Serbia *after* the democratic changes in 2000.

Second, if one accepts the $80 million price tag attributed to the Serbian aid effort, it is worth remembering that a large portion of that—as much as one third—would have been dedicated to overhead and administrative expenses. Of the roughly $55 million remaining, a large portion went to expensive but unsuccessful initiatives such as Ring Around Serbia. This meant that of all the resources dedicated to Milošević's ouster, those awarded to Serbian organizations and parties themselves remained remarkably modest. The Serbian-related budgets of IRI and NDI, for instance, were $1.8 million and $2.2 million, respectively.[130] NED, which sponsored some of the work of the institutes and offered grants to Otpor, spent a grand total of close to $3 million in Serbia from 1997 through 2000.

As has previously been argued, the provision of such assistance was helpful for Serbia's democrats. But as Morton Abramowitz, an NED board member explains, "It's not like we were giving vast millions . . . everything was

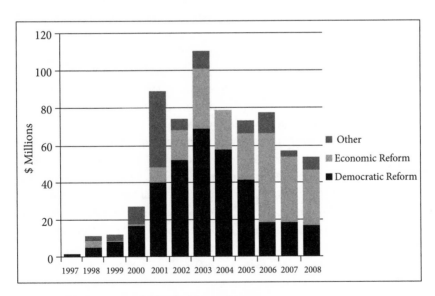

Figure 3. U.S. Democracy Aid to Serbia, 1998–2009
Source: Adapted from SEED reports.

small." Though highly useful, the grants NDI and IRI doled out to parties did not exceed $40,000 at a time. The same was true for grants from European aid providers. Organizations like the AMS offered small financial allotments to DOS and Otpor—just enough to pay for leaflets and other promotional materials.[131] These grants were ultimately effective not because they were so immense, but precisely because they were modest yet targeted.

Otpor and the Get-Out-the-Vote Campaign

Another facet of the aid agenda that has been exaggerated was the determinative role played by Otpor and the ultimate utility of the GOTV effort. Given the high voter threshold required to win the presidency—more than 50 percent of the vote—getting out the vote on election day was viewed as critical to Koštunica's victory. Democracy assistance targeted a variety of GOTV campaigns, spearheaded by Otpor and CeSID. The GOTV has since been heralded as a major success, ranking among aid's most effective initiatives in Serbia. The voter outreach efforts of Otpor in particular have been widely credited for the impressive turnout on election day—a whopping 71.5 percent. But although the narrative of Otpor's activism has won adherents and enthusiasts on either side of the Atlantic, an analysis of voter turnout throughout the 1990s shows that the results of the 2000 elections were far from unprecedented. Nor can the role of Otpor be said to have been determinative.

Figure 4 shows that voter turnout for both presidential and parliamentary elections was remarkably stable throughout the 1990s and in the year 2000. Though electoral participation dipped in 1997, this was a result of the electoral boycott of Serbia's opposition parties; 1997 aside, voter turnout for presidential elections averaged roughly 70 percent. Although high, the electoral turnout in September 2000 was hardly out of character for the Serbian electorate.

Moreover, the turnout for parliamentary elections held in December 2000—less than three months after Milošević's ouster—exhibited no upswing in turnout, despite an amply funded GOTV effort and the active role of Otpor. To the contrary, voter turnout in December 2000—like that of September 1997—was significantly lower than in either 1990 or 1992—two years in which Milošević is not believed to have engaged in substantial electoral fraud. Such evidence indicates that GOTV assistance may have been less influential than analysts have suggested.

So too was the role of Otpor. The legacy of Otpor has been promoted

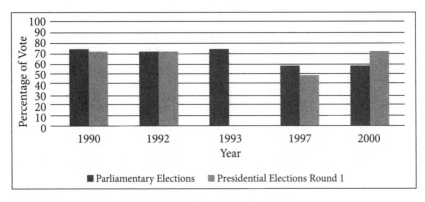

Figure 4. Voter Turnout in Serbian and Yugoslav Elections, 1990–2000
Source: Goati 2004.

heavily in the post-Milošević period, particularly in the wake of the Arab Spring, and it has given rise to a mythology that celebrates this youth-led movement for singlehandedly bringing down a dictator. As its founders tell it, Otpor was more powerful than all the eighteen parties of DOS combined.[132]

The reality is more complex, however. Otpor *was* an important part of the democratic opposition against Milošević. It helped to change the climate of the discussion on Serbia and it also injected new energy into the drive to unseat Milošević, increasing excitement within the electorate, and lowering the barrier of fear that might otherwise have dissuaded political activism. Yet Otpor was just one part of a multifaceted opposition.

And it was certainly not the best funded, at least not until after Milošević had been ousted. Although some within the U.S. government quickly caught on to Otpor's appeal (thanks in large part to the political instincts of U.S. envoy Robert Gelbard), many donors were wary of supporting these brazen youths. According to one NED representative, Otpor "scared the hell out of people in Washington."[133] Many believed that Otpor's members—who were by no means all anti-nationalist—simply "wanted to replace Milošević's socialism with quasi-fascism."[134] Others thought Otpor's clear emphasis on bringing down a dictator was simply too controversial. Said one CIPE representative involved in Serbia at the time, "We didn't want to fund Otpor's work. My feeling is that you shouldn't fund revolutionaries. . . . That's not the role of democracy assistance. . . . I don't want to be in this business of regime change."[135] Although Otpor did receive grants and training from the United

States and EU member states—funds that helped bankroll their work through-out late 1999 and 2000—it was not the darling of the international aid com-munity until *after* Milošević's fall from power.

Transatlantic Collaboration

Another factor frequently credited for the October 2000 changes is collabo-ration between donors and diplomats on either side of the Atlantic. According to Carothers (2001: 5), "U.S. and European aid worked from the same script" in seeking Milošević's ouster. William Montgomery, the former U.S. ambas-sador to the Federal Republic of Yugoslavia, argues that "there was a high degree of coordination and a high degree of agreement on the need to support the opposition. And a good division of labor."[136] Such statements are, to a large extent, true. Both European and American foreign aid was crafted with an eye on defeating Milošević. European and American officials met and spoke fre-quently throughout the months preceding October 2000, trading thoughts on their relationships with various opposition leaders, readjusting the sanctions regime, and coordinating policy statements.[137] But although the transatlantic aid community stood aligned on the mission to remove Milošević, European and American policy makers differed (sometimes significantly) on how to do so. Most important, so too did practitioners, many of whom had little inter-action with their colleagues from across the pond.

American policy makers were, for example, staunchly opposed to what was the cornerstone of the European aid effort: Energy for Democracy. They viewed the European initiative as violating the oil embargo they had placed on Serbia. According to Gelbard, the United States opposed the program "not because we object to helping opposition-run municipalities, but because oil is a fungible commodity and its distribution would inevitably benefit Milošević's regime."[138] The same was increasingly true for the sanctions regimen, which many European leaders were poised to disband on the eve of Milošević's elec-toral defeat.[139]

Yet the divide among European and American aid communities was most patently evident not within diplomatic circles but on the ground in Serbia. Europeans working in Belgrade had little direct contact with either their American colleagues working in Budapest or their Serbian colleagues working for Americans. As a consequence, neither was particularly well informed of the other's undertakings, particularly as concerned the provision of party aid.

Public Opinion Polling

Another facet of the aid agenda greatly oversold by practitioners has been that of U.S.-sponsored public opinion polling. Douglas Schoen (2007: 105), the Clinton administration's pollster at the time, writes that the opposition's use of his public opinion polls are "[w]hat ultimately ousted Milošević in 2000." Patton makes the case that U.S. polling "was crucial" to the institutes' success in Serbia. The perceived importance of such polling plays into a larger narrative in which U.S. support is perceived as having been crucial, first, for the selection of Koštunica as DOS presidential candidate and, second, for underscoring the need for opposition unity. It is a narrative that is also used to validate the investment in public opinion polling in dozens of countries across the world. In Serbia, at least, the evidence suggests that its impact is marginal. Indeed, American polls were neither the most widely used nor the most enlightening in 2000. To the contrary, they merely elucidated what domestic analysts and many party members already knew: that Koštunica and opposition unity would be key to Milošević's undoing.

In the years since October 2000, DOS's selection of Vojislav Koštunica has been attributed to American public opinion polling. Yet the selection of Koštunica was less a result of the wisdom of American pollsters than of the foresight of a handful of Serbian politicians, most notably Zoran Đinđić. A savvy politico with a passion for modern campaign techniques, Đinđić was well aware that his popularity in Serbia was insufficient to topple Milošević.[140] Having tried and failed to lead coalition alliances in the past, it was Đinđić who suggested Koštunica be the DOS front man—encouraging U.S. pollsters to include him in their polls (Schoen 2007: 137).

Apart from Đinđić—who regularly took note of polling data—most Serbian politicians placed little credence in pollsters' advice.[141] Vuk Drašković, for example, questioned the veracity of American polls and dismissed their findings when they conflicted with his intuition. Recalls Drašković, "It was very strange to believe those figures without doubt."[142] Many DOS members felt similarly, privately confiding skepticism in U.S. pollsters. According to a former NDI employee who worked closely with DOS politicians in 2000, "Nobody believed his [Schoen's] polls. . . . People did not believe in polls, mostly going with gut feeling."

There is also no reason to assume that *American* polls were the most compelling. As GSS's Gamser says, there were many opinion polls he and his colleagues consulted in the months leading to October 2000.[143] Serbian polling institutes like the Center for Policy Analysis and the Serbia Institute for Social Science "provided the opposition with the information necessary to mount a successful campaign" (Bieber 2003: 86). Domestic research institutes had conducted public opinion polls for most of the decade, well before NDI became involved in Serbia. Moreover, much of their data was indistinguishable from that released by the U.S. party institutes. As a consequence, DOS members were exposed to any number of polls, of which those supported by the Americans were but a minority.

U.S.-sponsored opinion polls have also been credited with DOS's unity. As Eli Lake explains, "The initial event that spawned the normally fractious opposition to unify . . . was not high-stakes espionage, but rather an opinion poll."[144] Yet the need for opposition unity was all but an unfamiliar concept for Serbia's opposition. By the time diplomats and aid providers offered their polls extolling the virtues of coalition politics, Serbia's opposition had already attempted a total of eight different coalitions (Table 9). Serbia's opposition had in fact formed the Alliance for Change—which would go on to form the foundation of DOS—before Schoen and his colleagues began sharing their polls. The GSS's Pešić explains, "The idea of uniting existed from the beginning, it did not come from the Americans. We had the message from the beginning. The idea of unification was very old."

The polling data offered was not particularly groundbreaking. Few Serbian politicians, for example, recall NDI polling as having been significantly different from the polls conducted by domestic analysts. Thus, although polls may have bolstered aid recipients' confidence in unity and Koštunica, such suggestions reinforced what parties already knew. It did not tell them something fundamentally new.

The problem with American polling in Serbia was not unique to the Balkans. Rather, it embodied a problem American pollsters face everywhere: Their polls are rarely regarded as neutral indicators of the state of public opinion. Instead, U.S. polling is often treated as suspect. Funded by a foreign government, its objectivity is frequently called into question and inevitably draws controversy. Moreover, polling itself often faces a hostile environment in nondemocratic and newly democratic settings, where instincts often outweigh statistics. Still, aid providers have made polling a staple of the party aid toolkit, one that they are reticent to abandon in light of current funding strategies.

Table 9. Coalitions Attempted in Serbia from 1990 to 2000

Coalition	Date Formed	Duration	Members
AOS	June 1990	6 months	DS, SPO, NRP, DF, LP, SSP
USDO	May 1991	3 months	SPO, SLS, ND–MS, DF
DEPOS	May 1992	18 months	SPO, SLS, ND–MS, SSS, DSS
DEKO	Nov. 1992	a few days	SPO, SLS, ND–MS, SSS, DSS, DS, GSS, SD
DEPOS II	Nov. 1993	3 months	SPO, ND, GSS
DA	Dec. 1995	4 months	DS, DSS, SLS, SNS
Zajedno	Nov. 1996	5 months	SPO, DS, GSS, DSS
Alliance for Change	July 1998	18 months	DS, GSS, DHSS

Source: Spoerri 2008a.

Easing the Path to Regime Change

Foreign policy makers, donors, and party aid practitioners made a major about-face in the months that preceded Milošević's ouster. After close to a decade of little to no assistance for Serbia's anti-Milošević opposition, they dramatically reversed course. As Goran Svilanović, the former president of GSS joked, the bombing of Serbia was followed by a bombardment of aid. Party aid played an important role in Milošević's ouster, helping to pay for DOS office rentals, campaign commercials, tour buses, public opinion polls, and a massive GOTV campaign that flooded the streets in cities large and small.

But party aid was not the only part of the foreign aid initiative. Assistance to Serbia's opposition parties was exceeded by an elaborate effort to build a radio tower. It was equaled by financial assistance to NGOs and youth movements like Otpor, many of which played a high-profile role in calling for Milošević's ouster. Democracy aid, in turn, was one part of a larger arsenal aimed at unseating Milošević. In the final months of Milošević's reign, economic sanctions were carefully targeted at Milošević's closest allies—making it impossible for them to enjoy the lifestyles to which they had grown accustomed. And diplomatic assistance, once conferred on Milošević, was now showered on the opposition.

The foreign policy reversal was a very important contributor to Milošević's fall. The full range of democracy assistance tools was also important. Political party assistance was just a small part of this, but it was not insignificant. Yet was assistance determinative? This chapter has argued that, ultimately, it was not. By 2000, Slobodan Milošević was a deeply unpopular and terribly flawed incumbent and Serbia's political opposition had a decade's worth of experience in combating Milošević's authoritarianism. It was this experience—their own experience—that encouraged them to unite behind Koštunica, to forge the DOS coalition, and to seek alliances with Serbia's security and paramilitary forces, which would ultimately prove critical in ensuring that public resistance against Milošević did not end in violence. Democracy assistance may have helped push Serbia's opposition to victory, but it by no means accounted for this victory.

Nor was democracy aid universally helpful. Plenty of the aid that went Serbia's way did little or no good—some may in fact have made things worse. The costly Ring Around Serbia project, for example, was money misspent. Photo opportunities between Western policy makers and Serbia's opposition were counterproductive. And a lengthy battle to prod Drašković into submission—to lure him into joining DOS—failed. Such missteps have gone ignored in the popular narrative of aid's success in Serbia. So intent on telling a story of democracy aid "done right," scholars and practitioners have failed to see what went wrong. This would prove particularly true in the post-Milošević era, as aid providers strove to secure Serbia's democratic gains—at times at the expense of democracy itself.

CHAPTER FOUR

Democracy Promotion in
Milošević's Shadow, 2001–2012

In the days that followed Serbia's "Bulldozer Revolution," donors and parties moved swiftly to secure the opposition's gains. For many, Milošević's defeat spoke to the transformation of the Serbian regime—an alteration widely hailed as "revolutionary and irreversible" (Pešić 2001: 175; see also Podunavac 2005: 12–13), a "turning point for the Yugoslav people" (Uzgel 2001: 1), the "end of an era" (Birch 2002: 499), and "the beginnings of the consolidation of democratic rule in the Balkans" (Nielsen 2001: 1). In many respects, this initial wave of enthusiasm appeared well founded.

Shortly after coming to office, DOS technocrats instituted a wide array of reforms, sweeping enough to convince analysts that post-Milošević authorities had gotten off "to a rapid and promising start" (ICG 2003: 7). As for those reforms still in need of adoption, many in the United States and the EU were eager to help. The newly democratic context thus gave way to the proliferation of foreign assistance. Democracy assistance, in particular, grew substantially, as did the budgets of party aid providers.

Yet if Serbia's transition was expected to follow a course similar to that taken elsewhere in Central and Eastern Europe, it soon disappointed. The early months of 2001 were followed by years of political stagnation and stalemate. Interparty rivalries, endemic corruption, clientelism, and the enduring presence of Milošević-era structures and norms quickly gave way to voter apathy and the resurgence of Serbia's far right. By the mid-2000s, scholars and analysts had denounced post-Milošević Serbia as a dysfunctional state. Milošević's ouster, one academic wrote, had "failed to change fundamental aspects of Serbian politics and the political system" (Pavlaković 2005: 47).

This chapter traces the obstacles confronting Serbia's budding democracy.

In so doing, it shines a light on the accomplishments and failings of both political parties and political party assistance. As will be seen, the laggardly fashion in which Serbia broached liberal democratic rule may in part be attributed to the gross democratic deficits still afflicting Serbia's political parties and party system more than a decade after the fall of Milošević. Yet rather than strive to redress such problems head-on, democracy aid providers have remained almost singularly focused on the political dichotomies that reigned in the 1990s. By 2004, staving off the looming threat of the far right's resurgence rose to the forefront of the democracy promotion agenda. Increasingly, political party assistance was used not merely to democratize Serbia's democratic forces but rather to bolster their electoral prospects at the expense of their so-called anti-democratic rivals. The mid-2000s thus witnessed a return to the highly partisan and politicized forms of political party aid that characterized Milošević-era aid. This did not always work to democracy's benefit.

Stumbling Toward Democracy

As is often the case in post-revolutionary contexts, the enthusiasm stirred by Milošević's ouster in October 2000 quickly descended into disappointment and political cynicism. Shortly after Milošević's defeat in Yugoslav presidential elections, in December 2000 Serbia held parliamentary elections, where DOS parties consolidated on Koštunica's victory, winning a parliamentary majority. But just several months later, the tenuous alliance forged between the newly appointed Serbian Prime Minister Đinđić and Yugoslav President Koštunica, gave way. When news spread that Đinđić's had negotiated a behind-the-scenes deal resulting in Milošević's arrest and extradition to the ICTY, Koštunica was incensed. The public falling out between Đinđić and Koštunica proved irreparable. Tensions between the two party leaders reached such a fever pitch that in 2001 Koštunica withdrew his party's backing from the DOS government. The result was a political stalemate that left political and economic reform at a standstill.

Prospects for democratic reform dimmed further when in March 2003 Đinđić was assassinated by the secret services. Threatened by Đinđić's new zeal in tackling organized crime, the very same group that Milošević had used to eliminate political opponents in Serbia and to carry out special operations missions in Croatia, Bosnia-Herzegovina, and later Kosovo set its sights on the Serbian prime minister. The assassination of Đinđić—who had hitherto been heralded by Western policy makers as Serbia's best chance for reform—immediately dimmed the prospects for a quick and calm transition. Yet the true extent of Serbia's problems would not manifest themselves until months afterward, when rumors of political corruption within Serbia's democratically elected leadership would send the country's political system into a tailspin.

For months after Đinđić's assassination, government officials instituted a state of emergency and accompanying crackdown on organized crime, known as "Operation Sword." The controversial effort succeeded in disentangling some criminal networks, and even succeeded in foiling a number of alleged assassination plots. Yet it ultimately left the "backbone" of organized crime intact.[1] Moreover, it failed to bridge the burgeoning differences among coalition partners, and it did little to undermine government authorities' penchant for corruption. By late 2003, rumors were rife that Serbia's so-called pro-reformist parties had engaged in corrupt privatizations and political intrigue.[2] Serbia's far right was quick to capitalize during Serbia's 2003 parliamentary elections.

Running on an anticorruption platform, the Serbian Radical Party (SRS) staged a surprising upset. Spearheaded by the flamboyant and overtly nationalist Vojislav Šešelj (who in February 2003 was transferred to the ICTY in The Hague on charges of war crimes), the SRS won a large plurality of the vote in 2003's parliamentary elections—becoming the largest party in Serbia's 250-seat parliament. The result was not merely the stagnation of Serbia's democratic trajectory but a deep disillusionment with Serbia's reformist parties that would pervade well into the next decade.

The perceived failings of post-Milošević authorities left many both inside and outside of Serbia in doubt as to the direction and nature of Serbia's post-revolutionary transition. Though Serbia had successfully embraced the most basic attributes of democracy—including free, fair, and competitive elections, as well as a strengthening of political and civil rights, including freedoms of speech, assembly, and opinion—the deepening of that democracy would prove more difficult.

From 2003 onward, Serbian democracy would suffer from a lack of checks and balances, a weak judiciary, a politicized media, a lack of sufficient civilian oversight of the country's security apparatus, and pervasive political corruption (Trivunović et al. 2007: 38).

Political parties and their leaders were a large part of the problem. Parties' corrupt practices were so far reaching that by 2007 Vesna Pešić—then a politician herself—said parties had achieved what amounts to "state capture," a phenomenon in which groups external to the state establish influence over state institutions and policies. Throughout the post-Milošević period, persistent impediments to the rule of law, the separation of power, alternative sources of information, and civilian oversight of security forces continued to offer the most profound indicators of democracy's deficits.

Despite some important strides in the post-Milošević era, in the decade after October 2000 problems also remained which compromised the independence of Serbia's media. According to the ICG (2003: 8), "Upon coming to office, Đinđić and his colleagues discovered exactly how effective the Milošević-era media constraints were, and decided to use them for their own purposes." Indeed, leading newspapers and television stations such as *Politika* and RTS were made financially dependent on governing authorities, a fact that encouraged self-censorship and a lack of critical coverage of state-sponsored policies. The government's far-reaching role into media affairs was at no point further underscored than in early 2003, in the aftermath of Prime Minister Đinđić's assassination. DOS authorities used the self-imposed "state of emergency" to silence criticism regarding their handling of the crisis. Anyone who dared to question the state of emergency was slapped with a 500,000 dinar (800 Euro) fine (Pavlović 2004: 12).

Political parties were not at the sidelines of these decisions. To the contrary, given their location at the helm of the political process, political parties and their leaders were often the masterminds of such antidemocratic politics. As a result, they often played a prominent role in exacerbating the democratic deficits that plagued Serbia in the post-Milošević period.

Party Politics Post-Revolution

More than ten years after Milosevic's fall, democratic reformers in Serbia have been forced to confront an uncomfortable reality. Despite the country's swift transition to electoral democracy, liberal democracy remains out of reach. Far from easing the country's transition, political parties have served as "sources of political instability" throughout the post-Milošević period (Đurković 2006; Orlović 2008; Pešić 2007) and threaten to derail democratic development in Serbia.

Corruption and Internal Autocracy

Integral to parties' destructive role in the transition process was their inability to conform to the demands of internal-democratic practice. As Serbia's regime transitioned to democracy, parties found themselves ensnared in many of the same battles and rivalries that had plagued pluralistic politics throughout the previous decade. Rather than shed the vestiges of Milošević-era politics, parties replicated many of the more insidious practices that long frustrated their democratic prospects. They thus remained personality based and opaque. The party system itself remained highly divisive and polarized for most of the 2000s, plagued by rapidly evolving cleavages that further augmented parties' differences and undermined the prospect for compromise.

Serbia's parties also suffered from a "poor ability to develop programs, a barely existent anchoring in society and strong foundations in individual personalities" (BTI 2003:8). Rather than root themselves in ideologically coherent programs, Serbia's parties remained dominated by charismatic individuals (Bardos 2003: 3). Of particular concern in the post-Milošević period was parties' dependence on illicit funding sources, particularly those stemming from Serbia's well-endowed tycoons (Milosavljević 2005; Savić 2011).

Indeed, at the heart of the problems confronting Serbian politics after revolution lay political corruption, which proved endemic throughout the political party scene in the post-Milošević period. In Milošević's absence, ostensibly reformist parties succeeded in divvying up the spoils of electoral coalitions and thereby controlled entire sectors, including public services and enterprises that were under their members' domain. This was facilitated by a dearth of independent control mechanisms, which allowed parties to exploit their political access to Serbian industries unfettered.

Throughout the 2000s, Serbia's political parties have had access to only moderate levels of state financing and paltry membership fees. Instead, their funding is alleged to be derived in part from questionable privatizations of state property and from criminals and organized crime networks (Center for the Study of Democracy 2004: 13). Serbian tycoons like Miroslav Mišković, Milan Beko, and Bogoljub Karić are suspected of having paid millions to political parties across the political spectrum in an effort to win their support on legislation critical to their financial interests.[3] These financial streams were made possible by weak legislative oversight of party financing, as well as by an elaborate array of parallel organizational structures that parties erected to enable such contributions.

These dubious financial arrangements propelled the EU to call on Serbia to enact better legislation through which to monitor party financing. In 2011, Serbia's parliament passed a highly anticipated Law on Financing of Political Parties, which required transparency of political party donations in excess of the average Serbian salary (about 360 euros). But not all of Serbia's eighty-one registered political parties ultimately agreed to release these data. Of those that did, according to Serbia's Anti-Corruption Agency, the vast majority hid their largest donations through a variety of business arrangements or by channeling such money through party-affiliated entities. Analysts estimate that as much as 40 percent of the money contributed to Serbian parties enters via a gray zone over which the law on financing of political parties will have little oversight.[4]

Illicit financing was not the only problem afflicting Serbia's parties, however. Another major problem was the lack of democratic process Serbian parties allowed within their own structures. With few exceptions, Serbia's parties remained opaque and top-down, with party leaders and an elite coterie determining everything from party policy and electoral strategy to party representatives and financing (Lutovac 2006; Spoerri 2008b). Rank-and-file party members not only had little say in internal party politics, they had little recourse were their opinions to differ from those of their party leaders.

In fact, the hegemony of party over party member was reinforced in 2006, with the adoption of Serbia's post-Milošević constitution. Article 102 of the constitution created a legal mandate allowing Serbia's political parties to force parliamentarians to place their parliamentary mandates at their parties' disposal, thus institutionalizing the already widespread practice of so-called blank resignations. Although ostensibly designed to ensure "party discipline" (Radojević 2011: 89), blank resignations essentially served as a form of blackmail, ensuring that all parliamentarians could be kicked out of parliament were they to stray from party lines.[5] According to the March 2007 Opinion issued by the Council of Europe's Venice Commission on Serbia's constitution, the practice was inherently anti-democratic. According to the Venice Commission, it posed "a risk of an excessive influence of political parties since the mandate of members of parliament is made dependent on the will and whim of the political parties" (Council of Europe 2007: 11). Building on such sentiments, the European Commission made the elimination of the provision a condition for the acceptance of Serbia's EU candidacy, thanks to which the practice was ultimately repealed in 2011.

Though an important first step in generating internal democracy within Serbia's political parties, the barring of blank resignations was just one small part of a larger anti-democratic organizational structure that remains embedded in Serbia's political parties. Episodes of interparty strife leading to new breakaway parties or disgruntled party resignations remained rampant in the post-Milošević period. Party leaders continue to act as party tyrants, particularly within smaller parties like the Liberal Democratic Party (LDP) and the Serbian Renewal Movement (SPO). Indeed, internal party factions, like internal party democracy and transparent party financing, remained a taboo subject throughout the 2000s.

The Democratization of Serbia's Nationalists

Not all of Serbia's party landscape witnessed direct parallels to the 1990s, however. In the post-Milošević period, certain segments of the party scene experienced a gradual—but dramatic—transformation. This applied first and foremost to Serbia's far right.

Throughout much of the post-Milošević period, analysts contended that Serbian politics was divided between a pro-democratic and an anti-democratic bloc. Where the DS, G17 Plus, GSS, and others, were designated "democratic," the SRS and SPS were labeled anti-democratic. Although this analysis was applicable for the early years of transition, by 2004 it was not. Though still directly affiliated with their controversial leaders—who, by the 2000s, were serving time at the ICTY on charges of war crimes[6]—both the SPS and SRS played by the rules of the democratic game. Not only did they participate in local, republican, and federal elections, but they respected the results of these elections even when doing so meant admitting their own defeat. Both the SRS and SPS also supported the ratification of Serbia's first post-Milošević constitution, and in 2006 they both helped pass legislation *increasing* ethnic minority representation in parliament.

As a result, in 2007 William Montgomery, the former U.S. ambassador to Croatia and later to the Federal Republic of Yugoslavia, publicly dismissed the notion that either party was "anti-democratic." In his words, "All of the parties in the Serbian Parliament have actually, more or less, behaved democratically over at least the past seven years."[7] According to Montgomery, the SRS's vice president, Tomislav Nikolić, "actually came across in a better light than many of the 'democrats.'"[8] Indeed, when in 2008 Nikolić narrowly lost his presidential bid to Boris Tadić, he not only conceded his defeat that same night but also became Serbia's first politician to publicly congratulate his opponent upon securing a presidential victory.[9] As a consequence, by 2008 it was widely agreed that "no party seriously question[ed] the desirability of democratization" in Serbia (Edmunds 2008a: 129).

What is more, by the mid-2000s both the SRS and the SPS—but the SRS in particular—had succeeded in garnering a fair amount of political legitimacy within the political party landscape. They did so in part by catering to the needs and interests of a specific part of the Serbian population that much of the "democratic bloc" ignored: Serbian refugees and the local communities with whom they resided.

Of all the former Yugoslav states, Serbia is home to the highest number of war refugees and former refugees.[10] These individuals make up roughly one-tenth of Serbia's entire eligible voting population and their grievances are, understandably, many. As Konitzer and Gruijić (2009: 865) explain, by offering material support to incoming refugees, the SRS "tapped into a fundamental need of this population."

By contrast, Serbia's democratic bloc chose to "belittle the refugees' travails and contemptuously regard the population as an undesirable, 'radicalized,' and atavistic impediment to Serbia's entrance into the community of democratic states" (Konitzer and Grujić 2008: 867). Whereas Serbia's democratic bloc overlooked Serbia's refugees, the SRS and its successor the SNS, successfully spoke to their needs and thus fulfilled one of the most basic roles of political parties in any democratic setting: to identify and represent the interests of their citizens.[11]

Western aid providers were reluctant to acknowledge the far right's growing legitimacy, however. To the contrary, they continued to isolate Serbia's far right well into 2008. As the following section will argue, this policy not only hurt Serbian democracy but also hurt Western governments. Indeed, the inability of diplomats and aid providers to reach out directly to SRS and SPS members left them largely ignorant about these parties' nature and ambitions. As one USAID representative would recount, by isolating the SRS the West isolated itself.[12] The result, created what aid providers later described as "an idiotic mistake."[13] As 2010 drew to a close, the consensus appeared to be that the United States and Europe had mishandled the Radicals completely.

Aiding Parties After Regime Change

The manifold ailments afflicting political parties and party life in the post-Milošević period posed a significant challenge to democracy promoters. Bolstered by Milošević's ouster, however, party aid providers were eager to ensure that Serbia's democratic transition remained on course. In 2001, Serbia welcomed a surge in democracy assistance and political party aid. Offices and staff of the U.S. party institutes and German *Stiftungen* expanded, while new actors emerged on the scene. The proliferation of democracy-related projects soon commenced, all targeted at Serbia's newly elected authorities.

Continuing a Partisan Approach

Aid providers first returned to Serbia—following their extended absence during and after of the NATO bombing of Serbia—in the days following DOS's December 2000 parliamentary victory. A few, however, braved the uncertainty that followed immediately after Milošević's resignation in October 2000. The first among them—a handful of USAID and U.S. State Department staff—briefly assumed residence in Belgrade's Hyatt Hotel. From there, diplomats and aid providers contacted DOS representatives, responded to inquiries from the outside world, and rapidly approved what was to become an onslaught of democracy assistance projects.

In mid-October 2000, IRI's American staff conducted the first of two assessment missions to Serbia. They met with DOS mayors and leaders and finally reestablished the institute's Belgrade office just a few days later. In the following month, FES's first German resident director came on board, overseeing a rapid expansion of FES's Serbia programs and office.

It would be several months, however, before the rest of the party aid community would return to Belgrade. Until then, donors concentrated on translating Koštunica's successful presidential bid into a sweeping DOS victory in the forthcoming parliamentary elections, set for 28 December 2000. As it had in the run-up to the elections of September 2000, party aid focused on grassroots campaigning and GOTV efforts. Working closely with Otpor, IRI commissioned a series of focus groups testing the movement's television and radio commercials. It also paid for Otpor's printed advertisements and television broadcasts, as well as the 100 billboards Otpor placed throughout the country, urging voters to vote on election day.

NDI buttressed IRI's efforts by ramping up its training programs. Over the course of just three months, it trained 1,674 DOS activists, with its core group of regional trainers providing insight into everything from voter contact to the identification of supporters and political message development to rural campaigning and GOTV. NDI also continued its polling research, assessing the layout of voter sympathies toward DOS and providing strategic consultations with coalition leaders. Like its Republican counterpart, NDI also offered material assistance, awarding $29,000 in support of DOS's republic-wide bus tours and speaking engagements.

European donors followed suit. FES implemented what its representatives define as an ambitious program based on bolstering DOS infrastructure throughout Serbia. As before, European institutions, the AMS among them, channeled funds through the Belgrade-based FES office; staff members provided direct material assistance to the DOS parliamentary campaign.[14]

Today, party aid providers look back on this period as one of enormous enthusiasm and potential. FES's former resident director to Serbia recalls that it was a "very optimistic, forward-looking atmosphere—everybody wanted to do something."[15] The enthusiasm was shared by all of those involved in Serbian affairs in the immediate post-Milošević period. According to NDI's director of CEE programs, "We thought the Balkan powder keg had finally been resolved."[16] As a result, resources from both sides of the Atlantic poured into the country.

The budgets of party aid providers already working in Serbia thus increased substantially. FES, NDI, and IRI each acquired larger premises and a larger staff, including (additional) members of the expatriate community. For the German *Stiftungen*, the relative safety and security found in this new environment meant Germans could assume residence in Serbia. For the smaller European party foundations—among them, the WFD and the Dutch AMS, and the International Democracy Institute—the newly liberalized atmosphere meant training would no longer have to be accommodated in neighboring countries but could take place in cities and towns across Serbia. An NDI representative explains, only "after Milošević was ousted [could] we talk about 'typical' party assistance. The clandestine time was over."[17] Traditional political party assistance could now commence.

Yet the immediate post-Milošević period provided an atypical party landscape. Having abruptly transitioned from a fractious opposition to a majority-led government, the eighteen-member DOS alliance found itself wielding virtually limitless powers. The recipients of party assistance now held *all* government positions, with nonrecipients composing *all* of the opposition (Table 10). For the first time, it was thus incumbent upon those on the receiving end of democracy aid not merely to campaign against tyranny but to lead Serbia's transition from a semi-authoritarian to a liberal democratic state. This had several important implications for party aid.

Because most DOS parties had little or no executive experience, donors sought to enhance the government's performance. As a consequence, many of the activities supported by party aid did not in fact directly address political parties but rather sought to improve the capacities of institutions governed by those parties, such as Serbia's parliament, ministries, or local governments. IRI, for example, did not embark on party work until early 2002—more than a year after Serbia's transition got started. Instead, IRI focused its energies on the so-called management of reform; using public opinion data to help government ministries and DOS-run municipal governments better communicate with a Serbian public all too impatient for tangible improvements to their quality of life.

IRI also continued its support for Otpor. Its primary goal of regime change now accomplished, by early 2001, Otpor struggled to identify its raison d'être. Using focus groups, polling data, and organizational training, IRI sought to assist Otpor in identifying new goals. Ultimately, IRI sought to help Otpor transform from an organization intent on regime change to a nonpartisan "watchdog" agency capable of providing a necessary check on DOS authorities.

Though never going so far as to exclude party-based assistance from its work, NDI, too, made nonparty work an integral component of its post-Milošević programming. Like its republican counterpart, NDI worked closely with members of the DOS administration, opting to concentrate on

Table 10. Political Parties and Partnerships, 2000 to mid-2002

Party	% of Votes	In Government	PPA
DOS	64.40	Yes	Yes
SPS	13.50	No	No
SRS	8.50	No	No
Serbian Party of Unity	5.30	No	No

Source: Goati 2004.

facilitating the outreach capacities of Serbia's parliament. The institute also invested heavily in "Contact Serbia," a network of constituency-relations offices set up across Serbia that aimed to reach out to local communities and involve citizens directly in local government. In addition, NDI continued its activities with the election-monitoring group CeSID, which by now had gained legal accreditation to monitor Serbian elections and was quickly gaining a reputation as an NDI success story.

For the *Stiftungen*, too, assisting the DOS government was a major priority. FES and KAS, for example, offered consultations on government-related projects and organized roundtable discussions among leading Serbian politicians and academics, during which the progress and direction of reform was debated.[18]

But DOS's place in government had an additional consequence for party aid. Because Serbia's democratic forces made up a single electoral coalition, party aid providers were at first content to assist DOS as a whole, rather than focus their resources on specific member parties. Although this was not a surprising position for the American institutes to take (given their preference for multiparty work), it was somewhat unusual for their European counterparts, who typically work on a party-by-party basis. Yet as FES's Michael Weichert explains, ideological questions were not in the foreground in the immediate post-Milošević period. As the fissures in the DOS alliance grew increasingly apparent, however, so too did the need to differentiate partner parties and to map out partisan affiliations. By 2002, the race for ideological counterparts had begun.

Serbia's leading reformist parties were avidly courted by foundations of all ideological stripes. The DS—the former party of Serbia's politically savvy prime minister, Zoran Đinđić—was particularly in demand. Says DS's Oliver Dulić, Serbia's former speaker of parliament, "Everyone tried to cooperate with us,"[19] including both KAS and FES—two foundations that are ideological poles apart. In the early 2000s, Dulić says DS members clearly exhibited a preference for liberalism and therefore would have made a natural counterpart for the liberal FNS.[20] Yet Đinđić had ultimate say and in 2002 he decided that the DS should join forces with the far larger and better resourced FES, thereby adopting a Social Democratic profile. The decision to forgo the more natural alliance with FNS was thus the result of political necessity and pragmatism—not an innate preference for social democratic philosophy.

The party affiliations that arose in the early 2000s were often formed irre-

spective of any deeply rooted ideological kinship. Instead, strategic calculations often trumped ideological affinities. For the DS, a close relationship with
Europe's Social Democrats promised significant benefits given the latter's dominant position within European politics. AMS's director, whose Dutch Social
Democratic foundation cooperated closely with the DS throughout the 2000s,
explains Đinđić, "was definitely *not* a Social Democrat. But around the time he
decided to become a Social Democrat, social democracy was the strongest
force in European politics."[21] FES's Resident Director had a similar impression.
"There was a big portion of pragmatism in [Đinđić's] decision," he recalls. "In
those days, most or many of the governments in the EU were led by Social
Democratic coalitions." Đinđić's decision to adopt a center-left profile was an
attempt to use party affiliation to reintegrate into the EU family. Certainly,
strong ties to leading parties in the EU would seem to bode well for the DS.
Thus, strategic calculations—rather than ideological concerns—ensured that
by late 2002 lines of donor-party cooperation were firmly established (Table
11).

It was only after ideological allegiances were secured that party aid began
to focus on the standard array of party aid programs, incorporating training
like local branch development, member recruitment, negotiation, and coalition building. NDI, for example, launched a series of youth summer and

Table 11. Political Party Affiliations as of 2004

Party Aid Provider	Partner Parties
Alfred Mozer Stichting (AMS)	SDU, LSV, DS
British Conservative Party	DSS, G17
British Labour Party	DS
Friedrich-Ebert-Stiftung (FES)	DS, SDU
Friedrich-Naumann-Stiftung (FNS)	GSS/LDP, LS
Heinrich Böll Stiftung	LDP
International Democracy Institute (IDI)	GSS/LDP
International Republican Institute (IRI)	DS, DSS, G17, GSS/LDP, LSV, SD
Konrad-Adenauer-Stiftung (KAS)	DSS, G17
National Democratic Institute for International Affairs (NDI)	DS, DSS, G17, GSS/LDP, SD, SDU, DA, NS, ND, DHSS, LSV, SDP

winter schools for up-and-coming young party members. IRI brought in international public relations experts who offered party members training in
on-camera interviewing. FES provided support for a DS-affiliated training
center, the Center for Modern Skills. With FES assistance, the center expanded its Political Communication Skills Program, providing courses, training, and workshops in political marketing, conflict resolution, and
communication skills.

Campaign support was also provided to parties in anticipation of Serbia's
first free and fair presidential elections. DS and G17 activists met with Serbian
and international trainers, gaining insight into grassroots campaign skills and
the basics of campaign planning. DOS (successor) parties received training in
voter research and identification, political message development and dissemination, and GOTV methods. NDI, the WFD, and the Swedish Conservative
Party teamed up to train fifteen DSS heads of regional boards on election-
preparation techniques, with training covering the spectrum from campaign
management and team building to candidate promotion and the media (NDI
2002).

Yet even in this period the overwhelming focus lay on helping Serbia's first
post-Milošević government remain united and pro-reform. It was only after
a series of major setbacks—Đinđić's assassination, the fall of the DOS government, and the resurgence of the SRS—that party aid providers began to recon-
sider their approach. Indeed, if in January 2001 donors could be said to have
found themselves at the cusp of a new democratic era, then they were uncer-
emoniously awakened at that era's precipice just three years later.

Crossing the Line

By all accounts, the Serbia of January 2001 bore little resemblance to the Serbia of January 2004. The combination of Đinđić's assassination and the subsequent resurgence of Šešelj's SRS profoundly altered the political landscape
and, with it, donors' confidence in Serbia's democratic prospects. For party aid
providers, Đinđić's assassination came as a particularly unwelcome blow. "We
were completely shell-shocked," recalls an NDI director for CEE. "The international community had banked very much on one person, it took a while to
readjust."[22]

Uncertainties were further aroused in the wake of December 2003's parliamentary elections, when Serbia's SRS staged its monumental comeback.

Together the SRS and SPS accounted for more than 40 percent of the seats in Serbia's parliament—the SRS alone accounted for one in three parliamentarians. Taken aback by the SRS's strong showing, Western governments adopted a policy akin to disbelief. Rather than engage the newly empowered radicals, foreign policy makers erected a cordon sanitaire—forbidding diplomats and aid providers from engaging Serbia's far right. All contact with far-right party members—even something as seemingly innocuous as the writing of a letter to an SRS member—was prohibited. This policy of isolationism would define the work of party aid providers well into the 2000s—and cause no small amount of controversy within democracy aid circles.

The rebirth of Serbia's far-right parties was met by a full-scale realignment of foreign policy priorities and the parallel restructuring of international intervention in Serbia. As the goals of foreign policy changed, democracy assistance was recalibrated to fall in line with these new goals. The main objective after 2003 was simple: to ensure that the SRS did not make its way back into power and that the victors of October 2000 did not become the losers of Serbia's subsequent transition.

The crux of this realignment saw to a marked shift in spending, away from democracy aid to economic aid. Economic aid, it was thought, would help alleviate the hardship suffered by Serbian citizens during the transition period, thus offering the government a strong platform from which to demonstrate its effectiveness. Having proven themselves capable of job creation and economic growth, DOS successor parties would be better poised to win elections.

The logic underpinning this strategy was based on the presumption that the resurgence of the SRS could be explained by the hardship ordinary Serbians were experiencing during Serbia's political and economic transition. Support for the SRS, it was thought, was thanks not to the political positions it upheld, but rather to the post-revolutionary disenchantment that inevitably followed in the wake of transition. Serbia's so-called losers of transition were thus not so much attracted by the serenade of Šešelj or Milošević as they were repelled by the failings of Đinđić's successors. The strong electoral performance of the SRS in December 2003 reflected not the resurgence of the radicals but rather the waning of Serbia's democrats.[23] Indeed, throughout the post-Milošević period, donors were convinced that public opinion remained firmly on the side of DOS successor parties. The problem lay merely in getting them to the ballot box.

Serbia's pro-reform voters were undisciplined, unmotivated, and

disillusioned in the post-Milošević period. As a result, DOS parties have fallen
victim to unrealistic expectations—a phenomenon witnessed across the postcommunist space. The solution therefore lay not in reconceptualizing the
SRS's place in a newly democratic Serbia but in ensuring that DOS successor
parties would mount a more credible challenge in the coming years.

The policies that developed from 2004 onward were twofold. First, there
was an effort to raise the standard of living for Serbia's so-called losers of
transition. Employment and rising standards of living, it was hoped, would
ensure that confidence in Serbia's democrats was restored. The newly appointed U.S. ambassador to Serbia, Michael Polt, thus reallocated U.S. foreign
aid spending, effectively turning the ratio of economy-to-democracy aid
spending on its head (Figure 5).[24] As spending on traditional democracy assistance programs decreased, so too did funding for political party aid. By the
mid-2000s, the institutes each received roughly $1 million a year for their
Serbia programs—a marked decline from their 2001 highs of more than $2.5
million.[25]

Funding for the *Stiftungen* also decreased. By 2007, the largest of the
Stiftungen—FES—spent only about €300,000 on its Serbian programs, of
which just one-third was devoted to parties.[26] Although the decline in democracy assistance to Serbia mirrored a similar trend in foreign assistance budgets
more generally—reflecting, in part, a reprioritization of states' geostrategic
interests in the aftermath of the U.S.-led invasion of Iraq—the newfound emphasis on enabling economic development at democracy aid's expense provides a clear indicator of donors' altered mindsets after 2003.[27]

While economic development was widely thought of as an antidote to
Serbia's nationalist upswing, political party assistance was not wholly for-
saken. From 2004 onward, party aid providers lay renewed emphasis on helping Serbia's so-called "democratic" parties strengthen their internal structures
and modernize their electoral machinery. By enhancing the campaigning capacities of DOS successor parties, party aid providers believed that Serbs
would be less inclined to vote the remnants of the ancien régime back into
office.

Beginning in early 2004, party aid providers redrew the contours of their
efforts. Focus shifted away from the government-building exercises that had
characterized the immediate post-Milošević period and back to political parties. Like the assistance of 1999 and 2000, aid sought to bolster the electoral
prospects of Serbia's so-called democratic bloc, which consisted of DOS successor parties, most notably the DS, G17 Plus, and DSS. Skills-building

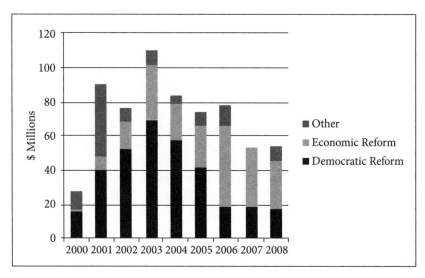

Figure 5. Breakdown of U.S. SEED Spending on Serbia, 2001–2008 (in millions of dollars)
Note: "Other" includes SEED funds dedicated to humanitarian assistance; security, regional, stability, and law-enforcement assistance; and cross-sectoral assistance.
Source: Compiled by author based on SEED Annual Reports FY 2000–2008.

training provided insight into voter targeting; public opinion polls helped parties refine their campaign messages; and the financing of "nonpartisan" GOTV campaigns helped ensure that voter turnout favored party aid recipients. The assistance effort that developed in the aftermath of the SRS's rise mimicked the overtly partisan and highly politicized character of pre-revolutionary aid, aiming not merely to bolster the electoral prospects of recipient parties but to undermine the prospects on nonrecipients. The next section maps out the key facets of such assistance, paying special attention to the mainstay of the party aid effort from 2004 on: electoral campaigning and voter targeting.

Electoral Campaigning and Voter Targeting

From the fall of 2002 onward, Serbs were awash in a near-constant frenzy of electoral campaigning. Over the course of just fifteen months—from September 2002 until December 2003—voters were asked to cast their ballots a total of five times in republican-level elections.[28] As a consequence, support for aid recipients' electoral campaigns became a central feature of party aid. As the 2000s progressed, such assistance became an increasingly critical part of an assistance agenda aimed not at democratizing Serbia's parties but at galvanizing the electoral prospects of aid recipients.

Campaign support came in several guises, one of which was the promotion of public opinion data. As in years past, aid providers encouraged parties to use opinion research to test voters' reactions to campaign messages, commercials, and tactics. Positive, substantive campaigns, the American institutes maintained, would better appeal to voters' sympathies (NDI 2004). Donors also relied on the traditional arsenal of campaign training and workshops. American and European aid providers thus offered partner parties—the DS, DSS, G17 Plus, GSS, Social Democratic Union (SDU), and SPO—their standard array of skills-building seminars, including training on campaign communication, member recruitment and the organization of volunteers, voter-contact techniques, and fundraising. Through the Center for Modern Skills, FES supported the efforts of young party members, who in many instances led the way in grassroots campaigning and voter contact. Working closely with G17 Plus, KAS sponsored seminars on campaign planning and tactics. Together with IRI, members of the British Conservative Party worked with DSS and G17 Plus to help guide the DSS campaign in a more positive direction, training members in message development and media communications.

But the hallmark of the party aid effort after 2000 was something fundamentally new to party aid in Serbia: voter targeting based on demographic analysis (NDI 2006a). In the months leading to the presidential elections in June 2004—which pitted DS candidate Boris Tadić and SRS candidate Tomislav Nikolić—NDI established a voter-targeting database, the first of its kind in Serbia. Designed to link detailed demographic data to highly targeted GOTV campaigns, the database became an integral part of a partisan aid initiative bent on maximizing the electoral prospects of favored parties.

By connecting past electoral results in polling stations throughout Serbia to current census data, the database was able to produce highly detailed lists containing individual voters' addresses, political preferences, economic statuses, gender, and age—polling station by polling station. The location, voting habits, and socioeconomic profiles of voters across Serbia were thus contained in a single database and, thanks to the American party institutes, placed in the hands of select recipients. For party aid providers, the utility of the voter-targeting database was twofold.

On the one hand, the database enabled partner parties to more accurately pinpoint likely or potential supporters.[29] With a more refined understanding of precisely where to concentrate their outreach efforts, parties could avoid expending time and resources on hopeless causes, while maximizing the likelihood of attracting potential supporters.

On the other hand, the database could be used to undermine the electoral prospects of nonrecipients, most notably the SRS and the SPS. As IRI reported in mid-2004, the outcome of that year's presidential election "depended heavily on voter turnout. Low turnout would have favored" the SRS (IRI 2004a). From the perspective of the party aid community, the solution was thus quite simple: Increase voter turnout by potential DOS sympathizers and decrease the likelihood that the SRS would win. "The key," as one former resident director of NDI noted, lay in "identifying segments of the electorate who were moving into and out of abstention."[30] This use of the voter-targeting database would raise voter turnout while undermining the electoral prospects of the SRS.

The voter-targeting database was first used in the presidential elections of 2004, when NDI, IRI, and Freedom House pooled their resources to sponsor a joint GOTV campaign headlined by CeSID. On the basis of demographic analysis drawn from NDI's voter-targeting database, CeSID used an extensive door-to-door outreach and a direct-mail campaign designed to encourage suspected DOS abstainers to come out and vote. Over several weeks, CeSID sent 300,000 pieces of GOTV literature to so-called "pro-reformist" households across Serbia. IRI sponsored focus groups to test voters' receptivity to CeSID's GOTV mass mailing, on the basis of which CeSID later revamped its GOTV mailing, sending out an additional 50,000 pieces of GOTV literature to individuals who had *not* voted for Tadić in the first round but were deemed likely to do so when given the prospect of an SRS-led presidency.

CeSID complemented the direct mailing with door-to-door outreach. In late June, 450 CeSID "volunteers"—each trained by NDI regional trainers and paid a stipend for their efforts—visited 35,000 homes throughout Serbia. As IRI explained, the hope was that CeSID's campaign "would reach the largest number of potential *reform* voters" (IRI 2004b, emphasis added). The effort was targeted toward the young and women ages 25 to 40—two demographics, IRI noted, that "generally have low rates of turnout and are considered essential to *reform*-party victories" (IRI 2004c, emphasis added). In addition, FES sponsored a large, but low-profile, voter outreach campaign of its own, funding the efforts of partner NGOs to send out hundreds of thousands of text messages to their supporters in the run-up to Tadić's election.[31]

This highly partisan GOTV campaign soon became a hallmark of the party aid community's work in post-Milošević Serbia and was later re-employed in the parliamentary elections of 2007. Like the months before the December 2003 elections, those preceding the 2007 elections were character-ized by severe political infighting. Wary of the DOS-successor government's perceived failings, a growing body in the electorate risked becoming frus-trated and apathetic. Thus, when in July 2006 an IRI poll "indicated that wide-spread apathy . . . will likely result in a low-turnout election, greatly benefiting the Radical elements in the country" the international aid community took note (IRI 2006a; see also NDI 2006a). Within weeks of the poll's release, USAID received signals from their DC headquarters to gear up for a major GOTV campaign. The party assistance programming that subsequently com-menced was, according to the former director of Democracy and Governance at USAID's Mission to Belgrade, "as close to overt political involvement as we've ever come."[32]

In the months that followed, NDI and IRI held a series of meetings with their USAID backers and supporters on the Hill. After heated negotiations, it was agreed that some $2 million—funds withheld until now because of Ser-bia's failure to comply with the ICTY—should be devoted to a massive GOTV campaign.[33] Of that total, $1.4 million would be evenly divided among the U.S. party institutes. In the coming weeks, IRI and NDI launched "robust" cam-paign capacity-building programs, linking public opinion research, party communications programming, and direct voter targeting (IRI 2006b). In December, they cosponsored a multipronged "nonpartisan" voter outreach campaign centered on a telephone survey, direct mailings, and door-to-door outreach. At the hand of voter lists generated from CeSID's voter-targeting database, a local public opinion firm conducted 75,000 automated telephone interviews with potential pro-reform voters in preselected polling districts throughout Serbia.

Based on those findings, NDI and IRI designed a series of party-specific spreadsheets for their partner parties (DS, DSS, G17 Plus, SPO, and LDP), laying out each party's "sure" voters, "leaning nonvoters," and former DOS coalition voters, as well as a general list of the "undecided" (IRI 2006b). With this information in hand, the institutes reengaged CeSID to conduct a mag-nified version of its 2004 GOTV campaign. As before, CeSID's campaign cen-tered on two large-scale efforts "aimed at boosting democratic voter turnout" (IRI 2007a). The first stage of the campaign involved 1.5 million direct mail-ings to high-propensity democratic polling areas (the "core" of the pro-reform bloc).[34] The second component involved hands-on door-to-door outreach. Using a script developed by the American party institutes (and a modest stipend paid for by NDI), CeSID canvassers knocked on roughly 50,000 doors in the two weeks prior to the 21 January 2007 elections.[35]

A similar dynamic was at play when parliamentary elections were repeated one year later. Convinced that these elections would serve as "a crucial litmus test of the nation's readiness to reject Milošević-era nationalism in favor of pro-Western democracy" (NDI 2008b), USAID earmarked $1 million to pre-electoral assistance. Of that figure, IRI and NDI received a total of $350,000 and $400,000, respectively.[36] The electoral assistance package that subsequently developed incorporated the standard CeSID-backed GOTV campaign, as well as an in-depth public opinion research component. In the run-up to the first round of presidential elections, CeSID thus distributed some 500,000 direct-mail pieces to households in "polling districts with high democratic turnout potential" (IRI 2008a). It followed this in the second round with an additional 750,000 such pieces. CeSID's highly partisan campaign was complemented by extensive door-to-door outreach, its paid "volunteers" once again receiving "a small fee to compensate for their time and incidentals" (NDI 2008b).

NDI's partisan voter-targeting campaign was bolstered by in-depth opinion research funded by IRI. In the eleven weeks prior to the election, IRI used a weekly series of tracking polls designed to test (potential) voter preferences. During the second round of the election—which featured Boris Tadić of the DS in a head-to-head contest with Tomislav Nikolić of the SRS—IRI also sponsored a series of dial-response focus groups, testing Tadić's video-clips and speeches, as well as those of his opponent. The results of both the polls and focus groups were, according to IRI, extremely "worrying" (IRI 2007b). For the first time, data indicated that support for the SRS vice president exceeded that of the DS incumbent by a margin of 39 to 36 percent. Moreover, of the DS president's supporters, some 44 percent believed the election's final outcome to be of little import. More daunting still, an increasing number of those polled found Nikolić to be an acceptable leader, characterizing the de facto SRS front man as "presidential," "intelligent," "capable of leading Serbia into the future, and trusted in a time of crisis" (IRI 2008a). Such evidence did not bode well for Tadić's reelection prospects.

To help enable Tadić's victory, IRI advised the DS to launch a number of hard-hitting commercials featuring footage of Šešelj and Nikolić making incendiary remarks. Such commercials, IRI advised, should be designed to remind Serbia's voters "who Nikolić actually is and what his real politics are" (IRI 2008a). To complement such imagery, IRI encouraged the Tadić campaign to run a series of positive commercials portraying a second Tadić presidency as one of stability and security, capable of ushering Serbia into Europe's fold.

These unabashedly partisan tactics were used again just three months later, in May 2008's parliamentary contest. These parliamentary elections were the second in two years—a reflection of the growing discord among former DOS parties, particularly with respect to the EU. As the 2000s progressed and the EU pushed for Kosovo's independence, the DSS became increasingly anti-EU. By early 2008, Koštunica even declared that EU accession was off his administration's agenda. By contrast, the DS and its supporters positioned themselves as pro-EU *and* pro-Kosovo—a position Koštunica viewed an untenable. As a result, according to NDI, the elections of May 2008 were "among the most decisive and contentious elections in a nation that has seen its share of both" (NDI 2008b).

Like the presidential election staged earlier that year, the electoral assistance effort centered on an NGO-led GOTV campaign built on door-to-door outreach, targeting 200,000 "reform-oriented" households.[37] Also like the presidential election, IRI sponsored a series of tracking polls for its partners in the "For a European Serbia" (ZES) coalition. As in years past, IRI advised ZES parties to strongly distinguish their own pro-EU platform from those of their opponents, whom, IRI warned, "paid lip service to the [EU] but would not be able to lead Serbia towards Europe" (IRI 2008b). To this end, the institute advocated yet another series of contrast advertisements featuring negative statements DSS and SRS candidates had made in reference to European integration. Such ads, IRI noted, would force "voters to reevaluate which political options were truly open to EU integration" (IRI 2008b).

Whether it was the massive GOTV campaign, the government's signing in late April 2008 of a provisional Stabilization and Association Agreement with the EU, a recent spate of visa relaxations for Serbian citizens, or Fiat's last-minute decision to build an auto-manufacturing plant in Serbia, the parliamentary elections of May 2008 ultimately saw to an impressive victory by the ZES coalition. Just several months later, the SRS collapsed amid a series of internal recriminations. The rise of the Serbian Progressive Movement (SNS), led by former SRS vice president Tomislav Nikolić, would mark the end of the highly partisan approach to party aid.

Party Building and Organization

With the post-2000 period marked by an incessant spate of electoral cycles, nonelectoral assistance aimed at furthering parties' organizational development often seemed to rank of only secondary importance.[38] Yet if electoral assistance proved to be the mainstay of party aid in the post-Milošević period, it was certainly not its sole part. From 2004 onward, party aid providers complemented their focus on campaign-related aid with an eye on parties' "long-term" development. This meant, among other things, providing assistance on capacity building to parties' local branches and party headquarters, supporting the establishment of in-house party training centers, and promoting greater inclusivity by encouraging the formation of youth and women's wings. Throughout the first decade of Serbia's transition, both American and European party aid providers worked on each of these issues to varying degrees but in similar manners.

The bulk of organizational aid during this period focused on enhancing the capacities of parties' local branches and headquarters. This meant educating party members and leaders on issues spanning from fundraising techniques to internal party communication to membership recruitment. More often than not, this was accomplished through multiparty and party-to-party training. At the forefront of the capacity-building effort lay the American party institutes, and NDI in particular. Through the expansion of its regional trainer program—which by 2009 had grown to include more than fifty party activists from across the political spectrum (with the exception of the SPS and SRS)—NDI led the way in skills and capacity-building training, teaching internal party activists how to train fellow (and opposing) party members using a variety of role-playing, debate, and SWOT analysis techniques.[39] The institute estimates that these NDI-trainers have gone on to train tens of thousands of party members throughout Serbia. IRI, by contrast, invested heavily in volunteer consultants, brought in primarily from the United States and Western Europe. These party "experts" consulted party members in the how-to of organizational development, often using their domestic experiences as party activists to inform their trainings. Both such efforts proved to be a hallmark of party aid in the post-2000 period. Indeed, as one party activist explained, the dissemination of "practical" or "technical" skills is "what Americans do best."[40]

Although the American party institutes (and NDI in particular) supported most of the capacity-building training, they were not the only actors

engaged in this field. To the contrary, the smaller European foundations each
sponsored several capacity-building training sessions each year. Thus in early
2007, for example, the Dutch AMS supported a multiparty training targeting
twenty-four "social democratic" activists from the SDU, LSDV, LDP, and DS
(AMS 2007: 60). Using SWOT analysis, participants debated possible organizational structures for their parties, the distribution of information within
their respective parties, and the need to build networks and communicate
with voters on the grassroots level. Likewise, the British Conservative Party
issued similar party-to-party training for DSS and G17 party activists, as did
the British Labour Party, with its allies the DS and GSS. Thus, in mid-2005 the
Westminster Foundation for Democracy offered seminars to the GSS in internal party communication, membership building, the development of printed
literature, and the use of photographs to promote party activities.

In addition to providing party training, party aid providers also sought to
initiate and strengthen parties' youth and women's wings. With respect to the
former, this was primarily achieved through the organization of annual summer and winter schools, as well as ad hoc educational programs. Through the
Center for Modern Skills, FES, for example, sponsored annual political
schools, incorporating courses, training, and workshops that introduced
young party members to political skills and to the techniques of political marketing (CMS 2006). Similarly, NDI sponsored summer and winter schools
that brought hundreds of young party activists together each year to learn
such skills as political-message development, public speaking techniques, the
best use of campaign resources, event planning and scheduling, and more.
Those individuals deemed the most responsive were later included in more
advanced skills-building seminars and schools and, in select instances, incor-
porated into the institutes' regional trainers program.

Party aid providers also reached out to female party members. As for the
youth, seminars and training were organized—sometimes in the form of
women's summer schools—targeting female members in both the higher and
lower echelons of partner parties. Meetings were also held to discuss the role
of women within party ranks and how to increase voter turnout among female
voters (see NDI 2006c). As a consequence, support for the DS women's forum
proved to be a critical component of the AMS's aid starting in 2006. The forum's participants, AMS trainers note, were "very active and enthusiastic"
(AMS 2006: 53) and responded well to the AMS's emphasis on female voter
targeting. Also in 2006, NDI worked with the same forum to establish a training program within the DS explicitly targeting female voters. The hope was

that the DS's education center would create special modules encouraging gen-der dialogue within the party and would thereby work to increase greater gender awareness, as well as to bolster the capacities of women activists and candidates (NDI 2007a). Similarly, in 2005 KAS co-organized a series of sem-inars in Belgrade titled "Women in Politics and Society," in which more than eighty female party members were educated on a spectrum of gender-related topics.

Ideology and Platform Development

As party aid providers have sought to shape the internal organization of po-litical parties, so too have they sought to shape the messages and platforms that parties uphold. Yet how practitioners have gone about pursuing such a goal has varied considerably across Serbia's diverse party aid landscape. Whereas the German *Stiftungen* have led the way in ideology-building semi-nars and conferences, the American institutes and other European founda-tions have concentrated far more on what they define simply as "message development." These competing emphases in many respects underscore the divergent trajectories American and German aid followed over the course of Serbia's transition.

For both the FES and KAS, arguably their chief ambition with respect to Serbia's political development has been the establishment of a clearly defined center left and center right (FES 2005). This has meant devoting resources toward further educating party members on the attributes of a given ideolog-ical profile. Most often, the *Stiftungen* have supported this by sponsoring con-ferences and seminars laying out the theory of political ideology. In April 2009, for example, KAS held a workshop titled "Conservatism and the Polit-ical Scene in Serbia," in which G17 Plus youth party members attended lec-tures delivered by political science professors from the University of Belgrade. Similarly, FES has sponsored a host of conferences, bringing together political party experts from Serbia's academic community. Together with party mem-bers, scholars discuss the theory underlying a social-democratic political ide-ology. FES has also provided funds for Serbian academics to conduct research on the subject of ideology formation, the findings of which it regularly pub-lishes in conjunction with the Belgrade-based Institute of Social Science. In this respect, FES also acts as a knowledge bank on political party development in Serbia.[41]

Unlike the German *Stiftungen*, the American party institutes have focused their efforts not on ideology building but on platform development. IRI took the main lead on this,[42] seeking to achieve programmatic coherence not through theory building (as the *Stiftungen* have preferred) but through a combination of public opinion research, platform-building training, and consultations. It thus encouraged partner parties to use polling data to help identify those issues of importance to the electorate and to determine the precise policy course party supporters prefer. IRI also advised parties to use "simpler, less theoretical, political language" when communicating their platforms and to accentuate "positive solutions to the country's problems" (IRI 2006b). In a rare instance of *Stiftung*–institute collaboration, IRI and KAS hosted a training session for the DSS in which IRI provided training in political-skills building, including how to integrate center-right conservative political thought and values into the DSS platform (IRI 2007a).

Cross-Border Links

A final—and for the *Stiftungen*, essential—facet of party assistance in the post-Milošević period has been programming that seeks to forge cross-border links between Serbian parties and their counterparts in the region on the one hand, and Serbian parties and their counterparts in Western Europe on the other. It is this latter goal that has defined the party assistance that the *Stiftungen* have provided and which most distinguishes their work from that of the American party institutes.

Fundamental to this has been the strengthening of Serbia-Germany bilateral relations. For well over a decade, the *Stiftungen* have fostered and facilitated meetings and contacts between Serbian politicians and German parliamentarians. On numerous occasions, the FES and KAS sponsored the travels of up-and-coming Serbian politicians to Germany, and brought leading Social Democratic and Conservative party Germans to Serbia. FES has been particularly active on this front, promoting the travels of Đinđić and Tadić and other DS officials throughout Germany, arranging meetings with German officials, and offering direct access to the levers of power in Brussels.

In addition, the *Stiftungen* have also sought to foster bilateral ties among young party members. A regional FES initiative titled "Promising Politicians" invited young party members to Brussels in an effort to create networks with

European politicians. "Welcome to Germany," a project jointly implemented by all of the German *Stiftungen*, encouraged promising Serbian students to travel to Germany and learn about the culture.

More than anything else, however, the purpose of the *Stiftungen* is to serve as conduits between German politicians and the Serbian political scene. Michael Ehrke of the FES explains, "One informal task of mine is to inform Germany of this region. We have the Bundestag and for them I am one of the first sources of information."[43] Given their close relationship with Serbian politicians, *Stiftungen* representatives provide on-the-ground insight into the political happenings in Serbia and are often a first point of contact for German officials seeking advice on Serbia policy. These contacts would prove critical in 2008, as European governments altered course in Serbia.

The Transition to a Post-Partisan Approach (2009–2012)

From 2000 to 2008, party aid providers unanimously refrained from working with Serbia's far-right elements. This was in spite of these parties' increasingly strong electoral showing within the context of free and fair elections. It was also in spite of these parties' increasingly democratic behavior. This changed at the close of 2008.

The 2008 parliamentary elections were met by ambiguous results. Though the pro-European ZES coalition had won a plurality of votes cast, it failed to win enough seats to form a government on its own. Serbia's nationalist parties, by contrast, were well situated to form a governing coalition as a DSS–SRS–SPS government. Having broken ties in previous months with the DSS because of its refusal to commit to EU membership, ZES had little choice but to lure the SPS into a coalition, awarding it the enviable position of "king maker."

Shortly after the formation of the government, the newly appointed FES resident director received a phone call from the office of DS president Boris Tadić, requesting that FES establish ties to the SPS. According to Tadić, "The stability of the coalition depends on them."[44] Tadić requested not only that FES incorporate the SPS within its programs, but that it actively promote SPS officials throughout Germany and back the SPS's bid to join the Socialist International. Ehrke was thereby asked to do what had been all but taboo throughout the past decade: overtly support a party once beholden to Milošević. It was a decision FES did not take lightly.[45] Yet it had little choice: the government's stability depended on FES's support. Thus, in late 2008 FES representatives accompanied SPS president, Ivica Dačić, on a high-level trip to Berlin, where the former Milošević ally was introduced to the governing board of the Social Party of Germany and where FES made the case for the SPS's place in the Serbian government and its inclusion in the Socialist International. In so doing, FES became the first party aid provider to actively reach out to the SPS.

Over the next several months, American and other European aid providers would follow suit. The diplomatic ban once placed on the institutes' relations with the SPS was rescinded, and informal negotiations on possible party programming commenced. When in the fall of 2008 Nikolić and his deputy Aleksander Vučić broke off from the SRS to form their own pro-EU SNS, donors had yet more reason to distance themselves from the partisanship of policies past. By April 2008, the institutes declared themselves "open to anybody that wants to work with us," including the SNS or SPS.[46] Already by 2010, SNS members were guests at the U.S. embassy's Fourth of July bash. Twelve months later, Serbian newspapers were filled with allegations that the former U.S. ambassador, William Montgomery, was a paid adviser to the SNS.[47] By April 2011, SNS's Nikolić was calling for closed-door meetings with the new U.S. ambassador, Mary Warlick. TThe era of partisan party aid had thus run its course.

Aid's Impact on Post-Milošević Serbia

When Milošević was ousted in the fall of 2000, the success of political party assistance—and democracy aid more generally—was widely acknowledged. Yet more than ten years into Serbia's democratic transition, an equally straightforward appraisal of party aid post-Milošević is patently lacking. To the contrary, aid providers and donors offer conflicting accounts of aid's effects, while aid recipients are ambivalent in their assessment of aid's utility.

Such ambiguity may well be the result of aid's competing (and, at times, conflicting) objectives in the post-Milošević period and, ultimately, its subservience to larger foreign policy goals. Although aid providers frequently professed their desire to see parties and the party system "democratized," their overriding concern was that of engineering the electoral defeat of nonrecipient parties. For aid recipients, too, the perceived purposes of aid have been wide ranging. For some, training and seminars were envisioned as a resource for gaining new skills and insights into the makings of professional politics.

For others, aid was a channel to the "Western world": a way to forge contacts with foreign dignitaries, a means to travel beyond Serbian borders, and an opportunity to establish international networks with non-Serbs. For only a small group of recipients is aid regarded as a tool of democratization: a vehicle to empower parties' grassroots and to help them gain a place within the power structure.

On each of these fronts, however, party aid has come up short. Serbia's political parties remain top-down structures, dominated by one or two personalities and programmatically indistinct. Parties themselves are reviled as corrupt and nepotistic, their dominance of Serbia's political and economic life so thorough that many believe parties rank among the greatest ills afflicting Serbia's democratic trajectory today. Nor is it clear that donors' desire to electorally eradicate the parties of the ancien régime has been realized. To the contrary, the SPS has played an important role in three post-Milošević governments. In 2012, the SNS—a party born from the ultra-right SRS—succeeded in forming a government with the SPS. Nikolić, the party's president, even achieved the surprising feat of beating the Western-backed Tadić in free and fair presidential elections. That both parties have resurfaced as credible opponents capable of combating the corruption witnessed over the course of the post-Milošević period is undoubtedly a rebuke of a foreign policy intent on rendering these parties irrelevant.

Yet the record has not been entirely lackluster. A former resident director of IRI argues that although there was "not necessarily systemic success," there was evidence of "anecdotal progress."[48] For example, IRI should be credited for steering President Tadić toward a more policy-based approach to governance. Nebojša Andrić, a member of DS and a regional trainer for NDI, is similarly convinced that "assistance from abroad does help."[49] A former resident director of NDI who went on to work in Georgia maintains that NDI "had a significant impact on the development of Serbia's democracy—not only in terms of parties but also civil society, development of youth and women, and the electoral process."[50]

The upcoming sections offer a more sober analysis of aid's effects in the post-Milošević period. While pointing to several instances in which aid has had a positive effect, evidence overwhelmingly suggests that aid has been ineffective in promoting the democratization of Serbia's parties and party scene, and it may in several instances have worked to democracy's detriment.

What Worked

Political party assistance in the post-Milošević period has had a troubled history. Yet several areas—however marginal to the overall development of political parties—speak to moderate success. Thus, although aid recipients were often hard-pressed to name concrete instances of aid's positive impact, they were widely supportive of its existence and welcomed donors' efforts to bolster democracy. Many also believed aid to be beneficial, occasionally very much so. Such perceptions are not entirely without merit. The five areas in which aid made a marked impact are the professionalization of aid recipients' electoral campaigns, aid recipients' GOTV efforts, an increase in the confidence of party members—particularly of young members,; the creation of internal party training centers, and the empowerment of minority parties. As in many other new democracies in Central and Eastern Europe and beyond, these types of activities represented areas where aid made a modest mark on the political landscape and made a small—but important—contribution to democracy.

PROFESSIONALIZING PARTIES

The most apparent manner in which aid made its mark was through the professionalization of Serbia's political party scene. Throughout the past decade, Serbia's political parties have become well-oiled political machines. They have repeatedly launched highly professional electoral campaigns, replete with multimedia outreach components (including television, radio, web-based, and newspaper advertisements), grassroots outreach (door-to-door campaigning, mass mailings, and local media), and a heavy reliance on public opinion polls. According to the OSCE (2007: 11), Serbian electoral campaigns are "vibrant," with parties making regular "use of media, organized street and in-door rallies and public events . . . billboards and posters . . . and door-to-door." The campaigns themselves have also become more positive, with candidates such as Tadić refraining from exclusively negative attacks on opponents in an effort to offer a more positive, forward-looking vision of Serbia's future.

Party assistance accounts for at least a small part of this. Top party brass has, on occasion, taken aid providers' advice to heart and taken their polls into consideration. For example, in 2008 the ZES coalition took IRI's advice to launch a two-tiered series of commercials, one offering a positive, pro-EU vision of the coalition, the other, attacking the opposition for being anti-EU. Party members themselves attest to the regular use of IRI polls, many maintaining that their parties "use them and take them seriously."[51] In fact, although a handful of parties remain wary of public opinion polls (most notably, Koštunica's DSS), the general consensus among those interviewed was that polling was a useful window into public opinion.

ACCEPTANCE OF DOOR-TO-DOOR CAMPAIGNING

The reliance on IRI polls—and confidence in public opinion polls more generally—has been matched by increasing acceptance of grassroots activism, in particular door-to-door campaigning. By 2008, the OSCE (2008: 10) remarked that Serbia's parties were engaging in "intense door-to-door visits." Though knocking on doors remains a struggle and many communities remain resistant—even in Belgrade, for example, parties fail to fulfill their self-imposed quotas—door-to-door campaigning is no longer taboo. In fact, almost all parties use some degree of door-to-door campaigning. Jovan Tatić, a former program coordinator at NDI, says, "Today, door-to-door is really accepted . . . but ten years ago it was thought to be impossible." He attributes this change to NDI: "I guarantee you that we [NDI] introduced it."[52] So too do many aid recipients. In fact, Marko Blagojević, an analyst at CeSID, says that party aid has been an important contributor to the professionalization of Serbia's parties, thanks to which their "tactics are much better developed" than they were in the 1990s.[53]

BUILDING CONFIDENCE

One area where party aid has had its greatest impact is with respect to confidence building. For many young and/or female party members, in particular, training has been an important resource, not necessarily for the skills it imparts (in fact, many of those skills are never put to use) but rather for building the self-confidence of party members as a professional party cadre.

Young and female party members have long been disempowered within their respective parties; training offers them an air of professionalism, providing at the very least the illusion that they are acquiring practical skills in public relations, door-to-door campaigning, and other electoral basics that may one day be put to use. Says one LDP member and NDI trainer, party aid training has "boosted young people's self-esteem and introduced them to the

world."[54] It is a claim reiterated by many aid recipients at the lowest echelons
of their parties.

For example, Dušan Kanazir, a member of LDP's youth wing, says that
NDI-sponsored "trainings built our confidence" and were "above all, good for
our self-esteem."[55] A political novice who had yet to participate in grassroots
campaigning, he viewed training as an indication that donors and parties
were confident of his abilities: "You go home with a sense that you received
something, that the party is investing in you."[56] Milena Stanković, an LDP
member and one of the few female members of parliament, feels similarly. She
says that training in public relations and public speaking "[was] very important" in the furthering of her career: "I learned a lot. . . . I saw that I was capable
on TV and it helped me to do this."[57] As a young and relatively inexperienced
politician, she says, "It's very important to have NDI trainings. I feel that I
need more trainings as an MP. I am learning new things everyday but by my-
self, I make mistakes. I need trainings to feel more confident."[58] Many young
party members were similarly convinced of aid's utility in this respect.

INCREASING VOTER TURNOUT

Another area where party aid providers concentrated heavily after 2000 was
that of voter turnout. Throughout the immediate post-Milošević period, voter
turnout was low, rarely exceeding 40 percent. This was problematic in two
respects. First, low voter turnout—particularly with respect to presidential
elections—risked halting Serbia's political process. Until 2004, Serbian law
mandated that presidential victors not only win more than 50 percent of the
national vote but that half of all registered voters turn out on election day. As
a consequence of this high turnout threshold, Serbian presidential elections
were repeated no less than four times before a president was ultimately
elected. Second, donors speculated that low voter turnout would increase the
odds of an SRS victory. Indeed, where voter turnout was at its lowest—as in
the presidential elections of November 2003, when less than 40 percent of
registered voters voted—SRS candidates outperformed their democratic
opponents.

In the light of such reservations, in 2004 party aid providers began spending millions of dollars on a concerted effort to raise voter turnout, repeatedly
sponsoring nationwide GOTV campaigns. These campaigns were a major
success in increasing voter turnout. From 2004 onward, voter turnout increased considerably, in both parliamentary and presidential elections alike

(Figure 6). Many, including the OSCE and USAID, attributed such results (at least partially) to the highly visible GOTV campaigns funded by USAID, the U.S. party institutes, and their domestic implementer, CeSID (OSCE 2004: 11).[59] Though it is difficult to measure the precise effect of such efforts, given that exit polls are not used in Serbia, communities targeted by the GOTV campaign—those of ethnic minorities, youth, and women—are all believed to have participated at higher volumes in the wake of GOTV efforts.

PARTY TRAINING CENTERS

In addition to increasing voter turnout, one of the long-term ambitions of party aid providers has been that of increasing the indigenous capacities of aid recipients. Key to this has been the creation of internal party training centers. As NDI, the AMS, and other aid providers have trained individual party members, they have sought to transfer some of the responsibility for that training onto parties themselves. Working closely with a select core of party activists, they have encouraged these individuals to lobby their party leaders to approve the creation of stand-alone training centers within their respective parties. They have, in several instances, succeeded.

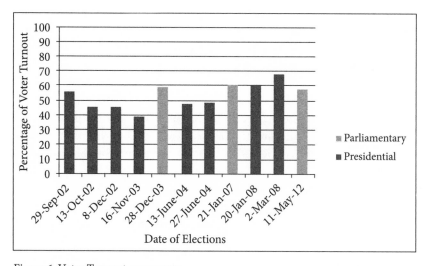

Figure 6. Voter Turnout, 2002–2012
Source: OSCE Office for Democratic Institutions and Human Rights Electoral Data on Serbia.

Vukosava Crnjanski is an example of a trainer who successfully lobbied party leaders to create such a center. A regional trainer for NDI, Crnjanski established an educational center within the GSS in 2005. At her request, NDI then trained fifteen additional GSS members to participate in the center as NDI-certified trainers. Now a member of LDP (which merged with GSS in 2007), Crnjanski is looking to repeat her efforts. As she explains, "If I want sustainability, we need to create new trainers."[60]

Like the GSS, both DS and DSS also developed in-house educational centers. In 2005, the DS formally assigned the Ljuba Davidović Foundation this function, and several months later the DSS erected what it called the Internal Trainings Department. In both instances, active party members adapted party aid training to suit their own parties' interests, crafting seminars on the basis of party aid literature and training materials provided by the institutes and foundations. As the institutes wind down their endeavors in Serbia, these training centers are poised to continue training party members.

MINORITY PARTIES

Finally, party aid providers have also had some success in strengthening the capacities of two key minority groups in Serbia: Hungarians and Bosniaks. Serbia is home to more than twenty ethnic and national minorities, making up just less than 20 percent of the total population. Given Serbia's troubled history of interethnic tensions, ethnic minority parties were a natural target of the foreign aid community. Serbia's minorities have traditionally had little say in the makings of their government. As late as 2003, the hefty 5-percent voter threshold required of all parties to enter parliament meant that not a single ethnic minority party was represented in Serbia's parliament. The elimination of that threshold in April 2004 changed the political outlook of minority parties and marked the start of a close relationship with aid providers and NDI in particular. This relationship only grew closer with the prospect of fiercely competitive parliamentary elections in 2004, 2007, and 2008, in which a handful of parliamentary seats threatened to determine the constitution of the next Serbian government. Within this context, donors believed that the ethnic vote could be an additional factor in determining the outcome of the elections.

As a result, from 2005 onward aid providers worked closely with ethnic minority parties, encouraging the formation of minority coalitions and teaching the basics of voter targeting. In late 2005, NDI launched a large-scale public opinion research venture, thanks to which ethnic minority party members gained insight into the voting habits of their electorate, including specific information on voter concerns in ethnic minority regions.

In part as a result of such efforts, several ethnic minority parties made parliamentary gains in the 2008 elections. Hungarian ethnic minority parties, for example, formed the Hungarian Coalition that included the Alliance of Vojvodina Hungarians, the Democratic Party of Vojvodina Hungarians, and the Democratic Fellowship of Vojvodina Hungarians. Their unity allowed Hungarians to maximize their vote in the 2008 parliamentary elections, enabling them to win a total of four seats in parliament.

The Bosniak minority living in Sandžak has also witnessed gains. The List for European Sandžak—representing the Party of Democratic Action of Sandžak, the Bosniak Democratic Party of Sandžak, and the Social Liberal Party of Sandžak—won two parliamentary seats in both 2007 and 2008 owing to their willingness to compete on a single ticket.

The record has been modestly positive with respect to donors' work with Albanian and Roma minority parties. In the months leading to the January 2007 parliamentary elections, information provided by NDI proved critical for the GOTV efforts of parties such as the the Union of Roma of Serbia (URS)—helping them to enter parliament for the first time. Indeed, Mentor Nuhiu of the Albanian Party for Democratic Action (PDD) says NDI "did a lot" to encourage Albanian parties to form electoral alliances and win a seat in Serbia's 250-seat parliament.[61] NDI's training for the Albanian Coalition from Preševo Valley and its extensive door-to-door campaign allowed the coalition (which included PDD) to win the 16,973 votes needed to enter parliament. NDI representatives even contacted Albanian Serbs in Belgrade, encouraging them to vote for the minority coalition. According to a member of the Democratic Union of the Valley, "Without NDI, we wouldn't be able to achieve this." In 2007, the electoral benefits of NDI's help were shared with the Roma. According to NDI, "the URS successfully identified voting districts with high numbers of Roma voters and as a result targeted campaign activities in these areas" (NDI 2007b).[62] Thanks in part to NDI, in 2007 the URS and the Roma Party (RP) each won one seat in Serbia's parliament.

But the good news did not last long. The increasingly rosy perspectives of Serbia's Roma parties came to an abrupt end in 2008 when, despite the repeated efforts of NDI and IRI, Roma parties failed to enter parliament. Like the Albanian parties of Serbia, they continued to suffer from weak organizational structures, corruption, personalized politics, and petty rivalries. Roma and Albanian party leaders, for example, often proved more interested in securing access to state coffers and self-enrichment than in best representing their communities. In 2008, the president of the Roma Party "Unity" (RPU) admitted to negotiating with both Nikolić's SNS and Tadić's DS on possible coalition formation. And in the electoral campaign of 2012, both the RP and Bosniak People's Party formed an electoral coalition with the SNS under the title "Let's Get Serbia Moving." According to NDI, it was obvious that many of Serbia's small ethnic minority parties were unwilling (or unable) to hold on to their own programmatic principles during negotiations with Serbia's large national parties.

In part as a consequence, donors' efforts to maintain Albanian and Roma ethnic coalitions have failed. The Albanian and Bosnian coalitions formed in 2007 fell apart once they assumed office, setting off a firestorm of recriminations within their respective communities. Thanks to this, the ethnic vote has remained divided, ensuring that no Roma party would enter parliament and just one Albanian party would enter in 2008—a major setback for minority rights in Serbia and for the institutes.[63] In the years that followed, allegations of corruption and internal party strife continued to haunt ethnic minority parties, making donor assistance impossible. The RP, for example, faced numerous accusations and trials for the misuse and theft of campaign funds. Likewise, the RPU's president was implicated in the misuse of donor funds during his involvement in a Roma television station, RTV Nišava.[64]

NDI's efforts to reach out to such parties after 2008 were often rebuffed, not because of a lack of interest on the parties' part but because of ineffective organizational structures. Baseline questionnaires administered by NDI often went unanswered, and few Roma leaders were able to articulate clear strategies and policies concerning their political engagement. The situation has been slightly more positive in the case of the Albanian minority parties, where NDI has been able to implement its trainer-of-trainers programs, but the results remain "modest."[65] Like the Roma parties, the Albanian ethnic minority parties rarely communicated with their members outside of the electoral arena and often succumbed to pressures exerted by larger parties like the DS or SNS, whose interests rarely extended beyond winning the vote of Serbia's minority communities.

Not surprisingly, donors have been forced to confront the fact that aiding ethnic minority political parties is capable of reaping only modest gains. Despite their best efforts, NDI's objectives to help Albanian and Roma ethnic minority parties "build their capacity and make a formal organizational and functional structure, to have several themes within the parties, not just the Presidency" have made only modest headway.[66]

LEVERAGING EU MEMBERSHIP

The EU's policy of conditionality, whereby it makes a prospective member's accession contingent on the realization of key benchmarks, is almost universally praised for inciting the adoption of democratic reforms throughout much of Central and Eastern Europe (Pridham 2005; Schimmelfennig and Scholtz 2008). These reforms extend from large-scale overhauls of political institutions to more narrow laws that govern things like campaign finance. Thus, although the EU does not itself dispense of political party assistance, its actions and decisions can directly and indirectly influence political party and party system development in aspiring member states. Such was certainly the case in Serbia, which has continuously sought EU membership since dispelling Milošević in October 2000. Throughout this period, EU conditionality has had a marked effect on ensuring the adoption of legal reforms that govern Serbia's political party system. Conditionality has had a notably less marked effect, however, on ensuring the implementation of those reforms and altering the corruptive practices ingrained in Serbia's political parties.

More than most (albeit not all) aspiring EU member states, Serbia has struggled throughout its European trajectory. For a long time, Serbia's failure to comply fully with the ICTY significantly hampered its accession process. As a result, until the arrest and extradition of Radovan Karadžić in 2008 and Ratko Mladić in 2011, Serbian authorities' European ambitions failed to gain real traction. Still, Serbia's EU trajectory has not been stagnant. Serbia's first major formal step toward EU membership took place in 2008, when the EU approved Serbia's Stabilization and Association Agreement (SAA). Then, in December 2009, the EU unfroze its trade agreement with Serbia and officially discarded the visa requirement previously needed for Serbian citizens to travel to the EU's "Schengen area." Serbia applied for EU membership around the same time and in March 2012 achieved a major feat: It became a full candidate for EU membership. Finally, in June 2013 Serbia was invited to open accession negotiations beginning the following January.

Throughout this process, the EU has profoundly influenced Serbian politics and has both directly and indirectly ensured the adoption of reforms governing the regulation of Serbia's party system. One example includes the passage of Serbia's 2011 Law on Financing of Political Parties—a major improvement on the political party legislation that had been enacted in 2004 to no effect. The law's adoption in June 2011 was a requirement for the successful attainment of Serbia's membership status, which Serbia finally won nine months later. According to then Prime Minister Mirko Cvetković, the law's passage—which set into place new regulations meant to increase transparency of party funding sources—was a direct result of EU-applied pressure (see Bertelsmann Stiftung 2012).[67]

The EU has also had a direct impact on parliamentarians' decision to end the practice of blank resignations enshrined in Serbia's post-Milošević constitution.[68] Throughout the 2000s, the use of blank resignations ensured that political parties had direct control over the voting habits of their members of parliament (MPs), enabling them to dismiss members who refused to follow the party line. By dismissing party members who did not vote according to the party leadership line, the party could simply appoint a new MP in their place. Not surprising, in early 2011 abolishing that practice emerged as a prerequisite for the European Commission's confirmation of Serbia's EU candidacy status. As a consequence, in May 2011 Serbia's parliament adopted a new law on the election of MPs that effectively abolished the practice of blank resignation letters, just weeks before the parliament also passed the law on party financing—both of which were needed to obtain EU candidacy status.

The passage of these laws represented an important step in shifting the legal boundaries of Serbia's party system. Without systematic implementation, however, the laws were unable to halt the corruptive practices that necessitated their adoption. Reporting on Serbia's progress in 2012, the European parliament noted that "the key to fight against systemic corruption lies in severing the bonds between political parties, private interests and public enterprises" and called on Serbian authorities to "make party financing transparent" and "implement the law on party financing"[69]—something Serbia's political parties had by and large failed to do in the elections of May 2012. Indeed, the source of almost half of party expenditures remained unknown following the 2012 elections, despite parties' legal obligation to share such information publicly. A report by Transparency International furthermore found the elections to suffer from "organized vote buying" and "indirect vote buying," which went uninvestigated, as prescribed by law.[70] To date, no party has ever been sanctioned in Serbia for violating party finance laws.

Like party aid providers, the EU may also have played a role in the success of reformist coalitions. In 2008, for example, the EU was widely suspected of having fast-tracked Serbia's signing of the Stabilization and Association

Agreement to benefit the DS-led coalition ahead of the parliamentary elections of May 2012.[71] Indeed, the signing of Serbia's SAA came just weeks before Serbians would go to the polls to elect their new parliament. Having taken years to reach this stage in its accession process, the feat was widely regarded as a coup for the DS. According to the *New York Times*, the EU's decision to hurry the SAA "helped bring a pro-Western political party to victory through Serbian elections."[72]

EU officials have not taken pains to deny such allegations. Speaking to reporters in August 2008, EU foreign policy spokesperson Cristina Gallach acknowledged "Everyone tells us, the polls tell us, that European support then gave a boost to Tadić that allowed him to win the elections."[73] According to the deputy director at the Center for European Reform, the EU's decision "was a gamble. There were people who said that the EU should not intervene in the internal affairs of Serbia. But it paid off."[74] Tadić's party, the DS, ultimately formed a pro-EU government that succeeded in arresting ICTY fugitive Karadžić, thus living up to the EU's hopes. Like the party institutes, however, the EU took a controversial step in seemingly bolstering the electoral prospects of some parties at the expense of others.

Finally, perhaps the most profound manner in which the EU has (inadvertently) influenced Serbia's political party scene is through the very prospect of EU membership. Parties' stance toward the desirability of EU accession was perhaps the most important political cleavage leading to the parliamentary elections of 2012. Indeed, until the emergence of the SNS, parties' support for or opposition to future EU membership was responsible for the creation of electoral coalitions and blocs and in large part defined party identities for most of the 2000s (Orlović 2011; Pavlović and Antonić 2007; Slavujević 2007). Ironically, this may have helped suppress the development of differentiated political platforms and ultimately slowed the programmatic maturation of Serbia's party scene.

What Did Not Work

Foreign assistance has helped Serbia's parties in a number of concrete, albeit modest, ways. Over the course of the past decade, party aid has helped party members gain confidence. It has enabled parties and civil society organizations to bring out the vote. And it has helped empower minority parties, even if this did not always translate into electoral success. But as in so many other new democracies, party aid has not facilitated a more substantive shift in party behavior. Serbia's parties continue to emulate many of the most corrosive qualities that define the "standard lament" and are regarded by many as among the chief ailments afflicting Serbian democracy today.

INTERNAL PARTY DEMOCRACY

One area where aid did not work was in democratizing Serbia's political parties internally. American donors traditionally place a great deal of emphasis on internal party democracy. USAID, in particular, has made the attainment of internal party democracy a priority for aid providers; as a consequence, the U.S. party institutes have been hard pressed to commend internal party democracy in their reports and proposals. In their quarterly reports to USAID, NDI and IRI both consistently list assisting parties in the development of internal democratic practices among their key long-term goals. In Serbia's case, there is little doubt that the democratization of parties' internal structures and procedures—through greater inclusivity, decentralization, and institutionalization—would benefit party members and democracy more generally (Lutovac 2006). Yet in practice, efforts to raise the profile of women and youth within partner parties was as close as donors came to promoting internal party democracy in Serbia. Apart from a handful of training centered on candidate selection, democratizing parties' decision-making processes simply did not rank high for most party aid practitioners.

Indeed, practitioners have been reluctant to broach the subject of internal party democracy. This applies across the party aid spectrum, to Americans and Europeans alike. "We can't push this," explains the resident director of FNS, using the iron fist in internal party politics is simply "the way to get things done here."[75] Similarly, a former resident director of NDI conceded that despite USAID's pushing, "Internal party democracy means nothing."[76]

Undoubtedly, party aid providers' discomfort in pursuing parties' non-democratic internal workings has stemmed largely from parties themselves. IRI representatives say internal democracy is "a tough sell, because you are essentially asking a party leader to relinquish some of their political power. It's counter to what they perceive to be their interest."[77] NDI program officers in Serbia agree. According to one, "Internal democracy is not realistic. I can't afford, as a professional, to have some set of goals that are not achievable."[78] Thus, although internal party democracy is often a stated goal found in NDI and IRI proposals, it is not one that has been attained in practice.

Serbia's political parties remain deeply undemocratic. Their organizational structures are top-down, their selection procedures are opaque, and their decision-making is exclusive (Goati 2005; Pavlović 2007; Spoerri 2008). Thus, in the ten-year period following regime change, just two major parties experienced a change in party leadership—the G17 Plus and the DS. Despite the DS's introduction of internal party elections in 2010, the party's electoral procedures are notoriously unfair (Savić 2011). The process of party fragmentation has also persisted unabated, as internal party factions have remained taboo. In fact, Serbia's post-Milošević constitution made parties even *less* tolerant of internal dissent by placing MP mandates at parties' disposal.

Not surprising, Serbian party members are palpably dissatisfied with the state of internal party politics. One young member of the DSS said, "I am frustrated that there is a lack of internal party democracy."[79] Supporters of the LDP have dubbed their party leader "a dictator" and an "autocrat." A former G17 member admitted to having left party politics because of internal party nepotism and a lack of mobility through merit.[80] The same is true of the SPO and SDU; their top-down politics have cost the two parties some of their most talented members.[81]

As in the 1990s, such frustrations have caused mass party disaffections, the exit of competent people from Serbia's political life, and fragility in electoral coalitions. For instance, an SDU member complained that the coalition partner LDP's president, Čedomir "Čeda" Jovanović, "didn't appreciate" his party's involvement in the coalition and made decisions without consultation. A former NDI trainer in Belgrade admitted, "Čeda's vigilance and energy is doing equal damage by turning people away. They are worked like slaves." Indeed, the donor-favorite LDP was widely cited as so authoritarian that some (incorrectly) predicted that it would fail to enter parliament in 2012.[82]

Turning Training to Practice

One consequence of the lack of internal democracy within Serbia's parties is that it renders many of the skills that party members learn useless. During the past decade, party aid providers have trained thousands of party members and activists. The majority of those trained have been members at the lowest echelons of parties' rank and file: the members of youth wings, the unpaid volunteers, and the young activists new to party politics. Yet training for these political novices has often focused on such skills as media relations, public speaking, and door-to-door voter contact—skills that only a select group of top-notch party members will ever use within the context of their top-down parties.

Aid recipients, for example, widely reported a lack of direct utilization of the skills acquired. Although members believed that training might be useful for a future career (including careers outside of politics), few admitted to having had the opportunity to put the training to use on behalf of their parties. Vukosava Crnjanski, an NDI regional trainer, admits that follow-up for training is often lacking, with much training being conducted for the sake of training rather than with a clear vision for how this may benefit the party. Nenad Čelarević of the Social Democratic Union Youth Board agrees, saying that follow-up is frequently absent.[83] Indeed, for all the money and resources invested in training, there is little evidence that the skills imparted are of significant use for political parties.

Part of the problem lies not merely in the content of party-related training but in the trainer-of-trainers program itself. Largely regarded as one of NDI Serbia's most innovative elements, trainer-of-trainers programs rest on the notion that training an embedded party member will facilitate sustainability by transforming individual members into indigenous resources with transferable skills. Most often, those trained as trainers are young, energetic party activists who, it is hoped, will rise through the party's ranks, bringing their acquired skills with them. But, as one practitioner admitted, precisely because these individuals are preexisting members and often young, many within the party—particularly older members—are reluctant to take them seriously. This suggests that the selection of trainer-of-trainers needs to be carefully considered.

Unfortunately, this does not always seem to be the case. NDI, for example, often relies on parties to recommend a small pool of candidates, from which NDI makes a final selection. But both party members and practitioners concede that candidates are often nominated by parties not on the basis of their talent or merit but by virtue of their association with a small number of elite decision makers. One practitioner explains, "There is no systematic vision of their future role and contribution to the party development."[84] Indeed, many of those who receive training do not go on to transfer their skills in the future, meaning that their skills often end with them.

Ideology Building

Another area in which democracy aid has failed to positively influence parties is with respect to their ideologies. Beginning in 2003, donors—in particular, the German *Stiftungen* and British party foundations—made ideology building a priority. Having so far worked on a multiparty basis, European party foundations sought to support a more clearly delineated ideological canvass, with parties neatly spread along a left-right spectrum. Pivotal to this goal was the creation of party-to-party relationships across European borders, with mother parties in Germany or the United Kingdom nurturing the ideological purity of their party kin in Serbia. Almost a decade after such initiatives were first put in place, however, practitioners widely acknowledge that their attempts to foster an ideological consensus have come to naught. Despite what are often close cross-border partnerships, ideological and programmatic coherence remains far from the norm in contemporary Serbia.

Serbia's largest political party, the DS, offers a case in point. The ideological reshaping of the party from liberal to social democratic was, by one member's own admission, "not so successful."[85] The member says, his party is divided roughly 50-50 between members preferring a social democratic line, and those who favor a liberal ideology.

Representatives of FES freely concur. FES's former resident director says that like most social democratic parties in Central and Eastern Europe, the DS is "purely neoliberal in [its] economic and social policies"; party leaders "don't even understand why there should be some social security" and exhibit no "sensitivity for the needs of the poor."[86] Given such ideological incoherence, it is hardly surprising that Serbia's Liberal Democratic Party cooperates with and receives assistance from both the Heinrich Böll Stiftung (HBS) and FNS. Neither *Stiftung* seemed particularly concerned that their alleged "sister" party was being courted by an ideological competitor. As one HBS representative shrugged, "There's no classical ideological spectrum in Serbia."[87]

Addressing Nationalism

If there has not been a clear ideological spectrum, there has certainly been a clear programmatic leaning to the far right. Arguably the defining feature of Serbian politics over the past two decades has been the preponderance of far-right parties and nationalism (see Bieber 2003; Dimitrijević 2008; Ramet 2007; Spoerri 2011). As a consequence, one of the primary ambitions of the foreign aid community in Serbia has been that of removing Serbia's so-called national question—issues pertaining to where parties stand on national sovereignty, Kosovo, and the ICTY—from the mainstream of Serbian politics.

In practice, however, party aid providers have spent far less of their time engaging Serbia's parties on the "national question" than one might suspect. Though aid providers repeatedly encouraged parties to concentrate on bread-and-butter issues, they were not always consistent in calling on parties to disavow nationalism. To the contrary, there were several instances in which aid providers actively encouraged partner parties to play up their nationalist credentials.

In the run-up to 2008's contentious parliamentary elections, for example, IRI advised the DS and its coalition partners to "present a strong defense on Kosovo," encouraging coalition members to reassure voters that "we will never recognize an independent Kosovo" (IRI 2008b). In the process, the institute encouraged aid recipients to put forward an ultimately untenable position that would leave Serbia's territorial composition unresolved, even as it attempted to gain membership to the EU.

Aid providers' failure to fully engage Serbia's parties on issues of nationalism was most prominently on display with respect to Vojislav Koštunica's DSS. Initially a center-right party (albeit one with incomparable nationalist credentials), the DSS received assistance in the form of training and public opinion polls from both the KAS and the American party institutes. Yet the party took a marked turn *away* from political moderation throughout the post-Milošević period. As the 2000s progressed, Koštunica upheld an increasingly hard-line position on Kosovo, cooperation with the United States, and the desirability of EU membership. His party's refusal to back EU membership led to the unraveling of the 2007 DS–DSS government and threatened to set forth a far-right coalition government.

Koštunica's DSS has not been the only so-called reformist party to struggle with nationalism. As Konitzer and Grujić (2009: 866) explain, parties like the DS "have shown an inability to strike a balance between Serbs' recent past and the current and future needs of a democratic Serbia" and "find it difficult simultaneously to maintain their dominant goal of 'facing the past' and to accept Serbian responsibility for past wrongdoings while still recognizing the suffering of Serbs at the hands of non-Serbs." Indeed, many so-called reformist parties have struggled to engage Serbia's "national question" head-on, and have yet to engage the general public in a meaningful conversation on Serbia's role during the Yugoslav wars and the consequences this has for Serbia's position on the international stage.

What Hurt

In the years that followed Milošević's unseating in October 2000, democracy assistance to political parties witnessed an ambiguous trajectory. Although helpful in certain respects, it failed to undo many of the most pernicious legacies parties accrued throughout Milošević's tenure. Not only did aid fail to live up to donors' stated goals, it may in several instances have worked against democratization processes in the post-Milošević period. One of aid's most troubling legacies was that it crossed the line into electoral meddling.

CROSSING THE LINE

Among the chief ambitions of political party aid in the post-Milošević period was that of ensuring that Serbia's politics did not revert back to the Milošević era. As NDI put it, its assistance strove "to stem the tide of radical political support"—in other words, to stem the tide of the SRS (NDI 2004b).[88] Key to this was ensuring that aid-recipient parties maintained sufficient electoral support to form coalition governments that excluded the SRS and SPS. Partisan GOTV efforts targeted the supporters of the so-called democratic bloc, while carefully avoiding supporters of the SRS and SPS. In entering the political fray in so partisan a manner, party aid providers effectively crossed the line into overt political meddling. In so doing, they raised troubling questions about the integrity of party assistance in the post-Milošević period.

There is little doubt that aid providers' GOTV efforts were designed to promote *targeted* participation in the electoral process. Indeed, the campaign was designed not to ensure that all eligible Serbian voters would come out to cast their ballots but rather to "ensure that the campaign would reach the largest number of potential reform voters" (IRI 2004a). Many believe such efforts worked for most of the 2000s. As IRI reported in 2004, "Democratic turnout in targeted areas was significantly higher than in past elections" (IRI 2004a). Indeed, post-election analysis revealed that Tadić's support nearly doubled in the 1,500 polling stations targeted by CeSID (NDI 2006d). NDI went so far as to boast that its voter-targeting assistance had changed the nature of electoral campaigning in Serbia and "made the difference in maintaining *democratic* voters at the polls" (NDI 2004c, emphasis added). According to Marko Blagojević, CeSID's director of operations, the impact of the database on Serbian politics was "revolutionary."[89]

The problem with partisan party aid was that it risked politicizing foreign aid in a democratic context. By the mid-2000s, Serbia had made considerable gains in transitioning toward democracy. A critical part of this transition was the gradual transformation and democratization of Serbia's far right, in particular the SRS and SPS. In the post-Milošević period, the democratic credentials of the SPS and SRS grew considerably. These parties succeeded in addressing the concerns and interests of legitimate segments of the Serbian population that "reformist" parties simply ignored (Konitzer and Grujić 2009). However, aid providers chose to disregard the far right's increasing legitimacy and democratic behavior. Most important, by exerting external influence on a domestic democratic process—by, for example, specifically targeting some voters and not others—aid providers played a direct role in tilting the electoral playing field in aid recipients' favor. Although favorable for those parties that sought to hasten Serbia's European trajectory, the results had dubious implications for the legitimacy of aid in a newly democratic environment.

One manifestation of this was that party aid providers began to root for lower voter participation and even nonparticipation among certain segments of Serbia's voting population, in particular supporters of Serbia's so-called non-reformist parties. In 2008, NDI resident director for Serbia, Tom Kelly, celebrated low voter turnout among anti-reformist voters, calling their decision to abstain from the democratic process "good news."[90] If aid providers' ambition is ultimately to ensure the realization of a substantive democratic process in which the views of all society members are heard and have equal weight, then such sentiments are unacceptable. Nor do they bode well for the legitimacy of party aid in newly democratic contexts. When orchestrated in so partisan a fashion, aid effectively crosses the line into direct electoral meddling, and gives credibility to detractors who question the intentions of democracy aid providers.

Direct intervention on partner parties' behalf was not only ethically questionable in a democratic context, but it was unsustainable. By the mid-2000s, donors were paying NGOs to do parties' work for them. Rather than encourage parties to build robust internal GOTV mechanisms, they paid so-called volunteers to do parties' work for them. Reporting to USAID on the state of 2004's targeted GOTV campaign, IRI confessed that although this strategy was "ultimately quite successful" in bringing out the vote for reformist parties,

IRI had serious "concerns about the manner in which the campaign was designed and implemented and about the viability of such efforts in the future" (IRI 2004a). In a memo to the U.S. Embassy in Belgrade, jointly written with NDI and Freedom House, IRI complained that the use of CeSID to bring out the vote undermined the sustainability of aid's impact, and encouraged parties to be less self-reliant.

According to IRI, "Political parties . . . are far better suited to run such a campaign than NGOs [because] a political party has an immediate self-interest in getting out the vote, making parties much more likely to mobilize and commit the resources to sustain GOTV in the long term." Furthermore, IRI complained that CeSID had "admitted they would not have been able to mobilize enough activists to carry out [door-to-door campaigning] had IRI and the other implementers not agreed to pay CeSID's door-to-door activists a stipend." IRI concluded that "future assistance, there, should be directed at enhancing the capacity of political parties and issue-oriented NGOs to conduct GOTV utilizing their own resources, to ensure the sustainability of GOTV long after international donors depart Serbia" (IRI 2004a).[91]

The concerns of IRI, NDI, and Freedom House fell on deaf ears, however. For the U.S. Embassy, the primary concern in Serbia was not empowering Serbia's parties to lead campaigns on their own but ensuring that non-reformist parties—the so-called anti-democratic bloc—did not assume power. As a result, relatively large sums of money continued to be infused into CeSID well into the 2000s.

Yet the problem with such assistance, as IRI noted, was that it did little to encourage political parties to mount the grassroots campaigns needed to build bonds between parties and their voters. To the contrary, by paying non-party activists to knock on doors on parties' behalf, such assistance perpetuated the divide between parties and their supporters and made any efforts to rely on dedicated, unpaid party activists more difficult. For many practitioners, such aid only risked fostering dependencies and made parties less inclined to run effective campaigns on their own.

By the late 2000s, growing numbers of practitioners were convinced that Serbia's parties might be better off without such support. Left on their own, they might have been less likely to win elections in the short-run, but they would have been more likely to develop the skills necessary to compete against highly effective parties like the SNS, which, in the absence of foreign support, had become a well-oiled political machine, more effective at grassroots campaigning and voter targeting than any Western-backed party in Serbia.

Party aid providers did not just help partner parties bring out the vote, however. They also helped parties win elections by encouraging them to take polarizing positions on important issues.

POLARIZATION

Polarization is an extremely politicized term in the democracy promotion community and, on the surface at least, it is something that party aid providers—particularly U.S. aid providers—claim they wish to avoid. In Serbia, for much of the 2000s, polarization was a major problem afflicting the party landscape, one that Serbian scholars blamed for delaying Serbia's democratic trajectory.[92] Despite this, however, party aid providers long sought to strengthen the divide between Serbian parties into two competing camps: those for and those against EU membership, thus exacerbating political polarization until at least 2009.

A critical part of that strategy was to center Serbian politics on a single issue: EU membership. Repeatedly through the 2000s, party aid providers encouraged so-called reformist parties and politicians to downplay their positions on other issues and instead hone in on their support for the EU. For example, in an effort to turn the subject of the 2007 parliamentary elections away from the issue of Kosovo's independence and back to the EU, IRI discouraged DS president, Boris Tadić, from acknowledging the possibility of an independent Kosovo (IRI 2007a). Instead, it advised his party to adopt a hard line on Kosovo and to promise "Europe and Kosovo"—both of which would later conflict with Serbia's efforts to join the EU.[93]

In the run-up to the 2008 presidential election, IRI advised the DS to launch a number of hard-hitting commercials featuring footage of Šešelj and Nikolić making incendiary remarks. Such commercials, IRI advised, should be designed to remind Serbia's voters "who Nikolić actually is and what his real politics are" (IRI 2008a).[94] To complement such imagery, IRI encouraged the Tadić campaign to run a series of positive commercials portraying a second Tadić presidency as one of stability and security, capable of ushering Serbia into Europe's fold.

IRI advised the DS-led coalition to strongly distinguish its own pro-EU platform from those of their opponents, whom, IRI warned, "paid lip service to the [EU] but would not be able to lead Serbia towards Europe" (IRI 2008b).[95] To this end, the institute advocated yet another series of contrast ads featuring negative statements DSS and SRS candidates had made in reference to European integration. Such ads, IRI noted, would force "voters to reevaluate which political options were truly open to EU integration" (IRI 2008b).

Closely related to their impact on polarization is donors' impact on party content. In their zeal to prevent an electoral victory by Serbia's far-right forces and to secure an electoral win for aid recipients, aid providers have inadvertently suppressed the development of meaningful political content. This has occurred in two ways: one, by overly relying on polling data as a means to encourage parties to develop their programs and, two, by encouraging political parties to form broad-based coalitions that cross ideological and programmatic boundaries. In both instances, aid providers have unconsciously encouraged parties to suppress the development of meaningful political content and, instead, encouraged them to concentrate on the one issue that unites them all: their pro-EU stance.

Over the course of its presence in Serbia, public opinion polling has emerged as a staple of the party institutes' work (much as it has in other newly democratic countries). Yet, despite aid providers' preference for polling, there is no consensus within expert circles that polling is in fact uniformly good for democracy. To the contrary, as Genovese and Streb (2004: 5) note, "Many worry that polls actually undermine democracy." The party institutes appear to have overlooked such concerns, however. In the process, their abiding faith in polling data has led them to advise parties to suppress certain positions and platforms that do not poll well within Serbia. Perhaps the most ominous example of this was with respect to gay and lesbian rights in Serbia.

As a predominantly Orthodox Christian country that adheres to conservative social mores, Serbia has long struggled to achieve gender and sexual equality. Anti-gay violence has been a problem in the postsocialist era, as exemplified by the anti-gay rioting that occurred during the 2010 Gay Pride Parade in Belgrade.[96] This violence was later used to justify the banning of the pride parade in 2011 through 2013. Yet despite this thorny legacy, some parties in Serbia's parliament have emerged as champions of sexual equality and gay rights. One party in particular—the LDP, which is led by Čedomir Jovanović— has taken on this issue. Throughout the 2000s, the LDP has made human rights and sexual equality a major part of its platform. Yet in 2007, IRI advised LDP to eliminate any mention of its support for "sexual freedom" from its campaign activities (IRI 2007a). This lone champion of sexual equality was thus encouraged to keep its position on this salient question silent and, instead, to present itself as a more middle-of-the-road party. Like all the so-called reformist parties that received party aid, the LDP was advised to stress its pro-European perspective.

The numerous electoral and governing coalitions supported by the international community were encouraged to do the same. Repeatedly through the 2000 period, external actors encouraged broad-based coalitions among ideologically disparate parties to be united on one point, and one point only: their support for Serbia's EU membership. Examples include the ZES coalition, which aid providers heavily supported in 2008, and the government that ZES formed shortly thereafter, which was a partnership with none other than the SPS.

These types of coalitions were meant to provide voters with a clear alternative: a pro-EU perspective versus an anti-EU perspective. In the process, however, these coalitions forced a partnership between parties that had little in common programmatically. ZES, for example, joined the monarchist SPO, with neo-liberal G17 Plus, and the self-proclaimed Social Democratic DS. These parties were encouraged to focus their campaigns almost solely on their pro-EU stance. Thus, when in late 2008 the SNS emerged on the political scene and adopted an explicitly pro-EU platform, these parties had little substance through which to differentiate themselves from one another and from the SNS in particular.

The result was that despite donors' efforts in 2012, the SNS won the plurality of the parliamentary vote and its president, Tomislav Nikolić, won the Serbian presidency. In the years since, Serbia's so-called pro-reformist parties have struggled to develop substantive political platforms that speak to clear segments of the Serbian population. No longer able to differentiate themselves from their opponents by their pro-EU positions, they have proven themselves incapable of explaining what it is that separates their parties from the pack, apart, of course, from the personalities of their leaders.

An Uninspiring Record

The world's democracy promotion community was met by enormous opportunity in the aftermath of Milošević's ouster. For the first time, donors' partners were committed democrats with the power to implement democratic change. Many believed Serbia had entered a new democratic era and would swiftly join the ranks of the EU. Such optimism did not last long. Within months of Milošević's resignation, the political parties that made up Serbia's democratic government reverted to their old ways—bickering among themselves, placing personal rivalry before the betterment of the state. Many also succumbed to the temptations of power, engaging in nepotism and corruption. Some overtly broke the law in an attempt to sidestep rivals.

Aid providers were slow to adapt to such realities. They were also slow to recognize the new Serbia that emerged in the aftermath of Đinđić's assassination. When they did, however, they responded not by erecting a new strategy of assistance but by re-employing the tried and trusted: a highly partisan strategy bent on ensuring stability, even at democracy's expense. From 2004 on, aid providers sought not to support internal democracy or the leveling of the political playing field but to ensure the electoral victories of partner parties. Donors were largely successful in this. Thanks in part to their efforts, Serbia's so-called reformists managed to maintain their grasp on the government until 2012, when they handed over the reins of both the Serbian presidency and prime ministry to none other than the SPS and the SNS.

Yet if external actors succeeded in upsetting the electoral ambitions of the SRS, they did not succeed in maintaining the legitimacy of their endeavors. By 2004, aid providers had effectively crossed the line into overt electoral meddling, brazenly targeting GOTV efforts that undermined the credibility of the party aid agenda. They also risked fostering dependencies among aid recipients and they inadvertently suppressed parties' ability to develop meaningful political content. Despite the warnings of IRI, NDI, and Freedom House, the U.S. State Department continued to fund NGOs to do the work of parties—bringing out the vote and knocking on doors on behalf of political parties. Perhaps more ominous still, they exacerbated a polarized party landscape that was ill suited to a democratic context. What explains this questionable record of achievement? Why were aid providers so unsuccessful in facilitating democratization in the post-Milošević period when they had defied the odds so recently before? The following chapter seeks to find out.

CHAPTER FIVE

Rethinking Aid's Legacy in Serbia

On 5 October 2000, Slobodan Milošević became the last quasi-dictator of the twentieth century to fall from power as a result of mass protests. Yet his largely nonviolent ouster was in many respects just the beginning. Three years later, on 23 November 2003, large-scale public protests over contested electoral results would force Georgia's president, Eduard Shevardnadze, to resign in what came to be known as Georgia's Rose Revolution. Then, in January 2005, allegations of massive corruption, voter intimidation, and electoral fraud led to a repeat presidential run-off between Ukrainian strongman Viktor Yanukovych and professed democrat Viktor Yushchenko. Like Serbia and Georgia before it, Ukraine's Orange Revolution saw the ouster of an authoritarian incumbent and the empowerment of a self-proclaimed democrat. Just two months later, the people of the Central Asian country of Kyrgyzstan would experience a similarly dramatic (albeit not wholly nonviolent) feat by overthrowing an entrenched dictator, President Askar Akayev, after parliamentary elections. Kyrgyzstan's Tulip Revolution was followed by the meteoric rise of opposition leader Kurmanbek Bakiyev, a man many hoped would help turn the troubled republic's tide toward democracy.

During each of the so-called color revolutions, parallels were drawn to the ouster of Milošević. In Georgia's case, it would be said that domestic activists looked at Serbia as a model for revolutionary success, while party aid providers would use lessons learned from Milošević's ouster to teach the basics of regime change (Mitchell 2012). Yet the enthusiasm spawned by the color revolutions was quickly met by a delay in these countries' projected democratic trajectories. As in Serbia, the countries of the color revolutions—Georgia, Ukraine, and Kyrgyzstan—soon faced a daunting array of political and economic challenges. The revolutionary zeal that inspired their democratic breakthroughs quickly gave way to apathy and disappointment. By the late

2000s, scholars pointed to the dim prospects for further democratization in Eastern Europe and elsewhere. Then, in 2011, the revolutions of the Arab Spring emerged.

Across the Middle East and North Africa, citizens mobilized in defiance of decades-long dictatorships. Protests emerged in Bahrain, Syria, Algeria, Iraq, Jordan, Kuwait, Morocco, and Sudan, as well as in Mauritania, Oman, Saudi Arabia, Djibouti, and Western Sahara. Mass protests in Tunisia, Egypt, and Yemen succeeded in ousting sitting heads of state. And in North Africa, a Western-backed military intervention helped Libyans dismantle the forty-two-year dictatorship of Muammar Gaddafi.

At the outset, the uprisings of the Arab Spring appeared only tangentially related to that witnessed in Serbia, a continent away and more than a decade before it. But within a few weeks of Zine El Abidine Ben Ali and Hosni Mubarak's departure on 14 January 2011 and 11 February 2001, respectively, direct connections between Serbia's ouster of Milošević were being drawn. The American international affairs magazine *Foreign Policy* featured an eight-page article titled "What Egypt Learned from the Students Who Overthrew Milošević."[1] That same year, *Foreign Policy* proclaimed Otpor founder Srdja Popovic an "Arab Revolutionary," and included him as one of the year's top 100 global thinkers. The magazine credited the U.S.-funded and U.S.-trained Serbian movement, Otpor, with "inspiring *Arab Spring* protestors directly and indirectly."[2]

As in Serbia, media reported the supposedly critical role Western democracy assistance had played in the felling of Middle Eastern strongmen. In a piece on the work of IRI and NDI in Egypt, the *New York Times* reported that "U.S. groups helped nurture Arab uprisings."[3] After decades and billions of U.S. dollars spent bolstering Middle Eastern military-backed dictatorships, it seemed a few short years of party aid had helped fell two of the Arab world's most entrenched dictatorships.

Once again, these analyses were based on an unquestioned assumption: that democracy aid could drive revolutionary change and that lessons learned from Serbia were broadly applicable to other authoritarian and post-authoritarian contexts. The previous chapters have argued that many of those lessons have been mis-learned. This chapter seeks to set the record straight by examining what worked and why, and what implications this has for aid's success elsewhere.

Two Decades of Mixed Results

Political party assistance in postsocialist Serbia has charted a course between success and failure. In the past twenty years of multiparty politics, party aid was both an enabler of and detractor from democracy. It helped parties build members' confidence. It facilitated parties' transformation into modern, technologically savvy electoral machines. It even helped parties unseat a quasi-dictator. Yet for all of aid's successes, there were also failures—some of them significant. For example, aid failed to ameliorate parties' most blatant democratic deficits. It did not address their penchant for corruption or encourage parties to promote a less nationalistic line of politics. Nor did aid make parties more receptive to member preferences or accepting of dissent.

Political party aid post-Milošević may in some cases actually have worked against democracy by further polarizing party politics, swaying electoral outcomes, and suppressing party content. Indeed, party aid in postsocialist Serbia leaves an ambiguous record of achievement, one that defies the simple categorization of either "success" or "failure."

What is abundantly clear, however, is that much of the 1990s—when assistance could have been most significant not only for bringing down Milošević but also for securing peace throughout the Balkans—was marked by a tragic legacy of missed opportunities.

Legacy of Missed Opportunities

If the months immediately preceding Milošević's ouster are worth noting for what aid providers *did* do, then the ten years leading to his removal are most notable for what they did *not* do. Serbia's transition from communist to pluralist rule was stained by numerous missed opportunities on the aid community's part. Despite Serbian parties' all-too-evident need (and, even, demand) for foreign aid, party aid was frequently absent or inappropriately allocated.

Indeed, when Milošević won Serbia's first multiparty elections in the winter of 1990, there were several opportunities for external actors to aid and support a nascent democratic opposition. As Chapter 2 explained, the SPO, DS, and GSS were just some of the parties that were working to defeat Milošević.

There is no question that these parties were imperfect: They suffered from ego-driven leaders, low party membership, poor organizational development, weak partisan identities, and personality-based profiles. Imperfect though they may have been, however, these parties regularly obtained more than a third of the popular vote and, in several instances, spearheaded major anti-Milošević protests that lasted weeks and sometimes months.[4] Several of these parties were avowedly antiwar and called for a stop to the bloody fighting that had engulfed the region for years.

Opposition parties were thus a defining feature of Serbia's political landscape and could have made important partners for the aid community. Yet donors and foreign policy makers repeatedly overlooked the domestic opposition to Milošević, underestimating both their opposition credentials and their fortitude throughout most of the 1990s. They also exaggerated their nationalism and ineptitude. As one donor noted, these parties simply did not live up to the "purity" that foreign policy makers demanded of aid recipients.

The legacy of missed opportunity did not end there. As Chapter 4 elucidated, party aid in the post-Milošević period failed to confront two key aspects of the Serbian party landscape: aid recipients' anti-democratic tendencies and the increasing legitimacy of the SPS and SRS. With regard to the former, practitioners of party aid overlooked the more glaring aspects of the "standard lament" throughout the 2000s. Rather than build on the goodwill they fomented in the run-up to Milošević's ouster, party aid providers missed the opportunity to effect substantive change within political party ranks, choosing to focus on parties' role in government rather than on their role within the electorate. Aid providers continued to neglect the more substantive aspects of aid recipients' behavior well into the 2000s, favoring a concern for parties' campaigning abilities instead.

Another shortcoming of aid providers was their failure to address the changing fortunes of Serbia's far-right elements in the post-Milošević period. Milošević's ouster was met by a wave of assistance that was showered on DOS parties. Serbia's "anti-reformist" forces—most notably the SRS and SPS—were consistently excluded from such assistance. Worse, aid providers actively aspired to orchestrate their electoral defeat, even as the democratic credentials of these parties became apparent. Aid providers' failure to foresee, let alone accommodate, the perceived legitimacy of Serbia's far-right elements among a large swath of the general public was a missed opportunity in the post-Milošević period.

The failure of aid to respond to this challenge is widely, albeit tacitly, acknowledged within aid circles. According to a former head of FES's Belgrade office, "We should have started earlier on to create opportunities where you can build bridges and establish contacts including with people in the Radical party or the socialist party." [5] In addition, he says, "There was such a focus on . . . our democratic friends in Serbia" that aid providers "neglected the relations with other parts of society and their organizations."[6] It would be close to a decade before the United States and its European allies would consider engaging Serbia's far right—a decade that saw Serbia stagnate in its transition and make little progress toward liberal democracy.

Helping Parties Do What They Want to Do, Better

The record on party aid was not all lackluster, however. When aid providers finally did get seriously involved in Serbia in late 1999, much of what they did was successful—some of it very much so. For example, aid helped parties launch the professional campaigns that ultimately ousted Milošević. Donor funds enabled parties to acquire the resources they needed to level the political playing field in the months before Milošević's removal. And aid enabled parties to modernize their infrastructures—supporting the creation of in-party training centers, youth wings, and women's wings. In fact, party aid was remarkably effective in helping parties improve in the areas they wanted to improve. Although this may not always have benefited democracy, aid did help parties do what they wanted to do, better.

Campaign assistance provided in the run-up to Milošević's ouster is a good example of this. Parties during this period were eager to launch campaigns that could rival that of the regime. They wanted convincing campaign commercials and were eager to make their case to potential voters across Serbia. They sought to bring out the vote on their own behalf and they wanted to be ready in the case of electoral fraud. Foreign assistance helped them do all these things, and do them better. Thus, aid providers supported focus groups to test parties' campaign commercials, advertisements, and billboards. Foreign funds paid for coalition buses, cars, and lodging. At campaign events, aid paid for high-quality sound systems. Foreign aid also helped put into motion a multifaceted GOTV effort that was fun, vibrant, and more appealing than any other that parties had previously initiated. As Chapter 3 explained, by catering to parties' wishes during these tenuous times, party aid made a positive contribution to Serbia's democratic trajectory.

Aid also helped parties realize their ambitions to professionalize in the years that followed Milošević's ouster. With donors' help, aid recipients launched a litany of highly professional electoral campaigns that included multimedia outreach components, grassroots outreach, and even public opinion polls. Thanks in part to foreign aid, Serbian electoral campaigns were highly professional and even "vibrant" (OSCE 2007: 11).

Party aid providers also helped forge links between Serbian parties and their self-professed ideological counterparts in Germany, the Netherlands, the United Kingdom, and beyond. Thanks to the German *Stiftungen*, parties like the DS were able to network and form alliances with the social democratic parties of Western Europe. These professional links were highly sought after by Serbian party members.[7]

Following Events, Not Leading Them

The aforementioned achievements—particularly those witnessed prior to October 2000—have convinced many of democracy aid's effectiveness in Serbia. Yet for all of party aid's utility, its significance is easily overstated. This is especially true if one considers the sequence in which events unfolded in Serbia. Throughout the postsocialist period, foreign aid frequently followed democratic developments rather than leading them. Most often, aid built on and strengthened what domestic actors themselves had already begun or it reinforced what domestic actors already knew; in some cases, it did both. This was true both for the initial launch of aid programs, as well as for the assistance that followed.

Indeed, when aid was first initiated in the spring of 1997, it arrived on the heels of—not the start of—the achievements of an organized anti-Milošević opposition. By March 1997, Serbia's democratic opposition controlled not only Belgrade but also most of the republic's largest cities. It was only at this point—after Serbian political parties had staged successive electoral feats, after they had united in a grand coalition that included four of Serbia's foremost political parties, and after they had succeeded in channeling public discontent into organized protests—that assistance was forthcoming. It was in fact only after Serbia's opposition had achieved demonstrable results and won democratic gains that aid began. Aid thus followed the self-made accomplishments of Serbia's democratic opposition—it did not create them.

A similar dynamic can be witnessed with respect to the West's support for opposition unity in late 1999 and 2000. Through a combination of carrots and

sticks, foreign aid providers sought to unite Serbia's fractious opposition behind a single electoral ticket. Their efforts have been cited as critical to aid's
achievements in Serbia and the ultimate unseating of Milošević (Schoen
2007). Yet the need for opposition unity was not, in fact, a foreign concept to
Serbia's opposition. Long before aid providers began working in Serbia, opposition parties had attempted to create a total of eight different coalitions—
some of which (most notably Zajedno) were arguably more inclusive than
DOS. In fact, when the aid community first began advocating unity, Serbia's
opposition had already formed the alliance that would go on to form the
foundation of DOS: the Alliance for Change. Nor was the decision to appoint
Koštunica as DOS's presidential candidate an idea that originated with external actors. To the contrary, as United States pollster Douglas Schoen (2007)
reflects, it was Đinđić who first floated the idea of a Koštunica candidacy.

That aid followed rather than led domestic transformations is also evident
in the post-Milošević period. It was, for example, only after the SPS had joined
an ostensibly democratic government, after the party had committed itself to
a pro-EU agenda, and after the party had suffered an internal reshuffling that
aid providers considered working to democratize the party. The same is true
for the SRS offshoot, Nikolić's SNS. Only after a majority of SRS party members opted to embrace a pro-EU agenda and distance themselves from Vojislav Šešelj, did aid providers seriously consider working with Serbia's far
right. Again, aid followed these trends toward moderation and democratization; it did not stimulate them.

Failing on Substance

In their two decades in Serbia, aid providers have sought not merely to facilitate Milošević's decline but also to facilitate democracy's ascent. This has
meant encouraging parties to pass democratic legislation and to behave democratically: to thwart corruption; to cater to the demands of their constituents;
to become less personality-centric; to engage in internal democracy; and,
where necessary, to lay partisan differences aside for the good of democracy.
Yet although party aid helped parties to craft the campaign that resulted in
Milošević's unseating, it failed to alter the pattern of party behavior that has
proven so destructive throughout the postsocialist period. Indeed, aid did not
stimulate meaningful changes within parties. This has been true in both the
late 1990s and throughout the 2000s.

With respect to the former, the most evident manner in which aid failed to change the behavior of Serbia's parties was in interparty relations. The most iconic example of this is, counterintuitively, represented by what many aid providers rank among their chief accomplishments: the creation of DOS and the semblance of the ever-elusive goal of "opposition unity." As described in Chapter 3, opposition unity is widely regarded as a prerequisite for regime change in authoritarian contexts; the establishment of DOS was viewed, however, as a major feat for the opposition and for aid providers. Although scholars have widely praised the unity of the DOS coalition in retrospect, the extent of the coalition's unity has been exaggerated with the passing of time.[8] Indeed, despite repeated efforts by the United States and DOS coalition partners, the opposition was never fully united behind Koštunica and the members of the opposition continued to bicker incessantly (albeit, on occasion, privately). In fact, Vuk Drašković—the leader of Serbia's largest opposition party—refused to join the alliance, electing instead to have his own candidate, Vojislav Mihailović, compete in the presidential elections *against* the DOS front man.

As a consequence, many journalists reporting in 2000 were unconvinced of DOS's unity well into early fall. Writing of Drašković's refusal to join DOS, the *New York Times* reported that "the split in the always fractious opposition virtually ensures that Mr. Milošević . . . will win another four years in power in September."[9] Just months before Milošević's ouster, analysts lamented the opposition's "inability to maintain a united front," arguing that DOS "rallies do not inspire, its leadership is divided, its support is waning, and its program is nonexistent" (Triantaphyllou 2000: vii). Though scholars would later deify DOS as an example par excellence of opposition unity, the coalition was more frail than analysts let on.

The ultimate consequence of this was the premature demise of the DOS government less than a year after Koštunica's presidential victory. The DSS's departure—and the subsequent bad blood between Đinđic and Koštunica— would bring the reform process in Serbia to a standstill (Bardos 2003: 13). Although DOS's demise and internal friction does not suggest that aid providers' efforts to support opposition unity were in vain, it does demonstrate that they were incapable of altering the more substantive dimensions of parties' behavior that would have allowed parties to collaborate—if not as members of a united coalition, than at least as allies committed to a democratic Serbia—for pro-reform legislation in the post-Milošević period.

Other limitations would also be evident in the years that followed DOS's collapse. One such example was that of ideology building. For years, the German *Stiftungen* worked to establish a clearly defined ideological spectrum in Serbia, with consistently center-left and center-right parties. But although the *Stiftungen* succeeded in encouraging parties to define themselves as such—with the DS bearing the mantle of the former and the DSS that of the latter—aid providers failed to propel a more substantive shift.

As Chapter 4 elucidated, the DS's decision to adopt a social democratic profile was almost entirely the result of foreign influences. But what external actors succeeded in doing in name, they failed to do in substance. Parties in the post-Milošević regime have shown little ideological coherence. They suffer from a "poor ability to develop programs, a barely existent anchoring in society and strong foundations in individuals personalities" (Bertelsmann Stiftung 2003:8). More than ten years after regime change, party leaders and their coterie of loyal allies—rather than party platforms, ideologies, or even party members—continue to dominate party life in Serbia (see Bertelsmann Stiftung 2007: 12; Đurković 2006; Pešić 2007). In this respect, Serbia's parties have changed little since the 1990s—despite the provision of assistance.

Indeed, an in-depth examination of party statutes and political platforms indicates great congruence throughout the past twenty years. Despite the stated ambitions of aid providers, parties remain top-down structures, with party leaders and an elite coterie determining everything from party policy to electoral strategy and party representatives (Spoerri 2008a). Rank-and-file party members not only have little say in internal party politics, they also have little recourse should their opinions differ from those of their party leaders. To the contrary, internal party factions remained a taboo subject throughout the 2000s. In part because of this, Serbia witnessed the proliferation of political parties during the post-Milošević period, with disgruntled party members responding to internal autocracy either by exiting Serbian politics or by launching their own (often equally autocratic) rival parties.

Working Against Democracy

Foreign aid's legacy in Serbia is further complicated by its negative repercussions. Previous chapters have shown that just as external actors helped democracy in Serbia, so too did they hurt democracy. Many of the interventions used on Serbia's behalf unwittingly worked against the very actors and processes that were vital to democracy's growth and maturation in Serbia. This pertained to both the 1990s and the 2000s.

As Chapter 2 showed, the United States and the EU were anything but helpful to Serbia's opposition in the immediate postcommunist period. Not only was aid not forthcoming but Western officials ignored the opposition entirely, treating anti-Milošević leaders like Drašković as similar to—if not worse than—Milošević himself. Yet external actors did not simply refrain from involving themselves in Serbia's affairs. Their interventions often worked against democracy. Holbrooke's repeated meetings with Milošević, for example, bolstered the Serbian leader's international credibility.[10] Many diplomats who were once engaged in Serbian affairs concede that Holbrooke's tactics played right into Milošević's hands, while working against Serbia's nascent democratic forces.

External actors hurt democracy in other respects as well. Sanctions, for example, cast an insidious legacy over Serbia's transition that would haunt democratic actors well into the 2000s. Not only did sanctions "cause enormous suffering" for millions of Serbs, they also "spurred the development of criminal organizations and corruption, and cemented the relationship between the state and organized crime" (Montgomery 2010: 37–38). Indeed, the economic isolation of Serbia would give rise to a vibrant gray economy and a culture of criminality that would imperil Serbia's democratic transition for years to come.

Party aid itself had a dubious legacy throughout the post-Milošević period. Donors' insistence on dousing the electoral prospects of Serbia's far right caused party aid to effectively cross the line into overt electoral meddling. Although such interventionism may have been understandable and, indeed, desirable during Milošević's violent authoritarianism, its legitimacy was far more questionable in its aftermath when elections were free and fair and the political playing field no longer worked to democrats' disadvantage. Indeed, in Serbia's newly democratic context, aid threatened to sway the political landscape in aid recipients' favor. In so doing, it risked undermining the credibility of electoral results within a newly democratic context.

One of the more deleterious consequences of political party aid was its impact on polarization. The emphasis on ensuring aid recipients' electoral winning at any cost fed into an us-versus-them mentality that added to the polarization of the political landscape. The exacerbation of polarization was not, however, aid's only downside. Donors also risked fostering aid dependencies in the post-Milošević period. The American party institutes and, to a

lesser extent, the European party foundations, did more than merely aid parties in their electoral campaigns. In several instances, they actually did the
work for them, going so far as to pay so-called volunteers to conduct door-to-
door advocacy on partner parties' behalf. Not surprisingly, such activities
have raised real concerns about parties' sustainability, even among aid
practitioners.[11]

Yet aid's negative effects in the post-Milošević period did not end there.
The U.S. party institutes' abiding faith in polling data led them to advise parties to support policies and campaigns of questionable democratic merit.
Throughout the 2000s, they encouraged parties to take hard lines on Kosovo
and to lessen their vocal support for sexual equality. Although such tactics
may have helped the parties at the ballot box, those tactics came into direct
conflict with donors' stated aims for democratization and the country's efforts
to join the EU.[12]

Reassessing Donor Motives and Practices

The conclusions drawn from Serbia have important implications for what
scholars know—or think they know—about political party aid, and democracy aid more generally. Perhaps the most important lesson we can draw from
the Serbian case concerns the motives of donors.

Party aid, like all democracy assistance, is premised on the assumption
that democracy is valuable and good. Because party aid seeks to support democracy, it, too, is good. Despite all of its acknowledged flaws, party aid has
thus been accepted as a mission of moral integrity. Its self-stated goals—"to
strengthen individual political parties, to promote peaceful interaction between parties and to help to create a more stable and democratic environment
for political parties in new, struggling, or flawed democracies" (Burnell and
Gerrits 2010: 1065)—have thus largely been accepted as true. Critical to this
acceptance have been two notions: one, that party aid is, within certain limits,
nonpartisan; and, two, that party aid is, essentially, a nongovernmental enterprise. Western donors' intervention in Serbia suggests that both such claims
may be flawed.

Let us begin with the assumption of nonpartisanship. Nonpartisanship
has long been a buzzword within the party aid community (see Carothers
2006a: 142; see also Burnell 2004b and Kumar 2005).[13] By spreading their
assistance across the ideological spectrum, "party assisters maintain that their

efforts avoid crossing the line into the more dubious terrain of electoral meddling" (Spoerri 2010: 1111). Thus, donors insist that their aid be provided without reference to specific policy positions taken by competing candidates or parties and be offered equitably to all groups committed to the democratic process, regardless of their specific platforms or programs.

The Serbian case suggests that such claims are not always acted upon. Whether in the 1990s or 2000s, party aid in Serbia followed a distinctly partisan approach. Although premised on the notion of promoting democracy, party aid aimed—at its core—to support the electoral prospects of partner parties and to undermine those of nonpartner parties. In the 1990s, for example, party aid was clearly geared toward facilitating regime change. It sought, on the one hand, to increase the electoral competitiveness of Koštunica and DOS while, on the other hand, it tried to undermine the power base of Milošević. This highly partisan agenda continued long into the 2000s, this time with the goal of securing democratic gains. Thus, aid sought to maintain the electoral competitiveness of DOS successor parties while decreasing the odds that nonrecipients would stage electoral comebacks—despite these parties' increasing democratic legitimacy. Evidence drawn from in-depth case studies in Georgia and Ukraine (Bader 2010), Bosnia and Kosovo (Nenadović 2012), and Russia (Mendelson 2001) suggests that partisanship may indeed be more common than aid providers suggest. If so, the problems associated with party aid in Serbia have troubling implications for party aid at large.

So too do issues regarding the nature of political party assistance. Just as donors have lauded their efforts as nonpartisan, they also have characterized themselves as nongovernmental. This characterization stems in part from their desire to portray themselves as independent sources of advice, uncorrupted by state concerns or preferences. Yet Serbia suggests that the reality is far more complex.

As demonstrated throughout the previous chapters, party aid to Serbia boasted extremely intimate links with foreign governments. It was, and remains, part and parcel of the foreign aid agenda. As such, it was designed to serve the self-defined interests of donors' home states. Indeed, as the former USAID mission director to Serbia, notes, "Foreign assistance is an instrument of . . . national policy, and an instrument of national security."[14] As a small but important facet of foreign assistance, party aid to Serbia was no exception to this rule. Time and again throughout the 1990s and 2000s, government directives dictated the aid agenda, setting the limits for what was and was not permissible within the sphere of party aid.

Governments' role in the work of party aid providers—especially large aid providers like the U.S. institutes and the German *Stiftungen*—suggests that the term "nongovernmental" is both inaccurate and misleading. Although these organizations are not governmental in the traditional sense of the term, neither are they independent of their government's reach. Organizations like FES and NDI are tools to further the interests of home states.[15] Often such interests lie in the promotion of democracy. At times, however, other concerns—whether an interest in stability or a desire for an ally's win—are more pressing.

Conclusion: Reconsidering the Serbian Model

When party aid practitioners first launched programs in Serbia in 1997, few could have foretold the sequence of events that would lead to Milošević's undoing just three years later. Poorly resourced, fractious, and resentful, Serbia's opposition appeared more quixotic than capable. The opposition hardly resembled the electoral tour de force that would unseat Milošević and effectively brand the term "electoral revolution." Yet if the aid community did not predict the ultimate strength of Serbia's opposition, neither did the international community predict the importance of party aid. In the weeks and months that followed Milošević's ouster, Serbia would "go down in history as the first poll-driven, focus group–tested revolution" in which "U.S.-funded consultants played a crucial role behind the scenes."[16] Democracy aid—and party aid in particular—was deemed critical.

This book has argued that such sentiments have, in many respects, been overstated. Democracy aid—while helpful—was far from crucial to parties' success. More often than not, party aid followed trends and came on the heels of internal reform. Yet this book has gone further still. Although most accounts of democracy aid have fixated on the seminal months leading to Milošević's ouster, this analysis has placed Serbia's political changes within a larger temporal perspective. In elucidating the decades that came before and after, it showed that party aid—and foreign aid more generally—boasts a thornier legacy than is commonly recognized.

Indeed, Serbia has been home to the best and worst of democracy promotion. Although its riveting story of democracy aid "done right" has been the subject of documentaries, articles, and scholarly manuscripts, its more nuanced story of democracy aid "gone right and wrong" has not. This book has sought to set the record straight: It has argued that aid's impact on Serbian parties has been surprisingly mixed. Repeatedly throughout the 1990s and 2000s, foreign aid has both helped Serbia's political parties and hurt democracy. In so doing, it has raised important questions about the legitimacy of party aid and about the untold consequences of an aid agenda intent on facilitating and securing regime change.

This book's overarching ambition has been to uncover those consequences. And there are many. As previous chapters argued, the ouster of Milošević in October 2000 represented the first time overt democracy assistance—rather than covert operations led by the Central Intelligence Agency or military interventions spearheaded by Western defense agencies—was credited with bringing down a dictator. Aid's perceived success in Serbia helped to spawn an aid industry bent on promoting democracy and bringing down dictators around the world. It also legitimized a crackdown on that aid by countries like Egypt and Russia, which have since cast democracy assistance as little more than veiled "attempts to influence political processes, including elections of various types, and institutions of civil society through the distribution of grants."[17]

During most of the 1990s, the priority of the international community in dealing with Serbia was not to transform it into a democracy but rather to help stabilize a deeply troubled and conflict-prone region. Whatever his domestic failings, Milošević was regarded as a "factor of stability" in the Balkans (particularly in the immediate post-Dayton period), and Western policy makers were not keen on helping his opposition initiate a democratic transition that would ultimately oust him. Similarly, in the period that followed Milošević's fall, foreign policy makers dictated the direction of democracy aid to ensure not necessarily that democracy itself was strengthened and promoted, but that Milošević's successors did not suffer Milošević's fate. After 2000, democracy assistance was thus geared toward ensuring that pro-Western parties remained in power. When and where these parties strayed from the ideals of democracy, aid providers chose to look the other way. More troubling still, they actively sought to bolster these parties' electoral prospects at the expense of other (anti-Western) parties, even within the confines of a newly democratic Serbia, when all of Serbia's major political parties abided by the rules of the democratic game. In the process, they contributed to deepening the polarization of an already dangerously divided country and they raised troubling questions about the legitimacy of democracy aid in countries experiencing a new democratic awakening.

Unfortunately, these dilemmas have gone unexplored by much of the democracy promotion community. Rather than honestly and openly tackling the valid concerns surrounding aid's relationship to the foreign policy pursuits of Western states—and how this affects aid's ability to support democracy abroad—aid providers and donors have treated such queries as accusations. Their silence has permitted the allegations uttered by the loudest critics of democracy assistance—like Russia—to retain far too much legitimacy. Moving forward, the democracy promotion community must engage in far more open discussion about the nature and consequences (both intended and unintended) of its interventions, its complex links to foreign policy, and the way the self-interests of home states do—and, occasionally, do not—work to support democracy abroad.

Interviewees

Abramowitz, Morton. Chairperson of NED.

Adams, Thomas C. Coordinator of U.S. assistance to Europe and Eurasia.

Anastasijević, Dejan. Journalist at *Vreme* magazine.

Andrews, Mary Catherine. Resident director of IRI.

Andrić, Nebojša. Member of DS and trainer for NDI.

Backović, Dejan. Member of SPS.

Balešić, Alma. Project assistant at the Alfred Mozer Stichting.

Belčević, Nenad. Program manager of NDI.

Bell, David. Resident director of IRI Serbia.

Benjamin, Robert. Regional director for CEE at NDI.

Berkvens, Arjen. Director of AMS.

Blagojević, Marko. Director of operations at CeSID.

Bogunović, Goran. General secretary at the SDU.

Bouwmeester, Gerolf. Party trainer for D66.

Braum, Bertram. Serbia desk officer at the U.S. State Department.

Calingaert, Daniel. Program director of Serbia for IRI.

Čamernik, Boris. NDI program officer.

Čelarević, Nenad. Member of the Youth Board of the SDU.

Cerović, Ivana. Director of programs for the Serbian Unity Congress.

Chenoweth, Eric. Director of the Institute for Democracy in Eastern Europe.

Countryman, Thomas. Director of the Office of South Central European Affairs.

Crnjanski, Vukosava. Member of the presidential board of the LDP.

De Vries, Ralph. Former international affairs officer for D66.

Dedović, Dragoslav. Regional director of HBS.

Demeš, Pavol. Director of Bratislava Office at the German Marshall Fund.

Dobbins, James. Special adviser to the U.S. secretary of state.

Đorđević, Ivan. Chief of staff of ND.

Drašković, Vuk. President of SPO.

Duik, Nadia. Senior program officer for NED.

Đukanović, Vladimir. General secretary of the SRS.

Dulić, Oliver. Member of DS and former speaker of the parliament.

Đurković, Miša. Scholar and political party expert.

DuVall, Jack. Director of the Center for Nonviolent Resistance.

Dzajić, Miloš. Founder of the Center for Modern Skills.

Ehrke, Michael. Resident director of FES Serbia.

Emmert, Jan Paul. Director of Democracy and Governance Office at USAID Belgrade.

Flanagan, Arthur. Senior adviser at Governance and Democracy USAID Belgrade.

Gamser, Dušan. Member of the presidency of the GSS and program officer for FNS.

Gaspari, Mirko. Political specialist at the U.S. Embassy Belgrade.

Gatzinska, Spaska. Assistant program officer for CEE at NED.

Grabow, Karsten. Project coordinator of political party programs at KAS.

Handrich, Thomas. Head of desk for South East Europe at HBS.

Hill, Nicholas. Political economy officer at the U.S. Embassy Belgrade.

Hooper, James. Director of the Balkan Action Council.

Howard, Ivana. CEE program officer for NED.

Hyman, Gerald. Director of Democracy and Governance Program at USAID.

Ilić, Borko. Member of DSS, trainer at NDI, and MP.

Ivanisević, Bogdan. Consultant for the International Center for Transitional Justice.

Jackson, Bruce. Director of the Project on Transitional Democracies.

Jelinčić, Jadranka. Executive director of the Fund for an Open Society Belgrade.

Jennings, Ray. Serbia country director for OTI.

Joksimović, Milena. Otpor activist.

Jovanović, Jovan. Member of G17 and adviser to Labus.

Kanazir, Dušan. Member of the local board of Stari Grad LDP.

Kanin, David. Retired CIA analyst.

Kassov, Allen. President of the Project on Ethnic Relations.

Kelly, Ellen. Senior rule-of-law adviser at USAID Belgrade.

Kelly, Tom. Resident director of NDI Serbia.

Kenney, George. Desk officer for U.S. State Department.

Kerim, Srđan. President of UN General Assembly.

Klijn, Hugo. Deputy head of mission at Dutch Embassy Belgrade.

Korth, Dakota. Program associate at the German Marshall Fund.

Krahe, Nadine. Evaluator for KAS.

Licht, Sonja. President of the Belgrade Fund for Political Excellence.

Lynch, Michael. Resident director for NDI Serbia.

Lynn, Stephanie. NDI program officer Belgrade.

Lyon, James. Special Balkans adviser for the International Crisis
    Group.

Magazin, Mia. International secretary of the youth wing of the DSS.

Manojlović, Ana. Program coordinator at FES.

McCarthy, Paul. Senior program officer for South East Europe at
    NED.

McMahon, Edward. Senior program officer NDI.

Miles, Richard Monroe. Chief of mission to U.S. Mission to
    Belgrade.

Milić, Danilo. Program coordinator at the Olof Palme International
    Center.

Milić, Rade. Member of Otpor and DS.

Milosavljević, Olga. Program assistant for NDI.

Mitchell, Lincoln. NDI resident director.

Momčilović, Mladen. Parliamentary program manager at NDI.

Montgomery, William. U.S. Ambassador to Federal Republic of
    Yugoslavia.

Moreira, John. Senior associate for Greenberg, Quinlan, and Rosner
    Research.

Napper, Larry. Director of SEED.

Nedeljkov, Raša. Member of the LSDV and trainer for NDI.

Nikolin, Sanja. Monitoring and evaluation specialist at USAID.

Norman, Robert. Deputy head of mission at U.S. Embassy Belgrade.

Nuhiu, Mentor. President of the Party for Democratic Action in
    Sandjak.

O'Brien, James. Special envoy to the Balkans for the U.S. government.

O'Hagan, Mary. Resident director of NDI.

Olsen, Trygve. IRI party trainer.

Orlović, Slaviša. Professor of political science at the University of Belgrade.

Parasiliti, Andrew. Vice president of Barbour, Griffith and Rogers International.

Patton, Kent. Resident director of IRI Serbia.

Pavlov, Vladimir. Member of Otpor and consul at the Serbian Consulate in New York.

Pavlović, Dušan. Professor of political science at the University of Belgrade.

Pejčić, Aleksandar. Member of the Executive Board of Leskovac GSS.

Pešić, Vesna. President of GSS.

Petrović, Mihailo. Vice president of the executive board of the youth wing of the DSS.

Pilipović, Gordana. Project coordinator at KAS.

Polt, Michael. U.S. Ambassador to Serbia.

Popović, Srđa. Member of Otpor.

Presnall, Aaron. Director of studies at the Jefferson Institute.

Prokić, Lidija. NDI senior program officer Belgrade.

Prostojević, Đorđe. SPO member and deputy minister for Diaspora,

Radičević, Ana. Project director Serbia for NDI.

Raj, Geeta. Country desk officer for Serbia at USAID.

Rexhepi, Atullah. Member of the presidential board of the Democratic Union in the Valley of Sandjak.

Ronner-Grubačić, Stella. Political officer for the Dutch Embassy Belgrade.

Rowland, Paul. NDI resident director Serbia.

Saraghan, Ann. Program officer of U.S. assistance to Europe and Eurasia.

Saxer, Marc. Coordinator of political party programs at FES.

Schoen, Douglas. Pollster for Penn Schoen Berland.

School Dorn, Ulrike. Senior program officer at NDI.

Schriefer, Paula. Director of programs at Freedom House.

Schroeder, David. Serbia desk officer for the U.S. State Department.

Semmel, Andrew. Congressional aide to Senator Richard Lugar of Indiana.

Serwer, Daniel. Vice president for the United States Institute of Peace.

Silber, Laura. Director of public affairs at the Open Society Foundations.

Simić, Marijana. Project coordinator at CeSID.

Simpson, Greg. Serbia resident director for IRI.

Skiles, Rhett. Serbia desk officer for IRI.

Slavujević, Zoran. Professor of political science at the University of Belgrade.

Sohns, Reinhold. International Dialogue department head of Department of Central and Eastern Europe for FES.

Sokolowski, Alexander. Senior political process adviser at USAID.

Stanisavljević, Dragana. Member of G17.

Stanković, Mašan. President of the youth board of LDP.

Stanković, Milena. Member of LDP Kragujevac office and MP.

Starešinić, Michael. Director of Freedom House.

Stephenson, James. USAID mission director.

Stratos, Kathryn. USAID spokesperson.

Šurbatović, Jovan. Member of DHSS and trainer for NDI.

Svilanović, Goran. President of GSS.

Swigert, Jim. Deputy assistant U.S. secretary of state for Southeast and Central Europe.

Taaks, Christian. Program officer for Central, Southeast, and Eastern European Desk for FNS.

Tatić, Jovan. Program coordinator of NDI Serbia.

Tatić, Tanja. Program administrator for NDI Serbia.

Tavčar, Milan. Member of LDP.

Thomas, Robert. International officer for the conservatives of the WFD.

Todorović, Đorđe. Program director for IRI.

Vejvoda, Ivan. Adviser to DS president, Boris Tadić.

Vučković, Nataša. Member of DS and MP.

Vuco, Beka. Regional director for the Balkans at the Open Society Foundations.

Vujić, Vojislav. President of the youth wing of DS.

Wahlers, Gerhard. Head of the Department of International Cooperation of KAS.

Weichert, Michael. Regional director of FES Serbia.

White, John. Press officer for the European Commission Delegation in Belgrade.

Whitman, Bernard. President of Whitman Insight Strategies.

Willert, Rainer. Program officer for Central, Southeast, and Eastern Europe at FNS.

Wilson, Andrew. Senior Program Officer for CIPE.

Yount, Ellen. Resident director of IRI.

Živković, Nikola. Teaching assistant at the Belgrade Open School.

Živković, Uroš. Member of the executive board at DSS.

NOTES

Introduction

1. International Center for Transitional Justice, "Transitional Justice in the Former Yugoslavia," available at http://ictj.org/publication/transitional-justice-former-yugoslavia, last accessed 12 April 2012.

2. This book focuses on Serbia. Today, the Republic of Serbia is an independent state. From 1992 until 2003, however, Serbia was part of the Federal Republic of Yugoslavia (FRY). In 2003, the FRY was reconstituted as the State Union of Serbia and Montenegro. In 2006, Montenegro officially seceded from the Union, forming its own independent state.

3. The years immediately leading to Milosevic's resignation in October 2000 were not, however, entirely nonviolent. The North Atlantic Treaty Organization (NATO) bombardment of Yugoslavia from 24 May 1999 to 10 June 1999 marked the second major combat operation in NATO history and, according to Human Rights Watch, resulted in the deaths of as many as 528 civilians. Although the NATO bombing was a clear act of military intervention, its role in contributing to Milošević's ouster remains highly contested—a matter that will be discussed at greater length in Chapter 3. It is noteworthy, however, that the campaign's explicit aim was not that of unseating Slobodan Milošević but rather that of ending the military conflict in Kosovo and forcing the withdrawal of Serbian forces from the province. Milošević would not, in fact, fall from power until seventeen months *after* the last NATO bombs fell over Serbia.

4. Just two deaths were reported in relation to the protests of 5 October 2000. Jasmina Jovanović reportedly fell beneath a truck, while Momčilo Stakić died of a heart attack. An additional sixty-five injuries were reported throughout the day's events. See "Otkriven spomenik Jasmini Jovanović," *B92*, 5 October 2002; "Momčilo Stakić umro na ulicama Beograda." *Glas javnosti*, 6 October 2000; and "Parties, Citizens Mark 5 October," *B92*, 5 October 2007.

5. M. Dobbs, "U.S. Advice Guided Milošević Opposition: Political Consultants Helped Yugoslav Opposition Topple Authoritarian Leader," *Washington Post*, 11 December 2000.

6. J. Von Hugrefe, "Hilfe Zur Revolution," *Der Speigel* 9 October 2000, available at http://www.spiegel.de/spiegel/print/d-17540534.html.

7. Kumar 2004: 24, See also Bunce and Wolchik 2011; Carothers 2001; Diamond 2008b: 116.

8. As the UNDP (2006: 5) acknowledges, "Assistance to political parties was considered as taboo."

9. Among the significant past studies focusing specifically on democracy promotion's effectiveness in Serbia are Carothers 2001, Gagnon 1998, Jennings 2009, and Presnall 2009. In their cross-country study of electoral revolutions, Bunce and Wolchik (2011) also deal with the democracy assistance agenda in Serbia. To date, however, no books have been published that are dedicated exclusively to democracy assistance in Serbia.

10. See, for example, *Bringing Down a Dictator*, the 2002 documentary that aired on PBS, or the article by Roger Cohen, "Who Really Brought Down Milosevic?" *New York Times*, 26 November 2000.

11. Wherever possible, the names of those interviewed have been cited. Where this was not possible because interviewees asked to remain anonymous, their names have been excluded.

Chapter 1. Aiding Democracy and Political Parties Abroad

1. M. Boot, "Exporting the Ukraine Miracle," *Washington Post*, 2 January 2005.

2. Chomsky on NED's 1993 intervention in Nicaragua, speech made at the Covert Action Quarterly Dinner, 10 December 1993, on CSPAN, available at http://www.c-spanvideo.org/program/52930-1, last accessed 3 March 2012.

3. For more on USAID's 2012 expenditures, please refer to http://www.usaid.gov/results-and-data/budget-spending/where-does-money-go.

4. In fact, one of the founders' first acts—embodied in the first article of the U.S. Constitution—was to forbid government officials from receiving foreign gifts.

5. Cf. Bunce and Wolchik 2006; Howard and Roessler 2006; Kuzio 2006; McFaul 2005; Petrova 2010; Schedler 2002; Wahman 2011.

6. See, for example, Transparency International (2013), "Corruption Barometer Index" showing which respondents in 51 of 107 countries across the globe listed political parties "to be among the institutions most affected by corruption," report available at http://www.transparency.org/gcb2013/results.

7. In 2010, IRI had a budget of about $85 million and NDI of about $120 million. KAS had a budget of about $168 million while FES had a budget of about $182 million. The German *Stiftungen* are not, strictly speaking, party aid providers. As Erdmann (2006) points out, party aid accounts for just 10–30 percent of the *Stiftungen* budgets. Most of their money is directed at nonparty actors (including civil society organization, educational facilities, local governments, media organizations, and so on).

8. For more on the modest effects of party aid, see Carothers 2006a; Kumar 2005; Burnell and Gerrits 2010.

Chapter 2. The Absence of Aid in Milošević's Serbia, 1990–1996

1. The International Crisis Group titled a 1999 report on Serbia, "Sidelining Slobodan: Getting Rid of Europe's Last Dictator" (ICG 1999). Just a few years later, Belarus's Alexander Lukashenko would inherent this ignoble title.

2. Milošević's father was a Serb Orthodox priest and his mother was a schoolteacher and stalwart communist. Both committed suicide before their son had established his political career.

3. JUL was the party presided over by Mirjana Marković, the wife of Slobodan Milošević.

4. For more on the SRS's links to war crimes, see Del Ponte 2008; Dodder and Branson 1999; Pribićević 1999.

5. In the words of Nenad Čanak, the leader of one of Serbia's most prominent regional parties, the SRS "was [the regime's] striking fist in the fight against political opponents. As quoted in Vjesnik, "Optužnica protiv Šešelja ključ je raspetljavanja krvavog balkanskog čvora," 22 February 2003: 3, available at http://www.vjesnik.hr/pdf/.

6. C. Sudetić, "Tens of Thousands Call for Removal of Serbia's Leader," *New York Times*, 1 June 1992.

7. C. Sudetić, "American Takes Helm in Belgrade," *New York Times*, 15 July 1992.

8. In English, *zajedno* means "together."

9. This included 5,000 communal organizations, 189 municipal and city committees, 29 district boards, 4 city and 2 regional committees, and a professional party apparatus composed of 750 employees (Bugajski 1995: 399; Slavujević 2008: 23).

10. The only case in which this happened was in 1994 when DS President Mićunović was ousted by his vice president, Zoran Đinđić, who went on to take the lead of his party until his assassination in 2003.

11. It is alleged that Milošević inserted regime loyalists into opposition parties in an effort to sow the seeds of discord from within opposition parties (see Antonić 2002). Milošević also frequently coaxed opposition leaders into forming alliances in an effort to discredit their standing among the public and opposition colleagues. Milošević is also accused of having orchestrated the construction of a false opposition, giving life to dozens of small parties that were opposition in name but not in substance.

12. In 1993, Pešić was awarded NED's prestigious Democracy Award in honor of her dedication to "another" Serbia. See NED's website at http://www.ned.org/events/democracy-award/1993.

13. In April, NED awarded IRI and NDI $75,000 and $92,549, respectively. Both institutes sent delegates to Yugoslavia to survey the prospects for future engagement.

14. "Yugoslavs Examine Government in a Multi-Ethnic State," NDI Report, Fall 1990/Spring 1991.

15. This included individuals such as Ibrahim Rugova from Kosovo, Stjepan Mesić from Croatia, Alija Izetbegović from Bosnia, and high-ranking members of the SPS.

16. Author's interview with former program officer for IRI, 14 April 2008, in Washington, D.C. (by phone).

17. Ibid.

18. Author's interview with former political officer at the Dutch Embassy to Yugoslavia, May 2007, in Amsterdam, the Netherlands.

19. C. Sudentic, "Yugoslav Premier Ousted by Foes 6 Months After Return from U.S.," *New York Times*, 30 December 1992.

20. D. Schoen, "How Milošević Stole the Election," *New York Times*, 14 February 1993.

21. As quoted in D. Binder, "U.S. Is Backing Serbian President's Internal Foes," *New York Times*, 19 November 1992.

22. R. Lugar, "Letter to Warren Christopher, Secretary of State," 25 October 1993. Document held on file by author.

23. Ibid.

24. Author's interview with NDI director of CEE programs, 15 April 2008, in Washington, D.C.

25. In his words, "I was a funder, but we were also advocates at the same time." interview with NED Senior Program Officer, 15 March 2009 (by phone).

26. Author's interview with USAID program officer, 7 April 2008, in Washington, D.C.

27. Ibid.

28. R. Lugar, "Key to Maintaining Peace in the Balkans," *Washington Times*, 24 May 1996.

29. See R. Lugar, "Letter to Warren Christopher, Secretary of State," 29 March 1996. Document held on file by author.

30. Ibid.

31. Ibid.

32. In response to the EU's statement, Đinđić, Drašković, and Pešić sent a joint letter to the EU complaining that its decision was "peculiar" (Antonić 2002: 195).

33. Radio Free Europe/Radio Liberty, No. 240, Part 2, 13 December 1996.

34. T. Wilkinson, "Serb Leader Brushes Off U.S. Criticism of Regime," 14 December 1996, available at http://articles.latimes.com/1996-12-14/news/mn-8882_1_opposition-leaders.

35. By late December 1996, it was clear that the public outpouring of support for the opposition was genuine. At the OSCE's request, on 20 December 1996 Filipe González, the former prime minister of Spain, traveled to Belgrade to determine the veracity of the opposition's claims. In a report released in January 1997, Gonzalez concluded that Zajedno had in fact won control of the fourteen cities in question and recommended that Milošević reinstate these victories without delay. In backing Gonzalez's mission, foreign governments had finally "made a decision . . . to disengage from Milošević, to engage instead with the opposition and to take some steps back from Milošević." Author's interview with former U.S. deputy assistant secretary of state, 19 April 2007. On 20 January 1997, the European Parliament would also backtrack considerably, adopting a resolution in which it "Insists that the results of the elections of 17 November 1996 are respected and calls on the President of the FRY and the competent electoral bodies to open a full investigation into the alleged irregularities by involving the representatives of the opposition parties for a re-examination of the complaints." European Parliament, Resolution on the situation in the Federal Republic of Yugoslavia (FRY), *Official Journal C 020 , 20/01/1997 P. 0053, available at: http://eur-lex.europa.eu/LexUriServ /LexUriServ.do?uri=CELEX:51996IP1356:EN:HTML, last accessed 25 January 2014.*

36. Author's interview with former GSS president, 28 June 2007, in Belgrade, Serbia.

37. Author's interview with former director of USAID Democracy and Governance Office, 10 April 2007, in Washington, D.C.

38. Ibid.

39. Author's interview with former USAID official, 7 April 2008 in Washington, DC.

40. Author's interview with former NDI employee, April 2009 (by phone).

41. Author's interview with an American aid provider, March 2009 (by phone).

42. John Major, the British prime minister at the time, repeatedly referred to the "bewildering roots" of the Yugoslav crisis and the "unraveling of ancient hatreds" (as quoted in Simms 2003: 17 and Knudsen 2008: 30).

43. Author's interview with former program officer for IRI, 19 March 2009 (by phone).

44. Author's interview with former director of USAID's Democracy and Governance Office, 10 April 2007, in Washington, D.C.

45. As quoted in D. Binder, "CIA Doubtful on Serbian Sanctions" *New York Times*, 22 December 1993.

46. As quoted in his memoir, Holbrooke 1999: 105.

47. Central Intelligence Agency, "Yugoslavia: End of a Nation-Building Experiment," 21 September 1990.

48. Author's interview with former political officer at the Dutch Embassy in Yugoslavia, May 2007, in Amsterdam, the Netherlands.

49. CIA, "Special Analysis: Threat to Stability Growing," 5 May 1989.

50. Author's interview with former senior program officer at NDI, 23 June 2009 (by phone).

51. Author's interview with senior director of NED's Europe and Eurasia Programs, 25 March 2009 (by phone).

52. Author's interview with Vuk Drašković, president of the SPO, 7 April 2009, in Belgrade, Serbia.

53. As quoted in A. Savill, "Drašković Back in the Fray for Greater Serbia," *Independent*, 23 September 1993.

54. As quoted in D. Binder, "U.S. Is Backing Serbian President's Internal Foes," *New York Times*, 19 November 1992.

55. Author's interview with Daniel Serwer, USIP, 9 April 2009, in Washington, D.C.

56. Author's interview with Vesna Pešić, president of GSS, 16 June 2007, in Belgrade, Serbia.

57. This included GSS, Milan Panić, and to a less consistent extent, DS.

58. His many years spent accruing a fortune in the United States left much to be desired in terms of his Serbian language skills; it also made him seem out of touch with ordinary Serbians.

Chapter 3. Preparing for Regime Change

1. For more on the Kolubara coal mine strike, see S. Erlanger, "Striking Serbian Coal Miners Maintain Solidarity," *New York Times*, 4 October 2000. See also S. Crawshaw, "Miners Take Milošević to the Edge of Meltdown," *The Independent*, 4 October 2000.

2. Chief targets consisted of TV *Studio B*; *Radio b92*; the newspapers *Blic*, *Danas*, *Dnevni Telegraf*, and *Naša Borba*; and the newsmagazines *Vreme* and *Evropljanin*.

3. Law on Public Information of 21 October 1998, Official Journal of the Serb Republic No. 36/98.

4. For example, the newsmagazine *Evropljanin* received a $240,000 fine and had its property confiscated after it published a letter of complaint addressed to Milošević. One of the letter's authors, Slavko Ćuruvija, was murdered in the months following the letter's publication. In early 2000, the newspaper *Danas* was forced to pay $14,300 for having printed the letter of a university dean whose sole transgression was having publicly accused the SRS leader, Vojislav Šešelj, of plagiarizing Vladimir Lenin. By the spring of 2000, the law had been invoked more than fifty-eight times and accumulated fines upward of $1.3 million.

5. A. Kričković, "Serbia: Milošević's Crackdown on Universities," *Radio Free Europe*, 3 February 1999.

6. An independent journalist, Ćuruvija had warned U.S. members of Congress that Milošević was waging war against his own people.

7. Vesna Pešić transferred authority to Goran Svilanović.

8. M. Milošević, "Srbija u razbijenom ogledalu: Šta čekaš, Vuče?" *Vreme* 491, 3 June 2000, available at http://www.vreme.com/arhiva_html/491/index.html.

9. Its members were soon joined by Dragoljub Mićunović's DC, Milan St. Protić's Social Democratic Club "Defense," Predrag Vuletić's Liberal Democratic Party, as well as several minority and regional parties and the Association of Free and Independent Trade Unions.

10. As quoted in Cohen 2001: 319.

11. S. Erlanger, "Foe Suggests Giving Milošević Immunity to Get Him to Quit," *New York Times*, 19 July 1999.

12. As quoted in S. Ast, "Intervju: Dragoljub Mićunović, predsednik Demokratskog Centra," *Vreme* no. 256, 1 October 1999, available at http://www.vreme.com/arhiva_html/456/1.html.

13. R. Nincić, "Opozicija na okupu: Kasno, možda ne i prekasno," *Vreme* 471, 15 January 2000.

14. M. Milošević, "Srbija u razbijenom ogledalu: Šta čekaš, Vuče?" *Vreme*, 491, 3 June 2000.

15. Author's interview with Vuk Drašković, SPO president, 7 April 2009, in Belgrade, Serbia.

16. See, for example, Drašković's interview in *Vreme* recorded shortly after the assassination attempt on his life: M. Milošević, "Srbija u razbijenom ogledalu: Vuk u meti," *Vreme*, 494, 24 June 2000.

17. As quoted in R. Ninčić, "Jugoslavija—Miloševićeva lična igračka, *Vreme* 497, 15 July 2000.

18. "Serbian Opposition Is Split over Candidate," *New York Times*, 7 August 2000.

19. This included Čačak, Kraljevo, Užice, Valjevo, Ljig, Milanovac, Takovo, Niš, Vranje, Leskovac, Pitor, Zaječar, Negotin, Bor, Majdanpek, Kragujevac, Subotica, Novi Sad, Vrbas, Bačka Palanka, Sombor, Šabac, Mitrovica, Loznica, Šid, Ljubovija, Zvornik, Pančevo, Zrenjanin, Kikinda, Bečej, Kovin, and Vršac.

20. The Red Berets are accused of having carried out political assassinations within Serbia, as well as war crimes across the former Yugoslavia. In 2005, Red Beret commander Milorad "Legija" Ulemek was found guilty of murdering Milošević ally-turned-critic, Ivan Stambolić. Two years later, Ulemek and eleven of his colleagues were convicted for their roles in organizing the assassination of Serbian Prime Minister Zoran Đinđić.

21. See also H. Griffiths, "Balkan Reconstruction Report: A Mafia Within the State," *Transitions Online*, 31 March 2003.

22. See S. Erlanger, "U.S. to Increase Fund for Anti-Milošević Media and Trade Unions," *New York Times*, 13 February 1997.

23. In a 1995 tour of the region, FES's Balkans director had met with leading figures of the Serbian opposition: Vesna Pešić, Žarko Korać, and Nenad Čanak, among others, and determined that aid should be forthcoming.

24. FES Resident Director Jelena Volić Hellbusch, as quoted in FES 2006: 11.

25. Author's interview with director of the Serbian Office of Transition Initiatives 1997–1999, 8 September 2007 (by phone).

26. The Center for Modern Skills was the first of many registered nonprofits that served as youth training centers for their respective parties. The fact that these organizations were (and remain) technically independent from their mother parties allows them to bypass the more stringent regulations that inhibit donor spending on political parties. The *Stiftungen*, for example, are not legally permitted to directly fund political parties. However, because these NGO party wings are technically independent, their acceptance of grants is regarded as less contentious.

27. It was only in March, at the explicit request of a member of DS's Belgrade city board, that NDI undertook training in the Serbian capital.

28. R. Lugar, "The Milošević Problem," *Washington Post*, 30 November 1998.

29. In addition to Lugar, this letter was signed by fellow Republicans Don Nickles, Larry E. Craig, Jesse Helms, and Gordon Smith, as well as Democrats Carl Levin, Joseph Lieberman, Robert Kerrey. Lugar et. al. "Letter to President William Jefferson Clinton, 22 December 1998.

30. Author's interview with former political counselor at the U.S. Embassy in Belgrade, 19 April 2007 in Washington, D.C.

31. Author's interview with former political economic officer for the U.S. Embassy in Belgrade, 16 March 2009 (by phone).

32. Panić testimony as provided in CSCE 1999.

33. As quoted in "The Milošević Regime Versus Serbian Democracy and Balkan Stability," Hearing before the Commission on Security and Cooperation in Europe (CSCE), 105th Congress Session, 10 December 1998.

34. S. Erlanger, "U.S. Ready to Resume Sanctions Against Serbs Over Kosovo Strife," *New York Times*, 6 June 1998.

35. Author's interview with diplomats and aid providers asked to leave Serbia in the run-up to the NATO bombing.

36. Though some did remain.

37. Author's interview with former NDI program officer to Serbia, 1 April 2009 (by phone).

38. T. Blair, "A New Moral Crusade: The British Prime Minister Looks Forward to Rebuilding the Balkans—Without Slobodan Milošević," *Newsweek*, 14 June 1999.

39. As quoted in I. Karacs, "The G8 Summit: Reconstruction: No Aid for Serbia Until Milošević Regime Goes," *Independent*, 21 June 1999.

40. Author's interview with Jim Dobbins, special adviser to U.S. Secretary of State Madeleine Albright, 8 April 2007, in Washington, D.C.

41. As quoted in E. Becker, "U.S. Quietly Resuming Aid for Some Anti-Milošević Groups," *New York Times*, 24 July 1999.

42. In the words of one former U.S. State Department officer, "After the bombing, U.S. policy changed to regime change. We were upset, we wanted him out. I had no problem with that." Author's interview with former Serbia desk officer with the U.S. State Department, 18 April 2007, in Washington, D.C.

43. Author's interview with Conservative Party International Office of the Westminster Foundation for Democracy, 25 January 2010 (by phone).

44. Hearing of the European Affairs Subcommittee of the Senate Foreign Relations Committee, "Prospects for Democracy in Yugoslavia," 29 July 1999.

45. Author's interview with former coordinator of U.S. assistance to Europe and Eurasia, 19 April 2007, in Washington, D.C.

46. Regional trainers were paid $400 a month for their first six months of work. After that period, they received $450 a month. After one year, they were paid $500, and by two years with NDI, they received $525 month. In addition, NDI's regional trainers were provided with mobile phones and were reimbursed for their mobile phone usage, up to $60 per month (NDI 2001)

47. Jim Hooper's testimony before the European Affairs Subcommittee of the Senate Foreign Relations Committee, *Prospects for Democracy in Yugoslavia*, 29 July 1999.

48. Much as it had for opposition forces in Nicaragua and Poland, NED had established a time-honored tradition of bypassing bans on party support to fund political coalitions composed of large swaths of opposition forces.

49. Author's interview with former IRI resident director for Serbia, 18 April 2007, in Washington, D.C.

50. Author's interview with Dutch diplomat in September 2009 (by phone).

51. Ibid.

52. Ibid.

53. The assessment was not unfounded. Avramović died just six months after Milošević's fall from power.

54. This was in contrast to a figure such as Zoran Đinđic who, although idealized following his death, was regarded as highly divisive during his lifetime. Throughout the 1990s, Đinđic was, moreover, regarded as a flip-flopper, particularly on the so-called national question.

55. From 1990 to 1995, the United States provided $600,000 to the International Media Fund to provide equipment to Serbian media partners. From 1993 to 1997, the EU devoted €1.7 million to the International Federation of Journalists; the money went directly to domestic partners.

56. Council of the European Union, "2232nd Council Meeting (General Affairs), Held in Brussels, on 6 December 1999," 17 January 2000, 13829/99.

57. As quoted in Albright 1999.

58. Author's interview with former director of the Office of South Central European Affairs, 19 March 2009 (by phone).

59. Author's interview with Dušan Gamser, member of the presidency of the GSS and FNS, resident director, 27 February 2007, in Belgrade, Serbia.

60. European Union, "EU Assistance to Serbia," available at http://www.delscg.ec.europa.eu/code/navigate.php?Id=195.

61. European Commission, "Serbia 2000: Action programme Part 2," available at http://ec.europa.eu/enlargement/archives/ear/serbia/main/ser-annual_programme_2000_part2.htm.

62. European Union, "EU Assistance to Serbia," available at http://www.delscg.ec.europa.eu/code/navigate.php?Id=195.

63. Were a candidate to fail to pass the 50-percent threshold, he or she would need to prepare for a second round of voting.

64. Author's interview with Dutch diplomat on 16 September 2009 (by phone).

65. NDI and the remaining German *Stiftungen* did not have a relationship with Otpor. Early into their efforts in Serbia, the U.S. party institutes had agreed that IRI would focus on youth groups and NDI would concentrate on nonpartisan vote counting. As pertains to the German *Stiftungen*, all except for FES decided not to support Otpor directly. KAS's Gordana Pilipović says, "We didn't work with Otpor because they had such good financial support, there was no need to support them." Author's interview with KAS project coordinator, 9 February 2007, in Belgrade, Serbia.

66. In fact, only $47,480 of this total was actually spent. The rest was returned to NED several years later. See NED 1999b.

67. Author's interview with former IRI director of Serbia programs, on 9 April 2008, in Washington, D.C.

68. As William Montgomery (2010), the U.S. ambassador to Croatia at the time, explains, "We all started from the assumption that Milošević would steal the elections."

69. CeSID served as NDI's nonparty partner, mirroring the relationship of Otpor with IRI.

70. Author's interview with former IRI program director for Serbia, on 9 April 2008, in Washington, D.C.

71. The EU later made exceptions to this in the form of its Energy for Democracy project launched in the winter of 1999–2000.

72. By the summer of 1999, some 800 names were included on this list. In June 1999, this so-called blacklist was synchronized with that of the United States.

73. Author's interview with James Lyon, International Crisis Group, 2 March 2007, in Belgrade, Serbia.

74. If sanctions were designed to undermine the loyalty of Milošević's economic power base, then covert operations were designed to undermine the loyalty of his political and security apparatus. There is ample reason to believe that the CIA and British Secret Intelligence Service (MI6) had informants embedded in Milošević's circle of allies. In March 2009, for example, retired CIA officer William Lofgren publicly acknowledged that Jovica Stanišić, the chief of Serbia's intelligence service, was a CIA informant throughout the 1990s, until his dismissal in 1998 (G. Miller, "Serbian Spy's Trial Lifts Cloak on His CIA Alliance," *Los Angeles Times*, 1 March 2009). George Busby and Anthony Monckton, covert operatives for the MI6, are said to have had particularly close ties to members of the SPS and would later stand accused of negotiating with Serbian tycoons, whose support was needed to ensure a peaceful transfer of power (See "MI6 smjenjuje špijune s Balkana" [MI6 Withdrawing Its Spies from the Balkans] *Nacional*, 31 August 2004, available at http://www.nacional.hr/

clanak/11109/mi6-smjenjuje-spijune-s-balkana, last accessed 26 April 2012). The British intelligence services have denied such allegations. However, British news agencies, including *The Guardian*, did cover the story, going so far as to release the names of the one alleged agent, Anthony Monckton, who was reported to have played an "important undercover role" in Serbia, as well as the rest of the region. See I. Traynor, "MI6 Involved in Balkan Spy Plot, Says Croatian Paper," *Guardian*, 27 August 2004. In his book, *Shadow Play* (2003), Tim Marshall, a foreign affairs correspondent for Sky News, provides an elaborate account of the covert initiatives led by the British MI6 and CIA in the months leading to 5 October 2000. Unfortunately, given that such evidence remains confidential, it is difficult to offer hard evidence of such allegations. At the very least, however, it is not farfetched to say that both the CIA and the MI6 were well informed of the initiatives undertaken by Zoran Đinđić, Čedomir Jovanović, Nebojša Čović, and other members of Serbia's democratic opposition to secure the allegiances of Serbia's police and JSO. Like key members of the DOS coalition, Western governments recognized that the centerpieces of Milošević's power base lay in the loyalty of his security apparatus. They thus did their utmost to ensure that such loyalty would not be forthcoming on 5 October 2000.

75. As stated in Albright's remarks at an opposition meeting in Berlin, Germany, on 17 December 1999. See Albright 1999.

76. This, according to the EU: European Union Assistance, "Federal Republic of Yugoslavia: The European Contribution," November 2000: 3.

77. Testimony of Special Envoy Robert Gelbard to the Senate Foreign Relations Committee (1999).

78. Ibid.

79. This figure is all the more striking when one considers that the Serbian population is roughly twelve times longer than that of Montenegro.

80. Author's interview with former Serbian NDI employee on 22 July 2011 (by phone).

81. Author's interview with NDI program officer for Serbia on 1 April 2009 (by phone).

82. Author's interview with former Serbian NDI employee on 22 July 2011 (by phone).

83. UNMIK was the UN mission established under UN Security Council resolution 1244 "to ensure conditions for a peaceful and normal life for all inhabitants of Kosovo and advance regional stability in the western Balkans."

84. Antonić (2002: 318) alleges that in the presidential elections of 1997, featuring Milošević-backed candidate Milan Milutinović, authorities succeeded in manufacturing 300,000 votes in Kosovo.

85. L. Kleveman, "UN Fears Milošević Rigged Kosovo Poll," *Telegraph*, 25 September 2000.

86. As quoted in N. Stefanović, "Intervju: dr Vojislav Koštunica, predsednički kandidat—Prazan džep i država," *Vreme*, 501, 12 August 2000, available at http://www.vreme.com/arhiva_html/501/index.html.

87. Author's interview with James Dobbins, special adviser to Secretary of State Madeleine Albright, 18 April 2007, in Washington, D.C.

88. Author's interview with Dušan Gamser, member of the presidency of the GSS, 27 February 2007, in Belgrade, Serbia.

89. Author's interview with NDI program coordinator, 4 April 2009, in Belgrade, Serbia.

90. Author's interview with NDI employee on 22 July 2011 (by phone).

91. Author's interview with Vesna Pešić, former GSS president, 16 June 2007 in Belgrade, Serbia.

92. Author's interview with former U.S. diplomat to Serbia, March 2009 (by phone).

93. David Costello, OTI resident director for Serbia, as quoted in Cook and Spalatin 2002: 11.

94. Clinton Presidential Library, "Records of Ring Around Serbia: Inventory on FOIA Request 2006-0206-F" p. 1, available at www.clintonlibrary.gov/_previous/.../Updated%20FOIA/2006-0206-F.pdf, *last accessed 22 July 2011.*

95. Author's interview with James O'Brien, special envoy to the Balkans, 10 April 2007, in Washington, D.C.

96. Ibid.

97. J. Rubin, "The Kids Who Confronted Milošević," *Mother Jones*, 22 September 2000.

98. "Serbian Opposition Is Split over Candidate," *New York Times*, 7 August 2000.

99. Author's interview with William Montgomery, U.S. ambassador to the Federal Republic of Yugoslavia, 2 December 2010 (by phone).

100. Author's interview with former resident director of IRI, 18 April 2007, in Washington, D.C.

101. Ibid.

102. Borba's Commentary, "Chosen to Give NATO Amnesty for Crimes," *Politika*, 10 January 2000, available at http://www.ex-yupress.com/politika/politika20.html.

103. As quoted in "Drašković Wants to Promote Himself to a Paid Traitor," *Politika*, 10 January 2000, available at http://www.ex-yupress.com/politika/politika20.html.

104. M. Milošević, "Srbija u razbijenom ogledalu: Brandenburška kapija," *Vreme* 468, 25 December 1999, available at http://www.vreme.com/arhiva_html/468/index.html.

105. Ibid.

106. Milan St. Protić, president of the DHSS, as quoted in W. Dozdiak, "U.S. Urged to Remove Sanctions in Yugoslavia," *Washington Post*, 26 October 1999.

107. Author's interview with James Lyon, ICG special Balkans adviser, 2 March 2007, in Belgrade, Serbia.

108. Author's interview with political specialist at the U.S. Embassy Belgrade, 13 March 2007, in Belgrade, Serbia.

109. Author's interview with James O'Brien, special envoy to the Balkans, 10 April 2007, in Washington, D.C.

110. Lungescu, O. "Serbia Sanctions under Review," *BBC*, 2 September 2000, available at http://news.bbc.co.uk/2/hi/europe/907534.stm.

111. As quoted in S. Castle, "EU May Lift 'Failed' Milošević Sanctions," *Independent* 11 July 2000.

112. As quoted in O. Lugescu, "Yugoslavia Sanctions 'Failing,'" BBC, 10 July 2000, available at http://news.bbc.co.uk/2/hi/europe/827836.stm.

113. In 2007, Serbia's organized-crime prosecutor, Slobodan Radovanović, launched an investigation into Milošević's son and widow, accusing them both of having participated in a European cigarette-smuggling ring.

114. As quoted in B. Harden, "The Milošević Generation," *New York Times*, 29 August 1999.

115. Hajdinjak (2002: 26–27) estimates that by the late 1990s, Montenegrin authorities were earning a whopping $700 million a year from illicit cigarette smuggling.

116. Author's interview with James O'Brien, special envoy to the Balkans, 10 April 2007, in Washington, D.C.

117. Author's interview with former coordinator for U.S. assistance to Central and Eastern Europe on 17 March 2009 (by phone).

118. Ibid.

119. European Council, "Proposal for a Council Decision Providing Exceptional Financial Assistance for Montenegro," 2000/C 337 E/03, submitted on 11 May 2000.

120. Author's interview with former coordinator for U.S. assistance to Central and Eastern Europe on 17 March 2009 (by phone).

121. Ibid.

122. All three were interviewed on the *PBS NewsHour* and all agreed that the NATO bombing contributed to Milošević's ouster. See "Milošević Ousted," *PBS Newshour*, 6 October 2010, available at http://www.pbs.org/newshour/bb/europe/july-dec00/yugo_10-6.html, last accessed 7 July 2013.

123. Author's interview with Vladimir Pavlov, former Otpor activist and current Serbian diplomat, 11 February 2009, in New York City.

124. M. Dobbs, "Serbian Nationalism Lifts Milošević," *Washington Post*, 30 March 1999.

125. Author's interview with Dušan Gamser, GSS members, and FNS director, 27 February 2007, in Belgrade, Serbia.

126. M. Dobbs, "Milošević Claims Victory, Lauds Army," *Washington Post*, 11 June 1999.

127. NDI, "Serbia Issues Poll," 24 October 1999, prepared by Penn Schoen & Berland.

128. Author's interview with Richard Monroe Miles, U.S. chief of mission to Belgrade 1996–1999, 26 April 2008 (by e-mail).

129. This figure included government and nongovernment expenditures. A similar figure of $41 million by the United States alone was given by Dobbs, "U.S. Advice Guided Milošević Opposition," *Washington Post*, 11 December 2000.

130. These figures are derived from the Grant Agreements forged between donors USAID and NED and the implementing agencies, NDI and IRI. The data for USAID funds to NDI were obtained through Freedom of Information Request F-00095-09, and that for IRI was provided directly by IRI staff. The data for NED's grants were provided through Freedom of Information Request FOIA2009NED-01.

131. Author's interview with Arjen Berkvens, AMS director, 27 January 2010 (by phone).

132. Author's interview with Srđa Popović, Otpor co-founder, 4 February 2007, in Belgrade, Serbia.

133. Author's interview with NED senior program officer, 15 March 2009 (by phone).

134. Ibid.

135. Author's interview with CIPE program officer, 20 April 2007, in Washington, D.C.

136. Author's interview with William Montgomery, U.S. ambassador to the Federal Republic of Yugoslavia, 2 December 2010 (by phone).

137. Author's interview with James Dobbins, special adviser to U.S. Secretary of State Madeleine Albright, 18 April 2007, in Washington, D.C. Dobbins says he had daily or bi-daily telephone calls with his colleagues in the British, French, and German foreign ministries. Albright was, he says, on the phone with her colleagues in Berlin and Paris at least once a week.

138. As quoted in Senate Foreign Relations Committee 1999.

139. See the previous section on sanctions.

140. James O'Brien notes, "To his credit, Đinđić himself said I may be a great campaign manager, but I know I can't win". Author's interview with James O'Brien, special envoy to the Balkans, 10 April 2007, in Washington, D.C.

141. Milošević was of the same opinion. He dismissed U.S. polls as "orchestrated and manipulated by the Americans and the Central Intelligence Agency, who help pay for them" (S. Erlanger, "Milošević, Trailing in Polls, Rails Against NATO," *New York Times*, 20 September 2000).

142. Author's interview with Vuk Drašković, SPO president, 7 April 2009, in Belgrade, Serbia.

143. Author's interview with Dušan Gamser, GSS member of the presidency, 27 February 2007, in Belgrade, Serbia.

144. E. Lake, "NGOs Form Front Line of U.S. Role in Yugoslav Polls," Centre for Peace in the Balkans, 7 October 2000, available at http://www.balkanpeace.org/index.php?index=article&article id=12752, last accessed 22 July 2011.

Chapter 4. In Milošević's Shadow

1. L. Cohen, "Democratic Consolidation in Serbia: Pitfalls of the Post-Djindjic Transition," Wilson Center, Meeting Report 294, 2004, available at http://www.wilsoncenter.org/publication/294-democratic-consolidation-serbia-pitfalls-the-post-djindjic-transition.

2. One example was the highly publicized "Bodrum Affair," which featured Otpor founder, Srđa Popović, and several of his DS colleagues who violated the parliamentary statute by voting on behalf of fellow member of parliament Neda Arnerić while she was vacationing in Bodrum Turkey. The vote was for the new governor of the National Bank of Serbia and the scandal made headlines for weeks.

3. "Insajder," "When Laws Don't Apply," B92, 29 June 2011, available at http://www.b92.net/eng/insajder/index.php?yyyy=2011&mm=06&dd=29&nav_id=75179, accessed 1 May 2012.

4. B. Pekušić, "Financing of Serbian Political Parties Questioned," SETimes, 1 March 2012.

5. "Speaker on MPs Blank Resignation Letters," B92, 27 October 2010, available at http://www.b92 .net/eng/news/politics-article.php?yyyy=2010&mm=10&dd=27&nav_id=70535, accessed 1 May 2012.

6. In 2001, Slobodan Milošević was extradited to The Hague on charges of war crimes. In 2003, Vojislav Šešelj voluntarily surrendered to Serbian authorities and was promptly extradited to The Hague, also to face charges of war crimes. Despite these extraditions, both the SPS and SRS opted to maintain direct links with Milošević and Šešelj, respectively, although individuals in Belgrade took on increasingly powerful roles within their parties. In 2004, Ivica Dačić won a highly contested race to become his party's president (despite strong opposition from Milošević). In the case of the SRS, Tomislav Nikolić and Aleksandar Vučić went on to take increasingly prominent roles within their parties as vice president and secretary general of the SRS, respectively. In 2008, differences between Nikolić and Šešelj led the former to forge his own party, the Serbian Progressive Party which, by May 2012, had emerged as the largest party in Serbia's parliament, receiving more votes than the Democratic Party of Boris Tadić.

7. William Montgomery, "Let's Stop Talking about a Democratic Block in Serbia," B92, 21 May 2007, available at http://www6.b92.net/eng/news/in_focus.php?id=152&start=0&nav_id=41324, last accessed 1 May 2012.

8. Ibid.

9. The speed of Nikolić's concession is all the more surprising when one takes into account the close nature of 2008's electoral contest. Nikolić lost by just two percentage points, after having won the first round of presidential elections held several weeks earlier. By contrast, it took Ukraine's Yulia Tymoshenko six days to concede her defeat to Viktor Yanukovych after it was learned that she had lost the 2010 presidential race by more than three percentage points.

10. Former refugees refer to individuals who have since taken Serbian citizenship.

11. It is noteworthy that the fulfillment of this achievement was one of the major goals of party aid providers in Serbia throughout the 2000s.

12. Author's interview with the director of democracy and governance unit at USAID Mission to Belgrade, 3 February 2007, in Belgrade, Serbia.

13. Author's interview with vice president of United States Institute of Peace, 9 April 2008, in Washington, D.C.

14. The practice, FES representatives admit, was highly unusual.

15. Author's interview with former FES regional director, 22 September 2009 (by phone).

16. Author's interview with NDI regional director for CEE, 19 April 2007, in Washington, D.C.

17. Ibid.

18. One output of such products was *(Re)Konstrukcija Institucija: Godinu Dana Tranzicije u Srbiji* [Re-constructing Institutions: One Year of Transition in Serbia], a 500-page look at domestic academics' perceptions of the state of reform in the country (Cvetković 2002).

19. Author's interview with DS party member and former speaker of parliament, 10 February 2007 in Belgrade, Serbia.

20. In his words, the DS "began as a clear liberal party with fresh liberal ideas."

21. Author's interview with the director of the Alfred Mozer Stichting, 27 January 2010 (by phone).

22. Author's interview with NDI regional director for CEE, 19 April 2007, in Washington, D.C.

23. Author's interview with IRI program director for Serbia, 8 April 2008, in Washington, D.C.

24. Thus, in 2003 for every $1.00 spent on economic development, $2.20 was spent on democratic development; by 2006 those numbers were reversed—for every $1.00 spent on democracy, $2.50 was dedicated to the economy.

25. This sum would increase if an important election were scheduled. These figures were confirmed by numerous interviewees.

26. Author's interview with FES program coordinator for Serbia, 3 June 2007, in Belgrade, Serbia.

27. Author's interview with U.S. ambassador to Serbia, 16 April 2008, in Washington, D.C.

28. Not surprising, voter apathy soon grew to epidemic proportions. By November 2003, less than 40 percent of voters bothered to make their electoral preferences known in the election of Serbia's first-ever democratically elected president—a number dwarfed by the 70 percent turnout that enabled the election of FRY president Vojislav Koštunica just three years prior.

29. As NDI's Quarterly Report from April–June 2004 explains, the database was in fact "tailored to help individual parties identify and target their potential supporters (abstainers and voters sympathetic to parties with similar platforms) and positive supporters (voters currently or formerly loyal to the party), while avoiding areas likely to be loyal to opponents" (NDI 2004b).

30. Author's interview with former NDI resident director for Serbia, 16 March 2009 (by e-mail).

31. Author's interview with FES program coordinator in Serbia, 3 June 2007, in Belgrade, Serbia.

32. Author's interview with the director of the Democracy and Governance Office at USAID's Mission to Belgrade, 2 March 2007, in Belgrade, Serbia.

33. Put in perspective, this figure would nearly have doubled the institute's annual budgets for Serbia.

34. This included seven different mailings: two of 150,000, targeting minorities: two of 150,000, targeting new and first-time voters; and three of 300,000 each, targeting "reform-oriented" households (IRI 2007a).

35. Two days prior to election day marks the so-called quiet period, after which Serbian law forbids parties from campaigning. Interestingly, although the initial aim was to reach some 100,000 reform-oriented households (IRI 2006b), in the end just 50,000 were approached.

36. The remaining $250,000 was awarded to the Institute for Sustainable Communities.

37. In this instance, although the effort in large part revolved around CeSID, several other NGOs were included in the effort, among them the Center for Development of Parliamentary Debate, Environmental Ambassadors, the liberal Network, the Youth Initiative for Human Rights, and the Zaječar Initiative (NDI 2008b).

38. Reporting on its activities in 2008, IRI noted that "the urgency of preparing for imminent parliamentary elections had upstaged the long-term effort of parties to develop and pursue comprehensive, wide-ranging party platforms and politics."

39. SWOT refers to strengths, weaknesses, opportunities, and threats.

40. Author's interview with a member of the General Secretary of the SDU, 7 March 2007, in Belgrade, Serbia.

41. Several of these publications were used throughout the author's research.

42. Although NDI also sought to integrate a platform-building component into its activities—by, for example, pressing aid recipients to conduct internal questionnaires designed to gauge members' policy preferences—it has done so on a far smaller scale than its Republican counterpart.

43. Author's interview with FES resident director Belgrade, 2 April 2009, in Belgrade, Serbia.

44. Ibid.

45. Not least because they were getting strong resistance from their Bosnian partner, the Socialist Democratic Party of Bosnia and Herzegovina.

46. Author's interview with resident director of NDI, 3 April 2009, in Belgrade, Serbia.

47. T. Spaić, "Nikolić placa 7.500 evra mesecno za Montgomerijeve savete," *Blic*, 18 February 2011, available at http://www.blic.rs/Vesti/Politika/236284/Nikolic-placa-7500--evra-mesecno-za-Montgomerijeve—savete, accessed 1 February 2014.

48. Author's interview with former resident director IRI, 8 April 2008, in Washington, D.C.

49. Author's interview with DS member and NDI regional trainer, 16 March 2007, in Belgrade, Serbia.

50. Author's interview with former NDI resident director, 16 March 2009 (by e-mail).

51. Author's interview with a former advisor to the G17 Plus, 22 June 2007, in Belgrade, Serbia.

52. Author's interview with former program coordinator at NDI, 4 April 2009, in Belgrade, Serbia.

53. Author's interview with Marko Blagojević, director of operations for CeSID, 26 February 2007, in Belgrade, Serbia.

54. Author's interview with LDP international secretary and NDI trainer, 26 June 2007, in Belgrade, Serbia.

55. Author's interview with member of LDP youth wing, 29 June 2007, in Belgrade, Serbia.

56. Ibid.

57. Author's interview with LDP member and MP, 5 July 2007, in Belgrade, Serbia.

58. Ibid.

59. USAID's views on this were confirmed by the author's interview with the USAID country desk officer for Serbia, 21 April 2007, in Washington, D.C.

60. Author's interview with NDI regional trainer and international secretary of the GSS, 26 June 2007, in Belgrade, Serbia.

61. Author's interview with member of the Party for Democratic Action, 3 July 2007, in Strasbourg, France.

62. Author's interview with member of the Democratic Union of the Valley, 3 July 2007, in Strasbourg, France.

63. Author's interview with NDI program manager, 28 September 2011, in Belgrade, Serbia.

64. Author's interview with NDI representative, 26 November 2011, in Belgrade, Serbia.

65. Author's interview with NDI program manager, 28 September 2011, in Belgrade, Serbia.

66. Author's interview with NDI representative, in Belgrade, Serbia.

67. "Party Financing, Blank Resignations on Agenda," *Tanjug*, 12 May 2011, available at http://www.invest-in-serbia.com/archive/politics/1305228300-party-financing-blank-resignations-on-agenda.html.

68. As explained earlier in this chapter, by forcing prospective MPs to sign blank resignations *before* they were elected to parliament, parties forced their members to sign away their mandate in the case of expulsion from the party, despite the fact that the Supreme Court declared that an MP, rather than the party, is the owner of the mandate.

69. European Parliament resolution on the 2012 Progress Report on Serbia (2012/2868/RSP).

70. Transparency International, "Presidential and Parliamentary Election Campaign Financing in Serbia: May 2012," USAID, July 2012.

71. I. Jovanović, "The EU Fast-Tracked Serbia's Signing to Boost Pro-Western Parties' Prospects Ahead of May 11th Elections," *SETimes*, 30 April 2008, available at http://www.setimes.com/cocoon/setimes/xhtml/en_GB/features/setimes/features/2008/04/30/feature-01.

72. S. Castle and S. Erlanger, "Quiet Pressure Behind EU Success," *New York Times*, 22 August 2008.

73. Ibid.

74. Ibid.

75. Author's interview with FNS resident director,12 February 2007, in Belgrade, Serbia.

76. Author's interview with former NDI resident director, 20 April 2007, in Washington, D.C.

77. Author's interview with IRI resident director, 8 April 2008, in Washington, D.C.

78. Author's interview with NDI program officer, 9 February 2007, in Belgrade, Serbia.

79. Author's interview with DSS member, 14 March 2007, in Belgrade, Serbia.

80. Author's interview with former G17 Plus member, 18 June 2007, in Belgrade, Serbia.

81. Author's interview with former SDU member, 29 February 2012 (by phone).

82. Ibid.

83. Author's interview with former SDU member, 2 February 2007, in Belgrade, Serbia.

84. Author's interview with NDI program manager, 28 September 2011, in Belgrade, Serbia.

85. Author's interview with DS member and former speaker of parliament, 10 February 2007, in Belgrade, Serbia.

86. Author's interview with FES resident director Serbia, 2 April 2009, in Berlin, Germany.

87. Author's interview with HBS resident director, 16 March 2007, in Belgrade, Serbia.

88. Likewise, IRI claimed it was hatching "strategies to convert Radical votes to democratic votes," while NDI noted that it was "striving to stem the tide of radical political support" (IRI 2006a).

89. Author's interview with the director of operations at CeSID, 26 February 2007, in Belgrade, Serbia.

90. Kelly's remarks were made at the NDI board meeting. See T. Kelly, "Review of Parliamentary Elections in Serbia," 15 May 2008.

91. Such concerns were reiterated by IRI staff members in interviews.

92. See, for example, the work of Goati, Orlović, Stojiljković, Slavujević, or Đurković.

93. In August 2011, for example, German Chancellor Angela Merkel would issue a heated rebuke of Serbia's position toward Kosovo, stating, "One of the preconditions for Serbia is Kosovo,

that relations between those states get normalised." See "Germany's Angela Merkel Ties Serbian Hopes to Kosovo," BBC, 23 August 2011, available at http://www.bbc.co.uk/news/world-europe-14631297, accessed 26 August 2011.

94. Conscious that such advice might be construed as little more than mudslinging, IRI encouraged the Tadić campaign to deflect such criticism with the following refrain: "We are merely showing the pictures and statements of the leaders of the SRS—*in their own words*—how can you call this a 'negative' ad?" (IRI 2008a).

95. This assertion would later prove false when the SPS and SNS did in fact lead Serbia toward Europe, by doing what the DS ultimately could not; agreeing to Kosovo's independence.

96. A. Vasovic, "Gay Rights March in Belgrade Triggers Violent Riots," *Reuters*, 10 October 2010, available at http://www.reuters.com/article/2010/10/10/oukwd-uk-serbia-gays-idAFTRE6990SJ 20101010, last accessed 1 February 2014.

Chapter 5. Rethinking Aid's Legacy in Serbia

1. T. Rosenberg, "What Egypt Learned from the Students Who Overthrew Milošević," *Foreign Policy*, 16 February 2011.

2. K. Pavgi, "The FP Top 100 Global Thinkers," *Foreign Policy*, 28 November 2011.

3. R. Nixon, "U.S. Groups Helped Nurture Arab Uprisings," *New York Times*, 14 April 2011.

4. Among these, March 1991's storming of "TV bastille," June 1992's antiwar rally, and June 1993's anti-regime protest stand out.

5. Author's interview with FES regional director, 22 September 2009 (by phone).

6. Ibid.

7. In 2008, for example, SPS president, Ivica Dačić, traveled to Athens, Greece, to lobby the president of the Socialist International, George Papandreou, to accept the SPS's membership—a request Papandreou agreed to accommodate once Dačić won Germany's backing. This was made possible thanks to the insistence of FES. See author's interview with Michael Ehrke, resident director of FES, 2 April 2009, in Belgrade, Serbia.

8. When in September 2000 Koštunica defeated Milošević, ample credit was given to Serbia's opposition political parties; see Sarah Birch (2002: 501); Bunce and Wolchik (2006: 56); Cevallos (2001: 8); and McFaul (2005: 9).

9. "Serbian Opposition Is Split over Candidate," *New York Times*, 7 August 2000.

10. This was reiterated throughout my interviews both with members of the diplomatic community and with aid recipients.

11. IRI, *Quarterly Report April–June 2004*. In a memo to the U.S. embassy, IRI staff noted that parties—not NGOs—"are the most appropriate and effective vehicles for GOTV" because they have "an immediate self-interest in getting out the vote, making parties much more likely to mobilize and commit the resources to sustain GOTV in the long-term." See IRI (2004a). This was also confirmed in discussions with IRI directors.

12. In August 2011, for example, German Chancellor Angela Merkel would issue a heated rebuke of Serbia's position toward Kosovo, stating, "One of the preconditions for Serbia is Kosovo, that relations between those states get normalised." See "Germany's Angela Merkel Ties Serbian Hopes to Kosovo," BBC, 23 August 2011, available at http://www.bbc.co.uk/news/world-europe-14631297, accessed 26 August 2011.

13. Possible exceptions here are the German *Stiftungen*, which maintain a fraternal approach to

party development. However, they too stress their ultimate impact as being nonpartisan (see the following section).

14. Author's interview with former USAID mission director to Serbia, 25 March 2009 (by phone).

15. An argument made in M. Spoerri, "Outrage over Egypt's Arrest of NGO Workers, but U.S. Would Have Done the Same," *Christian Science Monitor*, 13 February 2012.

16. M. Dobbs, "U.S. Advice Guided Milošević Opposition," *Washington Post*, 11 December 2000.

17. Russia's foreign ministry spokesperson Alexander Lukashevich, as quoted in T. Parfitt, "Russia Accuses U.S. of Funding Opposition as It Closes American Aid Agency," *Telegraph*, 19 September 2012.

BIBLIOGRAPHY

Ackerman, P., and J. DuVall. 2001. *A Force More Powerful: A Century on Nonviolent Conflict*. New York: Palgrave.

Adeney, K., and A. Wyatt. 2004. "Democracy in South Asia: Getting Beyond the Structure-Agency Dichotomy." *Political Studies* 52, no. 1: 1–18.

Agh, A. 1998. *Emerging Democracies in East Central Europe and the Balkans*. Northampton: Edward Elgar.

———. 2006. "East-Central Europe: Parties in Crisis and the External and Internal Europeanization of the Party Systems." In P. Burnell, ed., *Globalizing Democracy: Party Politics in Emerging Democracies*. London: Routledge.

Albright, M. 1999. "U.S. Support for Democracy in Serbia and Montenegro." Remarks at US-EU-Serbian Opposition Meeting, Berlin, Germany, 17 December 1999.

Almond, G., and S. Verba. 1963. *The Civic Culture: Political Attitudes and Democracy in Five Nations*. Princeton, N.J.: Princeton University Press.

AMS. 2006. *Annual Report 2006*. Amsterdam: Alfred Mozer Stichting.

———. 2007. *Annual Report 2007*. Amsterdam: Alfred Mozer Stichting.

Amundsen, I. 2007. *Donor Support to Political Parties: Status and Principles*. Bergen: Chr. Michelsen Institute.

Anderson, J. H., and C. W. Gray. 2006. *Anticorruption in Transition 3: Who Is Succeeding . . . and Why?* Washington, D.C.: World Bank.

Andreas, P. 2005. "Criminalizing Consequences of Sanctions: Embargo Busting and Its Legacy." *International Studies Quarterly* 49: 335–60.

Antonić, S. 2002. *Zarobljena Zemlja: Srbija za vlade Slobodana Miloševića* [A Closed Nation: Serbia under Slobodan Milošević]. Belgrade: Otkrovenje.

———. 2003a. "Political Systems and Elites in Serbia Before and After October 5th." In D. Vujadinović, L. Veljak, V. Goati, and V. Pavićević, eds., *Between Authoritarianism and Democracy: Serbia, Montenegro, Croatia. I: Institutional Framework*. Belgrade: CEDET.

———. 2003b. *Nacija u Strujama Prošlosti* [Nation in the Stream of the Past]. Belgrade: Cigoja Stampa.

———. 2006. *Elita, Gradjanstvo i Slaba Država: Srbija posle 2000* [Elite, Citizens, and the Weak State: Serbia After 2000]. Belgrade: JP Sluzbeni Glasnik.

Arksey, H., and P. Knight. 1999. *Interviewing for Social Scientists*. London: Sage.

Bader, M. 2010. *Against All Odds: Aiding Political Parties in Georgia and Ukraine*. Amsterdam: Amsterdam University Press.

Bajović, V., and S. Manoljović. 2013. "Corruption and Financing of Political Parties— Case of Serbia." Observatorio de Economia e Gestao de Fraude, Working Paper 21.

Bardos, G. 2003. "Serbia." In Freedom House, *Nations in Transit 2003: Democratization in East-Central Europe and Eurasia*. Washington, D.C.: Freedom House.

Barkan, J. D. 2000. "Protracted Transitions Among Africa's New Democracies." *Democratization* 7, no. 3: 227–43.

———. 2012. "Democracy Assistance: What Recipients Think." *Journal of Democracy* 23, no. 1: 129–37.

Bartolini, S., and Mair, P. 2001. "Challenges to Contemporary Political Parties." In L. Diamond and R. Gunther, eds., *Political Parties and Democracy*. Baltimore: Johns Hopkins University Press, pp. 327–43.

Beissinger, M. R. 2006. "Promoting Democracy: Is Exporting Revolution a Constructive Strategy?" *Dissent*, 53, no. 1.

———. 2007. "Structure and Example in Modular Political Phenomena: The Diffusion of Bulldozer/Rose/Orange/Tulip Revolutions." *Perspectives on Politics* 5: 259–76.

———. 2009. "An Interrelated Wave." *Journal of Democracy* 20, no. 1: 74–77.

Bennett, A. 2008. "Process Tracing: A Bayesian Perspective." In J. M. Box-Steffensmeier, H. E. Brady, and D. Collier, eds., *The Oxford Handbook of Political Methodology*. New York: Oxford University Press.

——— 2010. "Process Tracing and Causal Inference." In H. Brady and D. Collier, eds., *Rethinking Social Inquiry*. New York: Rowman and Littlefield.

Bennett, W. L. 1992. *The Governing Crisis: Media, Money and the Marketing in American Elections*. New York: St. Martin's.

Bertelsmann Stiftung. 2007. "BTI 2008 –Serbia Country Report." Gutersoh: Bertelsmann Stiftung.

———. 2012. "BTI 2008 –Serbia Country Report." Gutersoh: Bertelsmann Stiftung.

Bieber, F. 2003. "The Serbian Opposition and Civil Society: Roots of the Delayed Transition in Serbia." *International Journal of Politics,Culture and Society* 17, no. 1: 73–90.

———. 2005/2006. "Serbia: Minorities in a Reluctant State." *European Yearbook of Minority Issues* 5: 243–50.

———. 2006. "Serbia." In J. Goehring, ed., *Nations in Transit 2006: Democratization from Central Europe to Eurasia*. New York: Freedom House.

———. 2011. "Building Impossible States? State-Building Strategies and EU Membership in the Western Balkans." *Europe-Asia Studies* 63, no. 10: 1783–1802.

Binnendijk, A., and I. Marovic. 2006. "Power and Persuasion: Nonviolent Strategies to Influence State Security Forces in Serbia (2000) and Ukraine (2004)." *Communist and Post-Communist Studies* 39, no. 3: 411–29.

Birch, S. 2002. "The 2000 Elections in Yugoslavia: The Bulldozer Revolution." *Electoral Studies* 21, no. 3: 499–511.

BMZ. 2005. "Promoting Democracy in German Development Policy: Supporting Political Reform Processes and Popular Participation—A BMZ Position Paper." Special 137. Berlin: Federal Ministry for Economic Cooperation and Development.

Bochsler, D. 2010. "Regional Party Systems in Serbia." In V. Stojarová and P. Emerson. *Party Politics in the Western Balkans*. Abingdon: Routledge, pp. 131-50.

Bolleyer, N., and L. Storm. 2010. "Problems of Party Assistance in Hybrid Regimes: The Case of Morocco." *Democratization* 17, no. 6: 1202–24.

Brown, K. 2006. *Transacting Transition: The Micropolitics of Democracy Assistance in the Former Yugoslavia*. Sterling, Va.: Kumarian Press.

Brownlee, J. 2009. "Portents of Pluralism: How Hybrid Regimes Affect Democratic Transitions." *American Journal of Political Science* 53, no. 3: 515-32.

Brucker, M. 2007. "Trans-National Actors in Democratizing States: The Case of German Political Foundations in Ukraine." *Journal of Communist Studies and Transition Politics* 23, no. 2: 296-319.

Bryce, J. 1921. *Modern Democracies, II*. New York: Macmillan.

Bugajski, J. 1995. *Ethnic Politics in Eastern Europe: A Guide to Nationality Policies, Organizations, and Parties*. Washington, D.C.: Center for Strategic and International Studies.

———. 2004. *Cold Peace: Russia's New Imperialism*. Washington, D.C.: Center for Strategic and International Studies.

Bujošević, D., and I. Radovanović. 2001. *October 5: A Twenty-Four Hour Coup*. Belgrade: Media Center.

———. 2003. *The Fall of Milošević: The October 5th Revolution*. New York: Palgrave Macmillan.

Bunce, V. 2003. "Rethinking Recent Democratization: Lessons from the Postcommunist Experience." *World Politics* 55: 167-92.

Bunce, V., and S. Wolchik. 2006. "International Diffusion and Postcommunist Electoral Revolutions." *Communist and Post-Communist Studies* 39, no. 3: 283-304.

———. 2007. "Youth and Postcommunist Electoral Revolutions: Never Trust Anyone Over 30?" In Forbrig, J. and P. Demes, *Reclaiming Democracy: Civil Society and Electoral Change in Central and Eastern Europe*. Washington, D.C.: German Marshall Fund of the United States.

———. 2009. "Getting Real About Real Causes" *Journal of Democracy* 20, no. 1: 69-73.

———. 2011. *Defeating Authoritarian Leaders in Postcommunist Countries*. New York: Cambridge University Press.

Burnell, P. 2000a. "Promoting Parties and Party Systems in New Democracies: Is There Anything the International Community Can Do?" Paper presented at the Political Studies Association-UK 50th Annual Conference 10-13 April 2000, London.

———, ed. 2000b. *Democracy Assistance: International Cooperation for Democratization*. London: Frank Class.

———. 2004a. "The Domestic Political Impact of Foreign Aid: Recalibrating the Research Agenda." *European Journal of Development Research* 16, no. 2: 396-416.

———. 2004b. *Building Better Democracies: Why Political Parties Matter*. London: Westminster Foundation for Democracy.

———, ed. 2006. *Globalising Democracy: Party Politics in Emerging Democracies*. London: Routledge.

Burnell, P., and A. W. M. Gerrits. 2010. "Promoting Party Politics in Emerging Democracies." *Democratization* 7, no. 6:1065-86.

Bussey, J. 2000. "Campaign Finance Goes Global." *Foreign Policy*, 118: 74–84.

Calingaert, D. 2006. "Election Rigging and How to Fight it" *Journal of Democracy* 17 no. 3: 138–151.

Carothers, T. 1999. *Aiding Democracy Abroad: The Learning Curve*. Washington, D.C.: Carnegie Endowment for International Peace.

———. 2001. "Ousting Foreign Strongmen: Lessons from Serbia." In T. Carothers, ed., *Critical Mission: Essays on Democracy Promotion*. Washington, D.C.: Carnegie Endowment for International Peace.

———. 2002. "The End of the Transition Paradigm." *Journal of Democracy* 13, no. 1: 5–21.

———. 2006a. *Confronting the Weakest Link: Aiding Political Parties in New Democracies*. Washington, D.C.: Carnegie Endowment for International Peace.

———. 2006b. "Examining Political Party Aid." In P. Burnell, ed. *Globalising Democracy*. London: Routledge.

———. 2006c. "The Backlash Against Democracy Promotion." *Foreign Affairs* 85, no. 2: 55–68.

———. 2007. "How Democracies Emerge: The 'Sequencing' Fallacy." *Journal of Democracy* 18, no. 1: 12–27.

Catón, M. 2007. *Effective Party Assistance: Stronger Parties for Better Democracy*. Stockholm: International IDEA.

Center for the Study of Democracy. 2004. *Partners in Crime: The Risk of Symbiosis Between the Security Sector and Organized Crime in Southeast Europe*. Sofia: Center for the Study of Democracy.

Cevallos, A. 2001. "Whither the Bulldozer? Nonviolent Revolution and the Transition to Democracy in Serbia." Washington DC: United States Institute of Peace.

Checkel, J. T. 2001. "Why Comply? Social Learning and European Identity Change." *International Organization* 55, no. 3: 553–88.

Clinton Presidential Library. 2006. "Inventory for FOIA Request 2006-0206-F." Little Rock: Clinton Presidential Library.

CMS. 2006. *Annual Report 2006*. Belgrade: Center for Modern Skills.

Cohen, L. 1993. *Broken Bonds: The Disintegration of Yugoslavia*. Boulder, Colo.: Westview Press.

———. 2001. *Serpent in the Bosom: The Rise and Fall of Slobodan Milošević*. Boulder, Colo.: Westview Press.

———. 2005. "Political Violence and Organized Crime in Serbia: The Impact of Democratization." In W. J. Crotty, ed. *Democratic Development and Political Terrorism: The Global Perspective*. Boston: Northeastern University Press, pp. 396–419.

Cohen, M., and M. Kupcu. 2009. *Revitalizing U.S. Democracy Promotion: Comprehensive Plan for Reform*. Washington, D.C.: New America Foundation.

Committee on Evaluation of USAID Democracy Assistance Programs. 2008. *Improving*

Democracy Assistance: Building Knowledge Through Evaluations and Research. Washington, D.C.: National Academies Press.

Cook, T. J., and I. Spalatin. 2002. "Final Evaluation of OTI's Program in Serbia-Montenegro." Final Report. Arlington, Va.: Development Associates.

Cortright, D., and G. A. Lopez. 2000. *The Sanctions Decade: Assessing UN Strategies in the 1990s*. Boulder, Colo.: Lynne Reinner.

Cotta, M. 1996. "Structuring the New Party Systems After the Dictatorship: Coalitions, Alliances, Fusions and Splits During the Transition and Post-Transition Stages." In G. Pridam and P. G. Lewis. *Stabilizing Fragile Democracies: Comparing New Party Systems in Southern and Eastern Europe*. London: Routledge, pp. 69-99.

Council of Europe. 2000. "Annual Report CFSP 1999." Adopted by the Council on 10 April 2000.

———. 2007. "European Commission for Democracy Through Law: Venice Commission— Opinion on the Constitution of Serbia." Adopted by the European Commission at its seventieth plenary session.

Cox, M., G. J. Ikenberry, and T. Inoguchi. 2000. *American Democracy Promotion: Impulses, Strategies, and Impacts*. New York: Oxford University Press.

Craner, L.W. and Wollack, K. 2008. "New Directions for Democracy Promotion." Washington, D.C.: Better World Campaign, International Republican Institute, and National Democratic Institute, 2008.

Crawford, G. 2003. "Promoting Democracy from Without—Learning from Within: Part I." *Democratization* 10, no. 1: 77-98.

Crawford, G., and I. Kearton. 2002. *Evaluating Democracy and Governance Assistance*. United Kingdom, Center for Development Studies, Institute for Politics and International Studies, University of Leeds.

Crotty, W. J., ed. 2005. *Democratic Development and Political Terrorism: The Global Perspective*. Upne.

CSCE. 1999. "The Milošević Regime versus Serbian Democracy and Balkan Stability." Hearing before the Commission on Security and Cooperation in Europe, 105th Congress, 2nd session, 10 December 1998. Washington D.C.: U.S. Government Printing Office, 1999.

Cvejić, S. 1997. "Demokratija sa Kolektivnim Predumišljajem: Opšti karakter protesta 1996/97" [Democracy with Collective Premeditation: General Character of 1996/97 Protest]. In M. Babović, ed., *Ajmo, 'Ajde, Svi u Šetnju: Gradjanski i Studentski Protest 96/97* [Let's All Go Walking: Civil and Student Protest 96/97]. Belgrade: Medija Centar i Institut za Socioloska Istrazivanja Filozofskog Fakulteta u Beogradu.

Cvetković, V. 2002. *(Re)Konstrukcija Institucija: Godinu Dana Tranzicije u Srbiji* [Reconstructing Institutions: One Year of Transition in Serbia]. Belgrade: Institut za filozofiju i društvenu teoriju.

Dakowska, D. 2005. "German Political Foundations: Transnational Party Go-Betweens in the Process of EU Enlargement." In W. Kaiser and P. Starie. *Transnational European Union*. London: Routledge, pp. 150-69.

Dalacoura, K. 2005. "U.S. Democracy Promotion in the Arab Middle East Since 11 September 2011: A Critique." *International Affairs* 81, no. 5: 963-79.

Dalton, R. J., and M. P. Wattenberg. 2002. *Parties Without Partisans: Political Change in Advanced Industrial Democracies*. New York: Oxford University Press.

DANIDA. 2000. *Evaluation of Danish Support to Promotion of Human Rights and Democratization 1990-1998: 1 Synthesis Report*. Copenhagen: Danish Ministry of Foreign Affairs.

Dawisha, K., and B. Parrot. 1997. *Politics, Power, and the Struggle for Democracy in South-East Europe*. New York: Cambridge University Press.

De Zeeuw, J., ed. 2008. *From Soldiers to Politicians: Transforming Rebel Movements After Civil War*. Boulder: Lynne Rienner.

Del Ponte, C. 2008. *Madame Prosecutor: Confrontations with Humanity's Worst Criminals and the Culture of Impunity*. Milan: Feltrinelli Editore.

Democracy International. 2007. "A Study of Political Party Assistance in Eastern Europe and Eurasia." Washington, D.C.: USAID.

Di Palma, G. 1990. *To Craft Democracies: An Essay on Democratic Transitions*. Berkeley: University of California Press.

Diamond. L. 1997. *Consolidating the Third Wave of Democracies: Themes and Perspectives*. Baltimore: John Hopkins University Press.

———. 2002. "Thinking About Hybrid Regimes." *Journal of Democracy* 13, no. 2: 21-35.

———. 2003. "Can the Whole World Become Democratic? Democracy, Development, and International Policies." Working Paper, Berkeley: University of California, Center for the Study of Democracy.

———. 2006. *Squandered Victory: The American Occupation and the Bungled Effort to Bring Democracy to Iraq*. New York: Owl Books.

———. 2008a. "Democratization in the Twenty-First Century." In P. F. Nardulli, ed., *International Perspectives on Contemporary Democracy*. Urbana: University of Illinois Press.

———. 2008b. *The Spirit of Democracy: The Struggle to Build Free Societies Throughout the World*. New York: Henry Holt.

Diamond, L., and R. Gunther, eds. 2001. *Political Parties and Democracy*. Baltimore: Johns Hopkins University Press.

Dimitrijević, N. 2008. "Serbia After the Criminal Past: What Went Wrong and What Should be Done." *International Journal of Transitional Justice* 2, no. 1: 5-22.

Dobbins, J. 2007. "Who Lost Iraq? Lessons from the Debacle." *Foreign Affairs* 86, no. 5: 61-74.

Dodder, D., and L. Branson. 1999. *Milošević: Portrait of a Tyrant*. New York: Free Press.

Doorenspleet, R. 2004. "The Structural Context of Recent Transitions to Democracy." *European Journal of Political Research* 43, no. 3: 309-35.

Drašković, V. 2007. *Meta*. [Target]. Belgrade: Kompanija Novosti.

Drew, E. 1994. *On the Edge: The Clinton Presidency*. New York: Touchstone.

Đurković, M. 2006. "Political Parties in Serbia: Source of Political Instability." Oxford: Conflict Studies Research Centre.

———. 2007. "Problemi institucionalizacije partijskog sistema" [Problems of the Institutionalization of the Party System]. In *Srbija 2000-2006: Drzava, Drustvo, Privreda* [Serbia 2000-2006: State, Society, and Economy]. Belgrade: Institute for European Studies, pp. 39-62.

Duverger, M. 1959. *Political Parties: Their Organization and Activity in the Modern State.* London: John Wiley.

EC. 2011a. "Multi-Annual Indicative Planning Document: Instrument for Pre-Accession Assistance 2011-2013, Republic of Serbia." Brussels: European Commission.

———. 2011b. "Communication from the Commission to the European Parliament and the Council: Commission's Opinion on Serbia's Application for Membership of the European Union." Analytical Report, SEC 2011. 1208, Brussels, 10 December 2011.

Edmunds, T. 2008a. "Intelligence Agencies and Democratization: Continuity and Change in Serbia After Milošević." *Europe-Asia Studies* 60, no. 1: 25-48.

———. 2008b. *Security Sector Reform in Transforming Societies: Croatia, Serbia and Montenegro.* Manchester: Manchester University Press.

———. 2009. "Illiberal Resilience in Serbia." *Journal of Democracy* 20, no.1:128-42.

Eke, S. M., and T. Kuzio. 2000. "Sultanism in Eastern Europe: The Socio-Political Roots of Authoritarian Populism in Belarus." *Europe-Asia Studies* 52, no. 3: 523-47.

Emerson, M., and S. Aydin. 2005. *Democratization in the European Neighborhood.* Brussels: Center for European Policy Studies.

Enyedi, Z. 2006. "Party Politics in Post-Communist Transition." In R. S. Katz and W. Crotty, ed., *Handbook of Party Politics*, pp. 228-38.

Erdmann, G. 2006. "Hesitant Bedfellows: The German Stiftungen and Party Aid in Africa." In P. Burnell, ed., *Globalising Democracy: Party Politics in Emerging Democracies.* London: Routledge, pp. 181-99.

Erhardy, P. 2006. "Mapping the Activities of Democracy Assistance Foundations in the Western Balkans and the Black Sea Region." Olof Palme International Center.

Ethier, D. 2003. "Is Democracy Promotion Effective? Comparing Conditionality and Incentives." *Democratization* 10, no. 1: 99-120.

Fairbanks, C. H. 2007. "Revolution Reconsidered." *Journal of Democracy* 18, no. 1: 42-57.

Feldman, L. G. 2001. "Cooperative Differences in the U.S. and EU Balkans Policies: An American Perspective on the Political Dimension." *AICGS German Issues* 26/2001.

FES. 2005. "Democratic Party and European Social Democracy." Belgrade: Friedrich-Ebert-Stiftung.

———. 2006. *10 Godina u Srbiji* [10 Years in Serbia]. Belgrade: Friedrich-Ebert-Stiftung.

———. 2009. "Committed to Social Democracy: Political Education, International Cooperation, Scholarship Program, Research and Consulting." Berlin: Friedrich-Ebert-Stiftung.

Finnemore, M., and K. Sikkink, 1998. "International Norm Dynamics and Political Change." *International Organization* 52, no. 4: 887-917.

Fish, S. 2000. "The Executive Deception: Superpresidentialism and the Degradation of

Russian Politics." In Valerie Sperling, ed., "Building the Russian State: Institutional Crisis and the Quest for Democratic Governance." Oxford: Westview Press.

Forbrig, J., and P. Demeš, eds. 2007. *Reclaiming Democracy: Civil Society and Electoral Change in Central and Eastern Europe*. Washington, D.C.: German Marshall Fund of the United States.

Fukuyama, F., and M. McFaul. 2007 "Should Democracy Be Promoted or Demoted?" *The Washington Quarterly* 31, no. 1: 23–45.

Gagnon, C. 1994. "Serbia's Road to War." *Journal of Democracy* 5, no. 2: 117–31.

———. 1995. "Historical Roots of the Yugoslav Conflict." In Esman, M., and S. Telhami, eds., *International Organizations and Ethnic Conflict*. Ithaca, N.Y.: Cornell University Press, pp. 179–97.

———. 1998. "International Non-Governmental Organizations and 'Democracy Assistance' in Serbia." *Carnegie Project on Evaluating NGO Strategies for Democratization and Conflict Prevention in the Formerly Communist States*.

Gandhi, J., and A. Przeworski. 2007. "Authoritarian Institutions and the Survival of Autocrats." *Comparative Political Studies* 40, no. 11: 1279–1301.

Gandhi, J., and O. J. Reuter. 2008. "Opposition Coordination in Legislative Elections under Authoritarianism." Paper presented at the Annual Meeting of American Political Science Association, Boston, 28 August 2008.

Geddes, B. 2007. "Why Parties Are Created After Authoritarian Seizures of Power." Paper presented at the 2007 Annual Meeting of the American Political Science Association, Chicago, 30 August 2007.

———. 2008. "Party Creation as an Autocratic Survival Strategy." Presented at the Conference on Dictators, Princeton University, April 2008.

Gel'man, V. 2006, "From 'Feckless Pluralism' to 'Dominant Power Politics'? The Transformation of Russia's Party System." *Democratization* 13, no. 4: 545–61.

Genovese, M. A., and M. J. Streb. 2004. *Polls and Politics: The Dilemmas of Democracy*. New York: State University of New York Press.

George, A., and A. Bennett. 2004. *Case Studies and Theory Development in the Social Sciences*. Cambridge: MIT Press.

Gerring, J. 2001. *Social Science Methodology: A Critical Framework*. New York: Cambridge University Press.

———. 2006. *Case Study Research: Principles and Practices*. New York: Cambridge University Press.

Gershman, A. 2006. "The Assault on Democracy Assistance." *Journal of Democracy* 17, no. 2: 36–51.

Goati, V. 1995. "Peculiarities of the Serbian Political Scene." In V. Goati, ed., *Challenges of Parliamentarism: The Case of Serbia in the Early Nineties*. Belgrade: Institute of Social Science.

———. 2000. *Elections in FRY: From 1990 to 1998*. Belgrade: CeSID.

———. 2001. "The Nature of the Order and the October Overthrow in Serbia." In I.

Spasić and M. Subotić, eds., "Revolution and Order: Serbia After October 2000."
Belgrade: Institute for Philosophy and Social Theory, pp. 45-58.

———. 2004. *Partije i Partijski Sistem u Srbiji* [Parties and Party System in Serbia]. Belgrade: OGI Center.

———. 2005. "Internal Relations of Political Parties in Serbia." In W. Karasimeonov, ed., *Organizational Structures and Internal Party Democracy in South Eastern Europe.* Sofia: GorexPress, pp. 11-25.

———. 2006. *Partijske Borbe u Srbiji u Postoktobarskon Razdoblju* [Party Struggles in Post-October Serbia]. Belgrade: FES and the Institute for Social Science.

Gordy, E. 1999. *The Culture of Power in Serbia: Nationalism and the Destruction of Alternatives.* University Park, Pa.: Pennsylvania State University Press.

———. 2000. "Serbia's Bulldozer Revolution: Conditions and Prospects." *South European Politics* 1, no. 2: 78-89.

Government Accountability Office. 2009. "Democracy Assistance: U.S. Agencies Take Steps to Coordinate International Programs But Lack Information on Some U.S.-Funded Activities." Washington, D.C.: Report to Congressional Committees, September 2009.

Grabbe, H. 2006. *The EU's Transformative Power: Europeanization Through Conditionality in Central and Eastern Europe.* London: Palgrave.

Grabow, K. 2007. *KAS Democracy Report 2007: Parties and Democracy.* Berlin: Konrad Adenauer Stiftung.

Green, A. T., and R. D. Kohl. 2007. "Challenges of Evaluating Democracy Assistance: Perspectives from the Donor Side." *Democratization* 14, no. 1: 151-65.

Grugle, J. 2002. *Democratization: A Critical Introduction.* London: Routledge.

Gunther, R., and L. Diamond, L. 2003. "Species of Political Parties: A New Typology." *Party Politics* 9, no. 2 167-99.

G17 Plus. 2000. "Program of the Democratic Opposition of Serbia: For a Democratic Serbia." Belgrade: G17 Plus.

Hajdinjak, M. 2002. *Smuggling in Southeast Europe: The Yugoslav Wars and the Development of Regional Criminal Networks in the Balkans.* Sofia: Center for the Study of Democracy.

Hall, P. A., and R. C. R. Taylor. 2006. "Political Science and the Three New Institutionalisms." *Political Studies* 44, no. 5: 936-57.

Hammarberg, T. 2009. "Report by the Commissioner for Human Rights, Thomas Hammarberg, on His Visit to Serbia. 13-17 October 2008." Strasbourg, 11 March 2009.

Haselock. S. 2010. "Make It Theirs: The Imperative of Local Ownership in Communications and Media Initiatives." *United States Institute of Peace,* Special Report 253.

Hay, C. 2002. *Political Analysis: A Critical Introduction.* London: Routledge.

Hayden, R. M. 1992. "Constitutional Nationalism in the Formerly Yugoslav Republics." *Slavic Review* 51, no. 4: 654-73.

Haughton, T. 2007. "When Does the EU Make a Difference? Conditionality and the

Accession Process in Central and Eastern Europe." *Political Studies Review* 5, no. 2: 233–46.

Held, D. 1996. *Models of Democracy*. Cambridge: Polity Press.

Henderson, S. L. 2002. "Selling Civil Society: Western Aid and the Nongovernmental Organization Sector in Russia." *Comparative Political Science* 35: 139 –67.

Hockenos, P. 2003. *Homeland Calling: Exile Patriotism and the Balkan Wars*. New York: Cornell University Press.

Holbrooke, R. 1999. *To End a War*. New York: Random House.

Houngnikpo, M. 2003. "Pax Democratica: The Gospel According to Saint Democracy." *Australian Journal of Politics and History* 29, no. 3, 2003: 197–210.

Howard, M. M., and P. G. Roessler. 2006. "Liberalizing Electoral Outcomes in Competitive Authoritarian Regimes." *American Journal of Political Science* 50, no. 2: 365–81.

Huntington, S. 1968. *Political Order in Changing Societies*. New Haven, Conn.: Yale University Press.

———. 1991. *The Third Wave: Democratization in the Late Twentieth Century*. Norman: University of Oklahoma Press.

ICG. 1999. "Sidelining Slobodan: Getting Rid of Europe's Last Dictator." International Crisis Group, Europe Report no. 57.

———. 2000a. "Serbia on the Eve of the December Elections." International Crisis Group, Balkans Briefing, 20 December 2000.

———. 2000b. "Sanctions Against the Federal Republic of Yugoslavia (as of 10 October 2000)." Balkans Briefing, Washington/Brussels.

———. 2003. "Serbia After Đinđić." Balkans Report no. 141, Belgrade/Brussels.

Innes, A. 2002. "Party Competition in Postcommunist Europe: The Great Electoral Lottery." *Comparative Politics* 35, no. 1: 85–104.

IREX. 2001. "Serbia (Federal Republic of Yugoslavia)." In *Media Sustainability Index 2001*, International Research and Exchanges Board. Washington, D.C.: IREX, pp. 205–14.

———. 2002. "Serbia." In *Media Sustainability Index 2002*, IREX. Washington, D.C.: IREX, pp. 87–97.

IRI. 1997. "Quarterly Report July–September 1997: Serbia." USAID Cooperative Agreement Number EE-A-00-00028-00.

———. 1998. "Quarterly Report April–June 1998: Serbia." USAID Cooperative Agreement Number EE-A-00-00028-00.

———. 1999. "Quarterly Report July–September 1999: Serbia." USAID Cooperative Agreement Number EE-A-00-00028-00.

———. 2000. "Quarterly Report October–December 2000: Serbia." USAID Cooperative Agreement Number EE-A-00-0001300.

———. 2001. "Quarterly Report January–March 2001: Serbia." USAID Cooperative Agreement Number 169-G-00-00-00112-00.

———. 2004a. "Quarterly Report April–June 2004: Serbia." USAID Cooperative Agreement Number 169-A-00-01-00116-00.

———. 2004b. "Quarterly Report July–September 2004: Serbia." USAID Cooperative Agreement Number 169-A-00-0100116-00.

———. 2004c. "Quarterly Report January–March 2004: Serbia." USAID Cooperative Agreement Number 169-A-0001-00116-00.

———. 2006a. "Quarterly Report July–September 2006: Serbia." USAID Cooperative Agreement Number 169-A-00-01-00116-00.

———. 2006b. "Quarterly Report October–December 2006: Serbia." USAID 169-A-00-01-00116-00.

———. 2007a. "Quarterly Report January–March 2007: Serbia." USAID Cooperative Agreement Number 169-A-00-01-00116-00.

———. 2007b. "Quarterly Report October–December 2007: Serbia." USAID Cooperative Agreement Number 169-A-00-01-00116-00.

———. 2008a. "Quarterly Report January–March 2008: Serbia." USAID Cooperative Agreement Number 169-A-00-01-00116-00.

———. 2008b. "Quarterly Report April–June 2008: Serbia." USAID Cooperative Agreement Number 169-A-00-01-00116-00.

———. 2008c. "Serbia: Democratization and Stabilization Through Responsive Political Parties and Constituent Outreach—CEPPS/NDI Quarterly Report: April 1 to June 30, 2008." USAID Associate Award no. 169-A-00-06-0015-00 under the Leader Cooperative Agreement no. DGC-A-00-01-00004-00.

———. 2008d. "CEPPS/IRI Quarterly Report January–March 2008—Serbia: Strengthening the Democratic Political Process." USAID Cooperative Agreement no. 169-A-00-06-00103-00.

———. 2008e. "CEPPS/IRI Quarterly Report April–June 2008—Serbia: Strengthening the Democratic Political Process." USAID Cooperative Agreement no. 169-A-00-06-00103-00.

Ishiyama, J. 2008. "Political Party Development and Party 'Gravity' in Semi-Authoritarian States: The Cases of Azerbaijan, Kyrgyzstan, and Tajikistan." *Taiwan Journal of Democracy* 4, no. 1: 33–53.

Jacoby, W. 2004. *The Enlargement of the European Union and NATO: Ordering from the Menu in Central Europe.* New York: Cambridge University Press.

Jamieson, K. H. 1992. *Dirty Politics: Deception, Distraction, and Democracy.* New York: Oxford University Press.

Jennings, R. 2009. "Serbia's Bulldozer Revolution: Evaluating Internal and External Factors in Successful Democratic Breakthrough." CDDRL Working Paper, Stanford University.

Joksić, M. 2008. "Serbia's Bulldozer Revolution Reconsidered: Examining the Consequences of Pacted Transition in Cases of Regime Hybridity." The Hague: Master's thesis for the Graduate School of Development Studies at the Institute of Social Studies.

Jovanović, C. 2005. *Moj Sukob S Prošlošću: Srbija 2000-2005* [My Struggle with the Past: Serbia 2000-2005]. Belgrade: Dan Graf Danas.

Jovanović, M. 1997. *Izborni Sistemi: Izbori u Srbiji 1990-1996* [Electoral Systems: Elections in Serbia 1990-1996]. Belgrade: Sluzbeni Glasnik.

———. 2002. "Izborn Reforme—Slucaj Srbija" [Electoral Reforms—The Case of Serbia], *Nova Srpska Politicka Misao* 9, no. 1-4.

Kaldor, M. 2003. "Intervention in the Balkans: An Unfinished Learning Process." In P. Siani-Davies, ed., *International Intervention in the Balkans Since 1995*. London: Routledge.

Kaldor, M., and I. Vejvoda. 1997. "Democratization in Central and East European Countries." *International Affairs* 73, no. 1: 59-82.

Katz, R. S., and P. Mair. 1995. "Changing Models of Party Organization and Party Democracy: The Emergence of the Cartel Party." *Party Politics* 1, no.1: 5-28.

Kesić, O. 2005. "An Airplane with Eighteen Pilots: Serbia After Milošević." In S. Ramet and V. Pavlaković, eds., *Serbia Since 1989: Politics and Society Under Milošević and After*. Seattle: University of Washington Press, pp. 95-124.

Key, V. O. 1964. *Politics, Parties, and Pressure Groups*. New York: Crowell.

King, G., R. O. Keohane, and S. Verba. 1994. *Designing Social Inquiry: Scientific Inference in Qualitative Research*. Princeton, N.J.: Princeton University Press.

Kirchheimer, O. 1966. "The Transformation of the Western European Party System," In J. La Palombara and M. Weiner, *Political Parties and Political Development*. Princeton: Princeton University Press, pp. 184–192.

Kitschelt, H. 1995. "Party Systems in East Central Europe: Consolidation or Fluidity?" *Studies in Public Policy*. Glasgow: Center for the Study of Public Policy, University of Strathclyde, no. 241.

Kitschelt, H., Z. Mansfeldova, R. Markowski, and G. Toka. 1999. *Post-Communist Party Systems: Competition, Representation, and Inter-Party Cooperation*. New York: Cambridge University Press.

Knack, S. 2004. "Does Foreign Aid Promote Democracy?" *International Studies Quarterly* 48, no. 1: 251-66.

Knudsen, R. A. 2008. *The Comprehensive UN Sanctions Against the Federal Republic of Yugoslavia: Aims, Impact, and Legacy*. Norway: Kolofon.

Konitzer, A., and J. Grujic. 2009. "An Electorate Adrift: Refugees and Elections in Post-Milošević Serbia." *Europe-Asia Studies* 61, no. 5: 857–874.

Kopecký, P. 1995. "Developing Party Organizations in East-Central Europe." *Party Politics* 1, no. 4: 515-34.

Kopstein, J. 2006. "The Transatlantic Divide Over Democracy Promotion." *Washington Quarterly* 29, no. 2: 85-98.

Krnjević–Mišković, D. 2001. "Serbia's Prudent Revolution." *Journal of Democracy* 12, no. 3: 96-110.

Kumar, K. 2004. "International Political Party Assistance: An Overview and Analysis." Working Paper 33, Conflict Research Program, Netherlands Institute of International Relations, The Hague: Clingendael.

———. 2005. "Reflections on International Party Assistance." *Democratization* 12, no. 4: 506-28.

Kuzio, T. 2006. "Civil Society, Youth, and Societal Mobilization in Democratic Revolutions." *Communist and Post-Communist Studies* 39, no. 3: 365-86.

Laarhoven, J. V. 2008. "Political Party Building in Eastern Europe." *Eur View* 7: 75-80.

Ladrech, R. 2002. "Europeanization and Political Parties: Towards a Framework for Analysis." *Party Politics* 8, no. 4: 389-403.

Legro, J. W. 1997. "Which Norms Matter? Revisiting the Failure of Internationalism." *International Organization* 51, no. 1: 31-63.

Levitsky, S., and L. A. Way. 2002. "The Rise of Competitive Authoritarianism." *Journal of Democracy* 13. no. 2: 51-65.

———. 2010. *Competitive Authoritarianism: Hybrid Regimes After the Cold War.* New York: Cambridge University Press.

Lewis, P. G. 2001. "The 'Third Wave' of Democracy in Eastern Europe: Comparative Perspectives on Party Roles and Political Development." *Party Politics* 7, no. 5: 543-65.

———. 2003. *Political Parties in Post-Communist Eastern Europe.* London: Routledge.

———. 2006. "Party Systems in Post-Communist Central Europe: Patterns of Stability and Consolidation." *Democratization* 13, no. 4: 562-83.

Lewis, P. G., and Z. Mansfeldova, eds. 2007. *European Union and Party Politics in Central and Eastern Europe.* New York: Palgrave Macmillan.

Lipset. S. 1959. "Some Social Requisites of Democracy: Economic Development and Political Legitimacy." *American Political Science Review* 53, no. 1: 69-105.

———. 2000. "The Indispensability of Political Parties." *Journal of Democracy* 11, no. 1: 48-55.

Linz, J. J., and A. Stepan. 1996. *Problems of Democratic Transition and Consolidation: Southern Europe, South America, and Post-Communist Europe.* Baltimore: Johns Hopkins University Press.

Little, A., and L. Silber. 1995. *The Death of Yugoslavia.* London: Penguin.

Lust-Okar, E. 2005. *Structuring Conflict in the Arab World: Incumbents, Opponents, and Institutions.* New York: Cambridge University Press.

Lutovac, Z., ed. 2005. *Političke Stranke u Srbiji: Struktura i Funkcionisanje* [Political Parties in Serbia: Structure and Function]. Belgrade: Friedrich-Ebert-Stiftung/Institut društvenih nauka.

———. 2006. *Demokratija u Političkim Strankama Srbije* [Democracy in Political Parties of Serbia]. Belgrade: Friedrich-Ebert-Stiftung/Institut društvenih nauka.

———. 2007. "Nacionalne manjine u evropskim standardima i politickom životu Srbije" [National Minorities in European Standards and Political Life of Serbia]. In Z. Lutovac, ed., *Političke Stranke u Srbiji i Evropska unija* [Political Parties in Serbia and the EU]. Belgrade: Friedrich-Ebert-Stiftung/Fakultet politickih nauka, pp. 211-40.

Mahoney, J. 2001. "Path-Dependent Explanations of Regime Change: Central America in Comparative Perspective." *Studies in Comparative International Development* 36, no. 1: 111-41.

Mainwaring, S. 1998. "Party Systems in the Third Wave." *Journal of Democracy* 9, no. 3: 67-81.

Mainwaring, S., and T. Scully, eds. 1995. *Building Democratic Institutions: Party Systems in Latin America*. Stanford, Calif.: Stanford University Press.

Mair, S. 2000. "Germany's *Stiftungen* and Democracy Assistance: Comparative Advantages, New Challenges." In P. Burnell, ed., *Democracy Assistance: International Cooperation for Democratization*. London: Frank Cass.

Markovich, S. 2007. "Serbia." In K. D. Evenson and J. Geohring, *Nations in Transit 2007: Pause and Pushback for Democratization*. New York: Freedom House, pp. 603-28.

———. 2009. "Serbia." In V. D. Shkolnikov, *Nations in Transit 2009: Democracy's Dark Year*. New York: Freedom House, pp. 441-57.

Marshall, T. 2003. *Igra Senki* [Shadow Games]. Belgrade: B92.

McCarthy, P. 1997. "Serbia's Opposition Speaks." *Journal of Democracy* 8, no. 3, pp.3-16.

McClear, R., S. McClear, and P. Graves. 2003. "U.S. Media Assistance Programs in Serbia." Washington, D.C.: USAID Bureau for Policy and Program Coordination.

McFaul, M. 2004. "Democracy Promotion as a World Value." *Washington Quarterly* 28, no.1: 147-63.

———. 2005. "Transitions from Postcommunism." *Journal of Democracy* 16, no. 3: 5-19.

———. 2006. "The National Endowment for Democracy's Programs in Serbia Supporting the Breakthrough Elections of 2000." Report prepared for the National Endowment for Democracy, August 2006.

———. 2009. *Advancing Democracy Abroad: Why We Should and How We Can*. Stanford, Calif.: Rowman and Littlefield.

McFaul, M., A. Magen, and K. Stoner-Weiss. 2007. "Evaluating International Influences on Democratic Transitions: Concept Paper." Stanford, Calif.: Stanford University.

Mendelson, S. 2001. "Democracy Assistance and Political Transition in Russia: Between Success and Failure." *International Security* 25, no. 4: 68-106.

———. 2004. "The Seven Ingredients: When Democracy Promotion Works." *Harvard International Review* 26: 87-88.

Mendelson, S., and J. Glenn. 2002, *The Power and Limits of NGOs: A Critical Look at Building Democracy in Eastern Europe and Eurasia*. New York: Columbia University Press.

Mićunović, D. 2000. *Okrugli Sto Demokratske Opozicije Srbije* [Round Table of the Democratic Opposition of Serbia]. Belgrade: Democratic Center.

Miller, N. J. 1997. "A Failed Transition: The Case of Serbia." In K. Dawisha and B. Parrot. *Politics, Power, and the Struggle for Democracy in South-East Europe*. New York: Cambridge University Press, 1997.

Milosavljević, M. 2005. "Finansiranje političkih stranaka u Srbiji iz javnih izvora: norme i praksa" [Financing of Political Parties in Serbia from Public Sources: Norms and Practice]. In Z. Lutovac, ed., *Političke stranke u Srbiji. Struktura i Funkcionisanje* [Political Parties in Serbia: Structure and Functioning]. Belgrade: Friedrich-Ebert-Stiftung/Institut društvenih nauka, pp. 93-105.

Minić, J., and M. Dereta. 2007. "Izlaz 2000: An Exit to Democracy in Serbia." In J. Forbrig and P. Demeš, *Reclaiming Democracy: Civil Society and Electoral Change in Central and Eastern Europe*. Washington, D.C.: German Marshall Fund of the United States.

Mitchell, L. 2009. *Uncertain Democracy: U.S. Foreign Policy and Georgia's Rose Revolution*. Philadelphia: University of Pennsylvania Press.

———. 2012. *The Color Revolutions*. Philadelphia: University of Pennsylvania Press.

Montgomery, W. 2010. *Kad Ovacije Utihnu: Borba s demokratskom tranzicijom—Sećanja poslednjeg americkog ambasadora u Jugoslaviji* [*Struggling with Democratic Transition: After the Cheering Stops—Memoirs of the Last American Ambassador to Yugoslavia*]. Belgrade: Dan Graf Club Plus.

Moore, B. 1966. *Social Origins of Dictatorship: Lord and Peasant in the Making of the Modern World*. Boston: Beacon.

Nardulli, P. F., ed. 2008. *International Perspectives on Contemporary Democracy*. Urbana: University of Illinois Press.

Naylor, R. T. 1999. *Patriots and Profiteers: On Economic Warfare, Embargo Busting and State-Sponsored Crimes*. Toronto: McLelland and Stewart.

NDI. 1998. "Federal Republic of Yugoslavia: Political Party Building and Election Preparation." USAID Cooperative Agreement no. EUR-A-00-94-00028-00, August 1997 to June 1998.

———. 1999. "Serbia Issues Poll." 24 October 1999. Washington, D.C.: Penn Schoen Berland.

———. 2001. "NDI Serbia Regional Trainer Policy Handbook." Updated 23 June 2001.

———. 2002. "Quarterly Report Serbia: Political Party Building and Civil Society Development July1–September 30, 2002." USAID Cooperative Agreement no. 169-A-00-01-00115-00.

———. 2003. "Quarterly Report Serbia: Political Party Building and Civil Society Development April 1 to June 30, 2003." USAID Cooperative Agreement no. 169-A-00-01-00115-00.

———. 2004a. "Quarterly Report Serbia: Political Party Building and Civil Society Development April 1 to June 30, 2004." USAID Cooperative Agreement no. 169-A-00-01-00115-00.

———. 2004b. "Political Party Building, Good Governance, and Citizen Political Participation Workplan April 1, 2004–March 31, 2005."

———. 2004c. "Quarterly Report Serbia: Political Party Building and Civil Society Development October 1 to December 31, 2004." USAID Cooperative Agreement no. 169-A-00-01-00115-00.

———. 2005. "Quarterly Report Serbia: Political Party Building and Civil Society Development July 1 to September 30, 2004." USAID Cooperative Agreement no. 169-A-00-01-00115-00.

———. 2006a. "Serbia: Demographic Analysis for Voter Targeting—Final Report." NED Core Grant 2004-036. 04029, submitted March 2006.

———. 2006b. "Quarterly Report Serbia: Political Party Building and Civil Society

Development July 1 to September 30, 2006." USAID Cooperative Agreement no. 169-A-00-01-00115-00.

———. 2006c. "Quarterly Report Serbia: Political Party Building and Civil Society Development October 1 to December 31, 2006." USAID Cooperative Agreement no. 169-A-00-01-00115-00.

———. 2006d. "Political Party Building, Good Governance and Citizen Political Participation Workplan April 1, 2006–March 31, 2007." USAID Associate Award no. 169-A-00-06-00105-00.

———. 2007a. "Serbia: Democratization and Stabilization Through Repressive Political Parties and Constituent Outreach—CEPPS/NDI Quarterly Report: April 1 to June 30, 2007." USAID Associate Award no. 169-A-00-06-00105-00.

———. 2007b. "Serbia: Democratization and Stabilization Through Repressive Political Parties and Constituent Outreach—CEPPS/NDI Quarterly Report: January 1 to March 31, 2007." USAID Associate Award no. 169-A-00-06-00105-00.

———. 2008a. *A Guide to Political Party Development.* Washington, D.C.: National Democratic Institute for International Affairs.

———. 2008b. "Serbia: Political Party Building and Civil Society Development—NDI Quarterly Report: January 1 to March 31, 2008" USAID Cooperative Agreement no. 169-A-00-01-00115-00.

NED. 1999a. "Grant Agreement No. 99-948.0 Between the National Endowment for Democracy and the International Republican Institute." Effective date 16 August 1999 through 31 December 1999.

———. 1999b. "Grant Agreement No. 99-954.0 Between the National Endowment for Democracy and the International Republican Institute." Effective date 13 September 1999 through 31 December 1999.

———. 2006. *The Backlash Against Democracy Assistance: A Report Prepared by the NED for Senator Richard G. Lugar, Chairman, Committee on Foreign Relations United States Senate.* Washington, D.C.: National Endowment for Democracy.

Nenadović, M. 2012. *Installing Democracy in the Balkans: Analysis of Political Party Assistance in Bosnia–Herzegovina and Kosovo,* Ph.D. diss., University of Amsterdam.

Nielsen, C. A. 2001. "Normalizing Serbia." Madrid, Papeles del Este, January 2001.

Nikolayenko, O. 2012. "Nonviolent Youth Movements." Unpublished manuscript presented in New York City at Fordham University, 17 February 2012.

NIMD. 2008. "NIMD: Partner in Democracy." The Hague: Netherlands Institute for Multiparty Democracy.

Norad. 2010. "Evaluation of Norwegian Development Cooperation with the Western Balkans." Oslo, Evaluation Report 7/2010, No. 164.

Norris, P., ed. 1999. *Critical Citizens: Global Support for Democratic Governance.* New York: Oxford University Press.

———. 2004. *Election Engineering: Voting Rules and Political Behavior.* New York: Cambridge University Press.

NYU Law Review. 1999. "Constitutional Watch: A Country-by-Country Update on

Constitutional Politics in Eastern Europe and the ex-USSR." *East European Constitutional Review* 8, no. 4.

———. 2000. "Constitutional Watch: A Country-by-Country Update on Constitutional Politics in Eastern Europe and the ex-USSR." *East European Constitutional Review* 9, no. 1/2.

O'Donnell, G., and P. C. Schmitter. 1986. *Transitions from Authoritarian Rule: Tentative Conclusions About Uncertain Democracies.* Baltimore: Johns Hopkins University Press.

O'Donnell, G., P. Schmitter, and L. Whitehead, ed. 1986. *Transitions from Authoritarian Rule: Comparative Perspectives.* Baltimore: Johns Hopkins University Press.

Ohman, M., S. A. Oberh, B. Holstrom, H. Wochelberg, and V. Aberg. 2005 *Political Parties and Democracy Assistance: An Overview of the Support Provided by the Swedish Party Associated Organizations for Democracy Development in Developing Countries and Countries of Central and Eastern Europe,* Sida Evaluation 05/11. Stockholm: SIDA.

Olof Palme International Center. 2010. *Operating Policy of the Olof Palme International Center.* Stockholm: Olof Palme International Center.

Orlović, S. 2002. *Političke Partije i Moć* [Political Parties and Power]. Belgrade: Cigoja Stampa.

———. 2008. *Politički Život Srbije Izmedju Partokratije i Demokratije* [Political Life in Serbia Between Partitocracy and Democracy]. Belgrade: Sluzbeni Glasnik.

———, ed. 2011. *Partije i Izbori u Srbiji—20 godina* [Parties and Elections in Serbia—20 years]. Belgrade: Fondacija Friedrich-Ebert-Stiftung and Fakultet Političkih Nauka.

OSCE. 2001. "Republic of Serbia, Federal Republic of Yugoslavia: Parliamentary Elections 23 December 2000." Final Report, Warsaw.

———. 2004. "Republic of Serbia: Serbia and Montenegro—Presidential Election 13 June 2004." OSCE/ODIHR Needs Assessment Mission Report 29-30 April 2004.

———. 2007. "Parliamentary Elections 21 January 2007." OSCE/ODIHR Election Observation Mission Report, 26 April 2007.

———. 2008. "Republic of Serbia Presidential Election 20 January and 3 February 2008." OSCE/ODIHR Limited Election Observation Mission Final Report, Warsaw, 29 August 2008.

Ostojić, M. 2011. "International Judicial Intervention and Regime Change in Serbia 2000-2010." Ph.D. diss., Queen Mary, University of London.

Ottaway, M. 2003. *Democracy Challenged: The Rise of Semi-Authoritarianism.* Washington, D.C.: Carnegie Endowment for International Peace.

Owen, D. 1997. *Balkan Odyssey.* London: Houghton Mifflin Harcourt.

Pasquino, G. 1990. "Party Elites and Democratic Consolidation: Cross-National Comparison in Southern European Experience." In G. Pridham, ed., *Securing Democracy: Political Parties and Democratic Consolidation in Southern Europe.* London: Routledge, pp. 42-61.

Pavlaković, V. 2005. "Serbia Transformed? Political Dynamics in the Milošević Era and

After." In S. P. Ramet and V. Pavlaković, eds., *Serbia Since 1989: Politics and Society Under Milošević and After*. Seattle: University of Washington Press.

Pavlović, D. 2001. "Populist Lock." Belgrade: Institute for European Studies.

———. 2004. "Serbia During and After Milošević." Belgrade: Jefferson Institute.

———. 2007. "Political Parties and the Party System in Serbia After 2000." Paper presented at the international conference "Reshaping the Broken Image of Political Parties in South-Eastern Europe," held in Sofia, Bulgaria, 24–26 November 2006.

———, ed. 2008. *Konsolidacija Demokratskih Ustanova u Srbiji: Godinu Dana Posle* [Consolidation of Democratic Institutions in Serbia: One Year After]. Belgrade: Sluzbeni Glasnik.

Pavlović, D., and S. Antonić. 2007. *Konsolidacija Demokratskih Ustanova u Srbiji Posle 2000 Godine* [Consolidation of Democratic Institutions in Serbia After 2000]. Belgrade: Službeni Glasnik.

Pavlović, V., ed. 2006. *Političke Institucije i Demokratija* [Political Institutions and Democracy]. Belgrade: Fakultet Politickih Nauka.

Peceny, M. 1999. *Democracy at the Point of Bayonets*. University Park, PA: Penn State Press.

Pedersen, M. N. 1983. "Changing Patterns of Electoral Volatility in European Party Systems, 1948–1977: Explorations in Explanation." In H. Daalder and P. Mair, eds., *Western European Party Systems: Continuity and Change*. London: SAGE, pp. 29–66.

Penn Schoen Berland Associates. 2000. "Serbia Tracking Poll: Fourth Wave." Prepared for NDI, 20 September 2000.

Pešić, V. 2001. "The Scope of the Changes in Serbia After the October Revolution." In I. Spusić and M. Subotić. *Revolution and Order: Serbia After October 2000*. Belgrade: Institute for Philosophy and Social Theory, pp. 175–82.

———. 2007. "State Capture and Widespread Corruption in Serbia." CEPS Working Document no. 262.

Petrova, T. 2010. "Thinking About Transnational Diffusion and Cycles of Protest: The 1996–2005 Wave of Democratization in Eastern Europe." In S. Teune, ed., *The Transnational Condition: Protest Dynamics in an Entangled Europe*. Oxford: Berghahn Books, pp. 146–66.

———. 2011. "The New Role of Central and Eastern Europe in International Democracy Support." Washington, D.C.: Carnegie Endowment for International Peace.

Pevehouse, J. C. 2002. "Democracy from the Outside-In? International Organizations and Democratization." *International Organization* 56, no. 3: 515–49.

Pharr, S., and R. Putnam. 2000. *Disaffected Democracies: What's Troubling the Trilateral Countries?* Princeton, N.J.: Princeton University Press.

Pickering, P. 2010. "Assessing International Aid for Local Governance in the Western Balkans" *Democratization* 17, no. 5.

Pierson, P. 2000. "Increasing Returns, Path Dependence, and the Study of Politics." *American Political Science Review* 94, no. 2: 251–67.

Pinto-Duschinsky, M. 1991. "Foreign Political Aid: The German Political Foundations and their U.S. Counterparts." *International Affairs* 67, no. 1: 33-63.

Podunavac, M. 2005. *Srbija Izmedju Diktature i Demokratije* [Serbia Between Dictatorship and Democracy]. Belgrade: Socijaldemokratski Klub/Friedrich-Ebert-Stiftung.

Power, G. 2008. *Donor Support to Parliaments and Political Parties: An Analysis Prepared for DANIDA*. Copenhagen: DANIDA.

Powers, T. 1979. *The Man Who Kept the Secrets: Richard Helms and the CIA*. New York: Knopf.

Presnall, A. 2009. "Which Way the Wind Blows: Democracy Promotion and International Actors in Serbia." *Democratization* 16, no. 4: 661-81.

Pribićević, O. 1999. "Changing Fortunes of the Serbian Radical Party." In S. Ramet, ed., *The Radical Right in Central and Eastern Europe Since 1989*. University Park: Pennsylvania State University Press, pp. 193-212.

Pridham, G., ed. 1990. *Securing Democracy: Political Parties and Democratic Consolidation in Southern Europe*. London: Routledge.

———, ed. 1991. *Emerging Democracy: The International Context of Regime Transition in Southern Europe*. Leicester: Leicester University Press.

———. 2005. *Designing Democracy: EU Enlargement and Regime Change in Post-Communist Europe*. London: Palgrave MacMillan.

Pridham, G., and T. Verhanen, eds. *Democratization in Eastern Europe: Domestic and International Perspectives*. London: Routledge.

Przeworski, A. 1986. "Some Problems in the Study of the Transition to Democracy." In G. O'Donnell et al., *Transitions from Authoritarian Rule*. Baltimore: John Hopkins University Press, pp. 47-63.

Przeworski, A., M. Alvarez, J. A. Cheibub, and F. Limongi. 1996. "What Makes Democracies Endure?" *Journal of Democracy* 7, no. 1: 39-55.

Radojević, M. 2011. "European Standards and Constitutional Changes in Serbia." *Serbian Political Thought* 4: 81-101.

Ramet, S. 1991. "Serbia's Slobodan Milošević: A Profile." *Orbis, 1991*, pp. 93-105.

———. 2007. "The Denial Syndrome and Its Consequences: Serbian Political Culture Since 2000." *Communist and Postcommunist Studies* 40, no. 1: 41-58.

Ramet, S., and V. Pavlaković, eds. 2006. *Serbia Since 1989: Politics and Society Under Milošević and After*. Seattle: University of Washington Press.

Rand, J., J. G. McGinn, K. Crane, S. G. Jones, R. Lal, A. Rathmell, R. M. Swanger, and A. R. Timilsina. 2003. *America's Role in Nation-Building*. Washington, D.C.: RAND.

Randall, V. 2007. "Political Parties and Democratic Developmental States." *Development Policy Review* 25, no. 5: 633-52.

Randall, V., and L. Svåsand. 2002. "Party Institutionalization in New Democracies." *Party Politics* 8, no. 1: 5-29.

Ranelagh, J. 1986. *The Agency: The Rise and Decline of the CIA*. New York: Simon and Schuster.

Reeves, R. 1996. *Running in Place: How Bill Clinton Disappointed America*. New York: Andrews and McMeel.

Resende, M., and H. Kraetzschmar. 2005. "Parties of Power as Roadblocks to Democracy: The Cases of Ukraine and Egypt." In M. Emerson and S. Aydin, eds., *Democratization in the European Neighborhood*. Brussels: Center for European Policy Studies.

Reuter, O. J. 2010. "The Politics of Dominant Party Formation: United Russia and Russia's Governors." *Europe-Asia Studies* 62, no. 2: 293–327.

Reuter, O. J., and T. F. Remington. 2009. "Dominant Party Regimes and the Commitment Problem: The Case of United Russia." *Comparative Political Studies* 42, no. 4: 501–26.

Roberts, S. 2009. *Saving Democracy Promotion from Short-Term U.S. Policy Interests in Central Asia*. Washington, D.C.: Century Foundation.

Robinson, M. 1996. *Strengthening Civil Society Through Foreign Political Aid*. ESCOR Research Report R6234. Brighton: IDS.

Rosenberg, T. 2011a. "Revolution U: What Egypt Learned from the Students Who Overthrew Milošević." *Foreign Policy*. 16 February.

———. 2011b. *Join the Club: How Peer Pressure Can Transform the World*. New York: Norton.

Rueschemeyer, D., E. H. Stephens, and J. D. Stephens. 1992. *Capitalist Development and Democracy*. Chicago: University of Chicago Press.

Russet, B. 2008. "A Fourth Wave? The Role of International Actors in Democratization." In P. F. Nardulli, ed., *International Perspectives on Contemporary Democracy*. Urbana: University of Illinois Press.

Sartori, G. 1976. *Parties and Party Systems: A Framework for Analysis, 1*. Cambridge: Cambridge University Press.

Savić, M. 2011. "Serbia." In *Nations in Transit 2011: The Authoritarian Dead End in the Former Soviet Union*. Washington, D.C.: Freedom House.

Scarrow, S. 2005. *Political Parties and Democracy in Theoretical and Practical Perspectives: Implementing Intra-Party Democracy*. Washington, D.C.: NDI.

Schattschneider, E. E. 1942. *Party Government*. New York: Rinehart.

Schedler, A. 2002. "Elections Without Democracy: The Menu of Manipulation." *Journal of Democracy* 13, no. 2: 36–50.

———, ed. 2006. *Electoral Authoritarianism. The Dynamics of Free Competition*. Boulder, Colo.: Lynne Rienner.

Schimmelfennig, F. 2007. "European Regional Organizations, Political Conditionality, and Democratic Transformation in Eastern Europe." *East European Politics and Societies* 21, no. 1: 126–41.

Schimmelfennig, F., and H. Scholtz. 2008. "EU Democracy Promotion in the European Neighbourhood: Political Conditionality, Economic Development and Transnational Exchange." *European Union Politics* 9, no. 2: 187–215.

Schimmelfennig, F., and U. Sedelmeier. 2004. "Governance by Conditionality: EU Rule

Transfer to the Candidate Countries of Central and Eastern Europe." *Journal of European Public Policy* 11, no. 4: 661-79.

Schmitter, P. C., and T. L. Karl. 1994. "The Conceptual Travels of Transitologists and Consolidologists: How Far to the East Should They Attempt to Go?" *Slavic Review* 53, no. 1: 173-85.

Schoen, D. E. 2007. *The Power of the Vote: Electing Presidents, Overthrowing Dictators, and Promoting Democracy Around the World.* New York: Harper Collins.

Schoofs, S., and J. De Zeeuw. 2004. "Lessons Learned in Political Party Assistance." Seminar Report presented on 4 November 2004 at the Netherlands Institute of International Relations, Clingendael, Conflict Research Unit.

Schraeder, P. J. 2003. "The State of the Art in International Democracy Promotion: Results of a Joint European-North American Research Network." *Democratization* 10, no. 2: 21-44.

Schumpeter, J. 1942. *Socialism, Capitalism and Democracy.* New York: Harper and Bros.

SEED. 1998. "SEED Act Implementation Report: Support for East European Democracy—Fiscal Year 1997." Washington, D.C.: Bureau of Europe and Eurasia Affairs.

———. 2001. "SEED Act Implementation Report: Support for East European Democracy—Fiscal Year 2000." Washington, D.C.: Bureau of Europe and Eurasia Affairs.

———. 2002. "SEED Act Implementation Report: Support for East European Democracy—Fiscal Year 1997." Washington, D.C.: Bureau of Europe and Eurasia Affairs.

Sekelj, L. 2001. "Forced Democratization of a Criminal State." In Spasić, I. and M. Subotić, *Revolution and Order: Serbia After October 2000.* Belgrade: Institute for Philosophy and Social Theory, pp. 95-108.

Sell, L. 2002. *Slobodan Milosević and the Destruction of Yugoslavia.* Durham, N.C.: Duke University Press.

Senate Foreign Relations Committee. 1999. "Hearing of the European Affairs Subcommittee of the Senate Foreign Relations Committee, 'Prospects for Democracy in Yugoslavia.'" European Affairs Subcommittee, 29 July 1999, Washington, D.C.

Shin, D. C. 1994. "On the Third Wave of Democratization: A Synthesis and Evaluation of Recent Theory and Research." *World Politics* 47, no. 1: 135-70.

Shkolnikov, V. 2009. *Nations in Transit 2009: Democracy's Dark Year.* Washington, D.C.: Freedom House.

Siani-Davies, P. 2003. *International Intervention in the Balkans Since 1995.* London: Routledge.

Silitski, V. 2005. "Preempting Democracy: The Case of Belarus." *Journal of Democracy* 16: 83-97.

———. 2009. "What Are We Trying to Explain?" *Journal of Democracy* 20, no. 1: 86-89.

Simms, B. 2003. "The End of the 'Official Doctrine': The New Consensus on Britain and Bosnia." *Civil Wars* 6, no. 2: 53-69.

Skocpol, T. 1979. *States and Social Revolutions: A Comparative Analysis of France, Russia and China.* New York: Cambridge University Press.

Slavujević, Z. D. 2007. *Izborne Kampanje: Pohod na Birače—Slučaj Srbije od 1990 do 2007 godine* [Electoral Campaigns: Charge on the Voters—Case of Serbia from 1990 to 2007]. Belgrade: FES and the Institute of Social Science.

Snyder, J. 2002. *From Voting to Violence: Democratization and Nationalist Conflict.* New York: Norton.

Spirova, M. 2005. "Political Parties in Bulgaria." *Party Politics,* 11, no. 5: 601-22.

Spoerri, M. 2008a. "Uniting the Opposition in the Run-Up to Electoral Revolution: Lessons from Serbia 1990–2000." *Totalitarismus und Demokratie* 5, no. 1: 67-85.

———. 2008b. "Serbia's Parties on the Mend? The State of Intra-Party Democracy in Serbia Before and After Regime Change." *Balkanologie* 11, no. 1-2.

———. 2010. "Crossing the Line: Partisan Party Assistance in Post-Milošević Serbia." *Democratization,* 17, no. 6: 1108-31.

———. 2011. "Justice Imposed: How Policies of Conditionality Affect Transitional Justice in the Former Yugoslavia." *Europe-Asia Studies* 63, no. 10: 1827-51.

Spusić, I., and M. Subotić., eds. 2001. *Revolution and Order: Serbia After October 2000.* Belgrade: Institute for Philosophy and Social Theory.

Steinmo, S., K. Thelen, and F. Longstreth, F. 1992. *Structuring Politics: Historical Institutionalism in Comparative Analysis.* New York: Cambridge University Press.

Stefanović, D. 2008. "The Path to Weimar Serbia? Explaining the Resurgence of the Serbian Far Right After the Fall of Milošević." *Ethnic and Racial Studies* 31, no. 7: 1195-1221.

Stefanović, N., and I. Miklja. 2001. *5 oktobar: poslednja revolucija u Evropi* [October 5: The Last Revolution in Europe]. Belgrade: Dimedia.

Stojanović, S. 2001. "Democratic Revolution in Serbia." In I Spasić and M. Subotić, *Revolution and Order: Serbia After October 2000.* Belgrade: Institute for Philosophy and Social Theory, 2001.

Stojiljković, Z. 2006. *Partijski Sistem Srbije* [Party System of Serbia]. Belgrade: Sluzbeni Glasnik.

———. 2007. "Serbia." In K. Grabow, ed., *KAS Democracy Report 2007: Parties and Democracy.* Berlin: Konrad-Adenauer-Stiftung.

Stokes, S. C. 1999. "Political Parties and Democracy." *Annual Review of Political Science* 2: 243-67.

Swanson, D. L., and P. Mancini. 1996. *Politics, Money, and Modern Democracy: An International Study of Innovations in Electoral Campaigning and Their Consequences.* Westport, Conn.: Praeger.

Tansey, O. 2007. "Process Tracing and Elite Interviewing: A Case for Non-Probability Sampling." *Political Science and Politics* 40, no. 4: 765-72.

Thomas, R. 1999. *The Politics of Serbia in the 1990s.* New York: Columbia University Press.

Thompson, M. 1999. *Forging War: Media in Serbia, Croatia and Bosnia-Hercegovina.* Luton: University of Luton Press.

Thompson, M. R., and P. Kuntz. 2004. "Stolen Elections: The Case of the Serbian October." *Journal of Democracy* 15, no. 4: 159-72.

Tóka, G. 1997. "Political Parties and Democratic Consolidation in East Central Europe." Working Paper 279. Glasgow: University of Strathclyde.

Tordoff, W. 2002. *Government and Politics in Africa*, 4th ed. Bloomington: Indiana University Press.

Traub, J. 2008. *The Freedom Agenda: Why America Must Spread Democracy (Just Not the Way George Bush Did)*. New York: Farrar, Straus and Giroux.

Triantaphyllou, D. 2000. "Evaluating Serbia." Occasional Papers 19, the Institute for Security Studies/Western European Union.

Trivunović, M. 2004. "Status of Police Reforms After Four Years of Democratic Transition in Serbia." *Helsinki Monitor* 15, no. 3: 172-86.

Trivunović, M., V. Devine, and H. Mathisen. 2007. *Corruption in Serbia 2007: Overview of Problems and Status of Reforms*. Bergen, Norway: Chr. Michelsen Institute.

Tucker, J. 2007. "Enough! Electoral Fraud, Collective Action Problems, and Post-Communist Colored Revolutions." *Perspectives on Politics* 5: pp. 537–53.

Tures, J. A. 2005. "Operation Exporting Freedom: The Quest for Democratization via United States Military Operations." *Whitehead Journal of Diplomacy and International Relations* 47, no. 4: 490-519.

UNDP. 2006. "Handbook on Opportunities in Political Party Programming: UNDP Experiences and Perspectives." New York: UNDP.

———. 2010. "Serbia Corruption Benchmarking Survey: Analytical Report." Belgrade: UNDP and TNS Gallup.

USAID. 1991. "USAID Policy: Democracy and Governance." Washington, D.C.: U.S. Agency for International Development.

———. 2007. *A Study of Political Party Assistance in Eastern Europe and Eurasia*. Baltimore: Democracy International.

Uzgel, I. 2001. "Finishing the Unfinished Revolution: The Return of Yugoslavia to Europe." *Journal of International Affairs* 6, no. 1.

Vachudova, M. A. 2005. *Europe Undivided: Democracy, Leverage, and Integration After Communism*. New York: Oxford University Press.

———. 2008. "Tempered by the EU? Political Parties and Party Systems Before and After Accession." *Journal of European Public Policy* 15, no. 6: 861-79.

Van Biezen, I. 2003. *Political Parties in New Democracies: Party Organization in Southern and East Central Europe*. New York: Palgrave Macmillan.

———. 2005. "On the Theory and Practice of Party Formation and Adaptation in New Democracies." *European Journal of Political Research* 44, no. 1: 147-74.

Van Wersch, J., and J. De Zeeuw. 2005. "Mapping European Democracy Assistance: Tracing the Activities and Financial Flows of Political Foundations." Working Paper 36, Conflict Research Program, The Hague, Netherlands Institute for International Relations, Cingendael.

Vetta, T. 2009. " 'Democracy Building' in Serbia: The NGO Effect." *Southeastern Europe* 33, no. 1: 26-47.

Wahman, M. 2011. "Offices and Policies: Why Do Opposition Parties Form Pre-Electoral

Coalitions in Competitive Authoritarian Regimes?" *Electoral Studies* 30, no. 4: 642–57.

Walecki, M. 2003. "Money and Politics in Central and Eastern Europe." In R. Austin and M. Tjernstrom, eds., *Funding of Political Parties and Election Campaigns*. Stockholm: IDEA.

Way, L. 2008. "The Real Causes of the Color Revolutions." *Journal of Democracy* 19, no. 3: 55–69.

Webb, P., and S. White. 2007. *Party Politics in New Democracies*. New York: Oxford University Press.

Weinthal, E., and P. J. Luong. 2002. "Environmental NGOs in Kazakhstan: Democratic Goals and Nondemocratic Outcomes." In S. Mendelson and J. Glenn, eds., *The Power and Limits of NGOs: A Critical Look at Building Democracy in Eastern Europe and Eurasia*. New York: Columbia University Press, pp. 152–76.

Weissenbach, K. 2010. "Political Party Assistance in Transition: The German *Stiftungen* in Sub-Saharan Africa." *Democratization* 17, no. 6: 1225–49.

Wejnert, B. 2005. "Diffusion, Development, and Democracy: 1800–1999." *American Sociological Review* 70, no. 1: 53–81.

Whitehead, L. 1986. "International Aspects of Democratization." In G. O'Donnell, P. Schmitter, and L. Whitehead, eds., *Transitions from Authoritarian Rule: Comparative Perspectives*. Baltimore: John Hopkins University Press.

———. 1996. *The International Dimensions of Democratization: Europe and the Americas*. New York: Oxford University Press.

———. 2002. *Democratization: Theory and Experience*. New York: Oxford University Press.

Wigell, M. "Mapping 'Hybrid Regimes': Regime Types and Concepts in Comparative Politics." *Democratization* 15, no. 2: 230–50.

Wild, L., and A. Hudson. 2009. *UK Support for Political Parties: A Stock-Take*. London: Overseas Development Institute.

WFD. 2003. *Annual Review 2002/3*. London: Westminster Foundation for Democracy.

Woodward, S. 1995. *Balkan Tragedy: Chaos and Dissolution After the Cold War*. Washington, D.C.: Brookings Institution.

York, S. 2001. *Bringing Down a Dictator* [Documentary]. Washington, D.C.: York Zimmerman.

Youngs, R. 2003. "European Approaches to Democracy Assistance: Learning the Right Lessons?" *Third World Quarterly* 24, no. 1: 127–38.

———, ed. 2010. *The European Union and Democracy Promotion: A Critical Global Assessment*. Baltimore: Johns Hopkins University Press.

Youngs, R., K. Kausch, D. Mathieson, and I. Menendez. 2006. *Survey of European Democracy Promotion Policies, 2000–2006*. Madrid: FRIDE.

Zakaria, F. 1997. "The Rise of Illiberal Democracy." *Foreign Affairs* 76, no. 6: 22–43.

Zimmermann, W. 1996. *Origins of a Catastrophe: Yugoslavia and Its Destroyers*. New York: Times Books.

INDEX

ACKNOWLEDGMENTS

As most scholars will attest, writing—but, above all, finishing—a book is as much a testament to perseverance as it is a labor of love. This one could not have been written without the support of the many friends, colleagues, and family members who offered advice, assistance, and encouragement along the way.

First, a special thank you goes to Professor André Gerrits and Professor Peter Burnell. It is due to their efforts that the field of party aid is getting the attention that it rightly deserves. My gratitude is also reserved for Professor Annette Freyberg-Inan and Professor Marieke de Goede, who read and reread early drafts of chapters and offered critical advice for how to move forward.

I am also indebted to Maja Nenadović and Max Bader. Our exchanges over theory, methodology, and the roots underlying party aid were not only a constant source of inspiration but also, more often than not, a great deal of fun. I am also grateful to Thomas Carothers, who not only laid the foundation of all that I know about democracy assistance but also generously devoted his time and attention to this project, offering numerous tips of the trade along the way.

Of course, as much as this book is the product of scholarship, it is ultimately the story of the thousands of civic activists, party members, and party-aid professionals who work long hours and devote years, if not entire careers, to the cause of democracy. This project would not have been possible without the more than 150 party aid practitioners, policy makers, diplomats, party members, and journalists who took time to speak with me about what really happened in Serbia. Without their willingness to expose the good and bad of their own endeavors I could not have completed this research. Their honesty, candor, and enthusiasm cannot be stressed enough.

Both my debt and my gratitude extend especially to Rade Milić, for whom no favor was too large and no request too demanding. Rade, like so many of the young men and women I've come to know throughout my travels in Serbia, embodies the very meaning of friendship and is the very best that Serbia has to offer.

And then there is Mladen Joksić. There is no question that without Mladen my passion for the Balkans would never have been realized. Mladen gave me the motivation and dedication and, above all, humor needed to confront the inner workings of post-socialist Serbia day in and day out. I am indebted to him for his strong intellect, patience, kindness, love, and unshakable belief in my abilities. I can only hope that all the late-night readings of errant chapters, the heated debates over Serbia's past and future, and the mind-numbing requests that I frequently demanded, were worthy of the time and effort that he graciously provided. I may not say it enough, but I truly could not and would not have done this without him.

Finally, my gratitude extends to the academic institutions that supported this research. Funding provided by the Netherlands Organization for Scientific Research (NWO) within the framework of the project "International Intervention, Democracy and Political Parties: The External Dimension of Democratization Processes in the Balkans and the Former Soviet Union" were instrumental for the years of fieldwork and research that went into this book. Grants, research opportunities, and speaking engagements provided by the National Endowment for the Humanities (NEH), the Kokkalis Program of Harvard University, the University of Urbana-Champaign, and the Association for Slavic, East European, and Eurasian Studies (ASEEES) enabled me to hone my research agenda and present my research in cities near and far. I also thank the Harriman Institute of Columbia University and the Political Science Department of Central European University, each of which hosted my research and granted me access to their stellar research facilities. My editor at the University of Pennsylvania Press was fantastic, and his belief in this book is what brought it to publication.